T0214900

Communications in Computer and Information Science 1176

Commenced Publication in 2007
Founding and Former Series Editors:
Phoebe Chen, Alfredo Cuzzocrea, Xiaoyong Du, Orhun Kara, Ting Liu,
Krishna M. Sivalingam, Dominik Ślęzak, Takashi Washio, Xiaokang Yang,
and Junsong Yuan

More information about this series at http://www.springer.com/series/7899

Xueming Si · Hai Jin · Yi Sun ·
Jianming Zhu · Liehuang Zhu ·
Xianhua Song · Zeguang Lu (Eds.)

Blockchain Technology and Application

Second CCF China Blockchain Conference, CBCC 2019
Chengdu, China, October 11–13, 2019
Revised Selected Papers

 Springer

Editors
Xueming Si
Fudan University
Shanghai, China

Yi Sun
Chinese Academy of Sciences
Beijing, China

Liehuang Zhu
Central University of Finance
and Economics
Beijing, China

Zeguang Lu
National Academy of Guo Ding
Harbin, China

Hai Jin
Huazhong University of Science
and Technology
Wuhan, China

Jianming Zhu
Central University of Finance
and Economics
Beijing, China

Xianhua Song
Harbin University of Science
and Technology
Harbin, China

ISSN 1865-0929   ISSN 1865-0937   (electronic)
Communications in Computer and Information Science
ISBN 978-981-15-3277-1   ISBN 978-981-15-3278-8   (eBook)
https://doi.org/10.1007/978-981-15-3278-8

This Springer imprint is published by the registered company Springer Nature Singapore Pte Ltd.
The registered company address is: 152 Beach Road, #21-01/04 Gateway East, Singapore 189721, Singapore

Preface

As the program chairs of the 2019 CCF China Blockchain Conference (CBCC 2019), it was our great pleasure to welcome you to the conference, which was held in Chengdu, China, October 11–13, 2019, hosted by China Computer Federation, Blockchain Committee of China Computer Federation, China Electronics Technology Cyber Security Co., Ltd, Southwestern University of Finance and Economics, and National Academy of Guo Ding Institute of Data Science. The goal of this conference was to provide a forum for blockchain scientists and engineers.

The conference attracted 112 paper submissions. After the hard work of the Program Committee, 16 papers were accepted to appear in the conference proceedings, with an acceptance rate of 14.3%. The major topic of this conference was blockchain science and technology.

We would like to thank all the Program Committee members (52 coming from 44 institutes) for their hard work in completing the review tasks. Their collective efforts made it possible to attain quality reviews for all the submissions within a few weeks. Their diverse expertise in each individual research area helped us to create an exciting program for the conference. Their comments and advice helped the authors to improve the quality of their papers and gain deeper insights.

Many thanks should also go to the authors and participants for their tremendous support in making the conference a success.

We thank Dr. Lanlan Chang and Jane Li from Springer, whose professional assistance was invaluable in the production of the proceedings.

Besides the technical program, CBCC 2019 offered different experiences to the participants and we hope that you enjoyed the conference.

November 2019

Hai Jin
Jianming Zhu

Organization

The 2019 CCF China Blockchain Conference (CBCC 2019), http://2019.cbcc.dbw. org.cn/, was held in Chengdu, China, October 11–13, 2019, hosted by China Computer Federation, Blockchain Committee of China Computer Federation, China Electronics Technology Cyber Security Co., Ltd, Southwestern University of Finance and Economics, and National Academy of Guo Ding Institute of Data Science.

General Chairs

Chun Chen   Chinese Academy of Engineering, China
Xueming Si   Fudan University, China

Program Chairs

Hai Jin   Huazhong University of Science and Technology,
                            China
Jianming Zhu   Central University of Finance and Economics, China

Organization Chairs

Liehuang Zhu   Beijing Institute of Technology, China
Hongzhang An   China Electronic Technology Group Corporation,
                            China

Forum Chairs

Liang Cai   Zhejiang University, China
Ke Xu   Tsinghua University, China

Publication Chairs

Zeguang Lu   National Academy of Guo Ding Institute of Data
                            Science, China
Xianhua Song   Harbin University of Science and Technology, China

Competition Chairs

Yi Sun   Chinese Academy of Sciences, China
Jiang Duan   Southwestern University of Finance and Economics,
                            China

Publicity Chairs

Jun Li   Bubi (Beijing) Network Technology Co., Ltd., China
Wei Li   Hangzhou Qulian Technology Co., Ltd., China

Sub Forum Chairs

Haibin Kan   Fudan University, China
Zaishuang Liu   China Electronic Technology Network Information
                        Security Co., Ltd., China
Wei Li   Hangzhou Qulian Technology Co., Ltd., China
Yu Zhou   China UnionPay Electronic Payment Research
                        Institute, China
Guozi Sun   Nanjing University of Posts and Telecommunications,
                        China
Pingping Wu   Tencent, China
Wei Liang   China Telecom Beijing Research Institute, China
Keting Yin   Zhenjiang University, China
Qianhong Wu   Beihang University, China
Bo Tang   Changhong Information Security Lighthouse
                        Laboratory, China
Debiao He   Wuhan University, China
Jian Bai   China Electronic Technology Network Information
                        Security Co., Ltd., China

Contents

OBBC: A Blockchain-Based Data Sharing Scheme for Open Banking

Qinnan Zhang[✉], Jianming Zhu, and Qingyang Ding[✉]

School of Information, Central University of Finance and Economics,
Beijing 100081, China
zhangqnp@163.com, dingqingyang66@163.com

Abstract. The concept of open banking has been a powerful trigger for the revolution in the financial services industry. When financial institutions disclose application programming interfaces (APIs) to third-party providers (TPPs), the biggest system risks concern issues such as malicious attack, data leakage and tampering, privacy disclosure and more. API is a new communication path for information systems, but it could be misused and tampered. To address this, we conceptualize a blockchain-based data sharing scheme for open banking named OBBC, in which the API's information can be saved in a blockchain, that no one can dominate it. We propose an API consensus mechanism aims to ensures that the open API can't be maliciously tampered. Moreover, zero knowledge proof and Merkel tree structure are used to realize that users' privacy protection. In particular, we give the framework of our scheme and compare with existing data sharing schemes. We further implement a software prototype on fabric framework with real-world dataset. Experiment results show the feasibility, usability and scalability of our proposed open banking system.

Keywords: Blockchain · Open banking · API consensus · Data sharing

1 Introduction

In recent years, with the involvement of internet companies in the financial industry, banks are facing unprecedented competitive pressures. According to Brett king[1], the innovation godfather of Bank of America, the global banking industry is moving from 3.0 era to 4.0 era, and open banking will guide to a new stage of banking reform. Open banking originated from PayPal API in 2004, and now it has gained considerable interest and adoption in many large banks all over the world, such as CITI Developer Center of Citibank, Banco Bilbao Vizcaya Argentaria in Spain, DBS Group in Singapore, Bank of China Open Platform and API Bank of Shanghai Pudong Development Bank. According to statistics, since PayPal adopted API cooperation mode in 2009, its net revenue growth rate has exceeded 30%, we can expect that this field will change the working style of bank significantly.

The existing open banking consists of three groups of roles: financial institutions, third-party providers (TPPs) and users (Fig. 1). Users submit request that include account information, payment instruction and so on to TPPs. TPPs log in to authenticate through the authentication system. If the identity is authenticated successfully,

X. Si et al. (Eds.): CBCC 2019, CCIS 1176, pp. 1–16, 2020.
https://doi.org/10.1007/978-981-15-3278-8_1

TPPs then invoke Financial institution B or C' API to get necessary information for this transaction. Finally, TPPs return solutions to the user. Token authentication means that after a financial institution authenticates a user, it generates data (token) indicating the range of data to be accessed to the TPPs and the range of available services, and then transmits the data to the TPPs. It is a method of sending and receiving data between TPPs and financial institutions. For users, registration of ID and password to TPPs becomes unnecessary, and data range accessible by TPPs can be controlled.

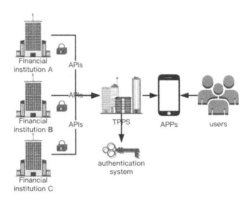

Fig. 1. The framework of existing open banking system model

However, despite the data range is controlled, there are still many security issues. First, traditional open banking is vulnerable to malicious attack such as distributed denial of service (DDoS) attacks, remote hijacking and so on, which makes the services unavailable. Three major Dutch banks had been subjected to DDoS attacks in 2018, resulting in the paralysis of websites and Internet banking services. Second, hackers forge illegal open API and provide for the TPPs, that may lead to data leakage and even paralysis of the entire financial platform. Once the open API is tampered and forged, the user data will be completely exposed and hackers can easily control data and make illegal transactions. Lastly, user's sensitive information (e.g. name, email address and phone number) and transaction solutions are saved in the database of bank systems, which has the risk of privacy disclosure and data loss. In October 2013, the Woo Yun Vulnerability Reporting Platform disclosed the vulnerability of Min sheng Bank's Android application could lead to the leakage of sensitive information. Moreover, the unauthorized access to an interface of China Merchants Bank leads to the disclosure of name and billing information in May 2016 [1].

Blockchain is a type of distributed accounting technology, which can realize data hard to forgery, hard to tampering and traceability [2], and blockchain has been used in many applications and services, such as identity management, protection of intellectual property, crowdsourcing [3], decentralized DNS services [4], and so on. In this paper, we propose a blockchain-based data sharing scheme for open banking to increase user's data security, service availability and prevent user privacy data from leakage.

To the end, our specific contributions are in the following:

- We apply blockchain to open banking scenarios and conceptualize a blockchain based data sharing schema for open banking named OBBC, which can prevent the tampering and forgery of open API. Moreover, we give a complete description about the framework of OBBC.
- We proposed an open API consensus mechanism, in which Practical Byzantine fault tolerance (PBFT) consensus algorithm is took to ensuring the reliability of API information. Among that, checkpoint protocol uses stable checkpoints to reduce memory usage; view switching protocol uses optimal block timeout monitoring to automate view switching.
- To protect data privacy, we use zero knowledge proof algorithm and the Merkel tree data structure to prevent user's privacy data from leakage by TPPs in financial transactions.
- Finally, we compare with existing data sharing schemes in other application scenarios and implement a software prototype about our scheme on fabric framework with real-world dataset. Experiment and analysis results show the feasibility, usability and scalability of our proposed open banking data sharing scheme.

2   Preliminaries

2.1   Blockchain

Blockchain is a decentralized, non-tampering distributed database, in which the data store in a block structure and verify by consensus of the participants in the system [5]. Nakamoto first proposed the concept of blockchain in 2008 and described a peer-to-peer version of the electronic cash named Bitcoin [6]. As the supporting technology of Bitcoin, blockchain has become an important research topic in the financial industry [7]. Blockchain technology uses distributed architecture, cryptography, consensus algorithm, smart contract and other technologies to achieve information tamper-proof, forgery-proof and traceability in the process of information collection, circulation and sharing. There are many application practices to apply blockchains to data sharing. For example, Enigma [8, 9] is a decentralized computing platform with privacy and extensibility.

Consensus mechanism is the core of blockchain, it can ensure that all nodes follow the same accounting rules without central control and achieve consistency of distributed data [10]. The earliest consensus problem is the probability distribution of consensus proposed by Eisenberg and Gale [11]. Dwork and Naor [12] proposed Proof-of-Work (PoW) algorithm, which ensure data consistency and consensus security by consuming computing resources of distributed nodes. King [13] first realized Proof-of-Stake (PoS) in paper, which obtained the right to account by supreme rights not consuming computing resources. Larimer [14] put forward the consensus mechanism of delegated-Proof-of-Stake (DPoS) in 2013. It not only solves the problem of PoW's calculating power competition, but also solves the problem of PoS's unwillingness to participate in accounting. DPoS relies on token coin, but there are no token coins in the open banking scenario. Schwartz [15] put forward the Ripple Protocol Consensus Algorithm (RPCA) in 2014. This algorithm combines PBFT and gets rid of the limitation of consensus through mining. Ripple is an open payment network to solve the problem of high remittance cost. Ongaro [16] proposed Raft consensus algorithm in 2013, which has been implemented in many open source languages. Liskov [17] proposed Practical Byzantine fault tolerance (PBFT) algorithm in 1999, which reduces the complexity of the original Byzantine fault tolerant algorithm. The project of Hyperledger launched by the Linux Foundation uses PBFT algorithm to reach the consensus of the whole network. PBFT algorithm can ensure that the blockchain can run normally when Byzantine fault tolerance occurs in less than one third of the nodes.

2.2   Open Banking

Open Banking is a platform cooperation mode [18], which uses open application programming interface (API) technology to realize data sharing between financial institutions and third-party providers, so as to improve customer experience. Open banking uses the form of Bank-as-a-Platform (BaaP) to instead of conveying products and services directly to customers [19]. In the BaaP platform, the banks serve customers by providing APIs and interface services to third-party financial technology companies. At present, in addition to the business challenges such as supervision, the biggest problem is the security of data and privacy protection. How to ensure the data security and privacy in the process of data sharing between banks and third parties is the primary problem for open banking.

Throughout the world, the open banking model shows a rapid development trend, and many regulatory policies and institutional innovation cases related to the open banking model have landed. In 2012, the first open data Institute (ODI) was established with the support of the British government. In 2014, the ODI studied the impact of open API data, that the conclusion shows that after opening data, the competitiveness of banks has been improved [20]. By early 2018, the larger retail banks operating within the UK will be obligated to create standards for APIs [21]. At the end of 2015, the EU promulgated a Payment Services Directive (PSD2) [22], which banks in the EEA are required to open their customer data to third-party institutions in the form of APIs by January 13, 2018. PSD2 is similar to the UK Open Bank Guidelines, which require all EU companies to complete technical compliance with PSD2 by September 2019. In 2016, Citibank launched CITI Developer Center around the world, opening seven kinds of API interfaces. Users can not only use Citibank's massive data, but also use API module to build their own financial service program. The Spanish Banco Bilbao Vizcaya Argentaria (BBVA) is the first bank in the world to open APIs commercially. It has long defined the platform development strategy and achieved win-win development through open data interface. In Asia, Singapore DBS Group has been at the forefront of the development of open banking. At the end of 2017, it launched an API platform, which has opened 155 APIs, including transfer, payment and incentives [23]. In china, Bank of China put forward the concept of open platform in 2012, and launched the Bank of China Open Platform in 2013, which opened 1600 API interfaces and integrated all kinds of bank business interfaces. 2018 is the first year of the of China Open Banking development, in which Pudong Development Bank launched the first API Bank in the industry. It is foreseeable that more policies will be introduced to support the development of open banking in the future.

2.3 System Overview

In order to solve the security problem in the process of data sharing for open banking, we conceptualize a blockchain-based data sharing schema named OBBC. Figure 2 gives an overview of OBBC. It includes a comprehensive set of Open API Consensus mechanism, detailed in Sect. 3. There are three main processes in the scheme: (1) Open API Consensus (detailed in Sect. 3), (2) Data Privacy Protection (detailed in Sect. 4), and (3) Data Encryption. Data encryption encrypts uses API key (API invoke credential private key) to encrypt invoke information and store ciphertext in a blockchain database, that avoids invoke information is tampered and identity fraud. Because blockchain data synchronization consumes time, all data should not be stored on the chain, so we can create distributed hash table (e.g. Kademlia [24]) to store data index and improve access efficiency.

The BaaP platform provides consensus open API information, accessible bank user info and data storage function for TPPs, which the consensus mechanism of blockchain ensures that API's information or bank data is difficult to tampered with, and the same time, the bank user privacy accessible by TPPs can be effectively protected by zero knowledge proof algorithm. Moreover, if the bank's system is attacked by hacker, the distributed blockchain data storage structure and platform service mode can guarantee the availability of services.

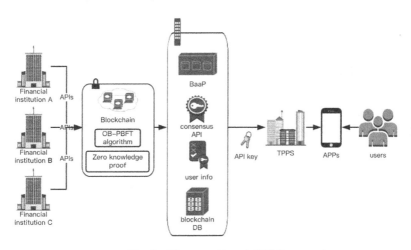

Fig. 2. The overview of OBBC

3   Open API Consensus Mechanism

Open banking generally includes three categories of open API, which including data services, user management and payment services. Among them, data services mainly include location of ATM and branch, public services, etc. User's management mainly includes account authorization, credit score, bank card management, etc. Payment services mainly include fund transfer and remittances, mobile Payment, integral payment and so on. Table 1 below presents a classification of existing open API from a well-known bank.

Table 1. Classification of existing open API from A well-known bank.

Category	API example	Features
data services	Location services	Provide location of bank service, such as ATM and branch
	Different services	Provide services according to different national and regional
User management	Authorization	Authorize third party access to data or services
	Credit score	Provide bank user's credit scores to third party
	Card management	Provide multiple credit and debit card management
Payment services	Transfer remittances	Implementing user transfers across institutions
	Mobile payment	Third party can call up mobile payment
	Integral payment	Third-party applications receive user bonus points for payment

Data source: McKinsey analysis

3.1   Open API Threat Type

Once the bank API is open to third parties, it will inevitably attract the attention of the attacker and gain profits by attacking or tampering with the API information. We define the open API's threat type which illustrates potential threats and malicious behaviors as follows:

- Malicious Writing: Attackers can forge bank identities, write illegal APIs and provide to third-party providers, thus obtaining user information and even making illegal transfers.
- Information tampering: By tampering with API information opened by banks, attackers can provide wrong APIs to third-party providers to obtain illegal profits.
- Malicious TPPs: By getting user privacy data for profit, which has the risk of privacy disclosure and data loss.

In order to deal with the above API threats, we propose the following API consensus mechanism and privacy protection scheme to reduce the risk of bank opening API. The specific definition and implementation of the open API consensus mechanism is as follows:

3.2 Basic Concepts

Definition 1 (Quorum). We definition the set of system nodes named Quorum, and the intersection of any two Quorums is not empty. Assuming that the set of system nodes is U, $\partial = \{Q1, Q2, \ldots, Qn\}$ and $Q1 \subseteq U$, the satisfiable formula (1) is called Q as a Quorum.

$$\forall Qi, \ldots Qj \in \partial \land Qi \cap Qj \neq \varnothing \tag{1}$$

Quorum has the following properties:

(1) Intersection: Any two Quorums have at least one common and correct replica.
(2) Availability: There must be Quorum without faulty replicas.

In this paper, we define a quorum as a set containing at least 2f + 1 replicas, where f represents the maximum number of tolerable error nodes in the system, so as to ensure that at least f + 1 node in a quorum has no error.

Definition 2 (View). In PBFT algorithm, the replicas move through a succession of configurations called views, which are numbered consecutively. R is a collection of all replicas, each replica is represented by an integer, followed by $\{0, 1, 2, \ldots, |R| - 1\}$, in which the primary node in a view is defined as replica p, that satisfies:

$$p = v \bmod |R| \tag{2}$$

The purpose of above formulas is to find primary node, which named initialize view. In this paper, if the primary node fails, we use View Change algorithm to get the primary node's number.

Definition 3 (Certificate). The system consensus process requires message transmission, which is called certificate. Among them, the certificate information contains the number of information. This paper takes the block number as the information number.

3.3 Open API Block Consensus

Transactions in blockchain are submitted in block data format and recorded permanently in blockchain. In our scheme, the open API block structure and the process of opening API consensus is as the follows Fig. 3:

(1) Bank generates open API block data, which is mainly composed of block header and block body. Block header includes previous block hash, timestamp of current request, block body hash and Merkle root. Block body includes current API unique identification (DID), API version, API request address, input and output parameters, and API calling entity (HTTP interface can be omitted);
(2) Banks use private keys for digital signatures to prevent block data tampering;
(3) Identity authentication system uses bank public key for digital signature verification;
(4) After successful digital signature verification, send API write request to primary node;
(5) Primary node broadcasts API block data;

(6) Consensus nodes verify the API information by consensus algorithms;
(7) After consensus verification, the API information is written to the blockchain network;

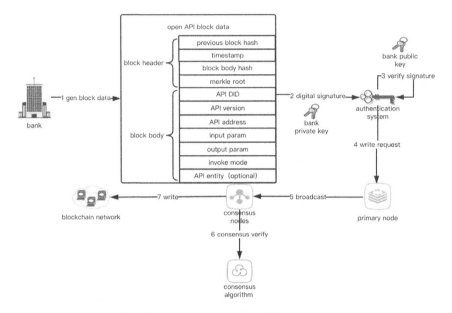

Fig. 3. The process of open API consensus

Block validity check includes block header and block body check. Block head information includes hash value of the previous block hash value, block body hash value and timestamp. If the current block information or the previous block information changes, it will inevitably cause the hash value of the current block to change. If an attacker modifies a block, the hash value of the block will change. In order for the latter block to be able to connect, all the later blocks must be modified in turn, otherwise the modified block will be separated from the block chain. Because hash computing takes time, it is almost impossible to modify multiple blocks in a short time, thus ensuring that API information on the block chain can't be tampered with. When open API information needs to be written or updated, the primary node writes API information to the block and broadcasts the block information. When more than one third of the nodes agree on the block, the block information is written into the block chain. The node ensures the orderliness of block addition by block number and the previous block hash recorded in block header.

In our scheme, PBFT algorithm is adopted as the consensus mechanism of open API. When the open API block information passes the consistency check of the three stages, it can enter the execution stage, delete the block from the buffer and add it to the blockchain. We use the stable checkpoint protocol to monitor the time of adding blocks. Stable checkpoints can reduce memory by recording the maximum request number that consensus completes. The previous number has been consensus completed by default. Moreover, we use performance and dynamic scoring to optimal construct node lists. When a view switch is successfully completed, the node score is added 1 and when the view switch fails, the node score is cut 1. The regular overtime automatic check of optimal node aims to automatically monitor whether the primary node fails or not. The node list is sorted regularly by performance parameters and dynamic scoring, the first node of the node list is regarded as the optimal block, which defines as optimal block initialization. For each view change task, there is a limited condition Quorum $(\forall Qi, \ldots Qj \in \partial \wedge Qi \cap Qj \neq \varnothing)$. The View Change algorithm is described as follows:

Algorithm 1: View Change

Input: block information and API cache list information
Output: the new primary node number
1: time ← Current Time
2: Repeat:
3: if API cache list ≠ ∅ then
4:    if optimal block's transaction information = ∅ then
5:      if Current Time - time > t then
6:        output: optimal block's number
7:    else
8:      time ← optimal block's time stamp
9:      if Current Time - time > t (optimal block timeout not responding) then
10:       output: optimal block's number + 1
11:     else
12:       Thread. sleep (t)
13:       time ← Current Time
14: until output

---

4   Data Privacy Protection

It's possible that user privacy data included in the user's account and transaction will be exposed to the risk of leakage via TPPs in the scenario of open banking. Zero knowledge proof is an algorithm based on cryptography, which can verify the validity of some information in the original information without exposing the original information. It can protect the privacy of data and ensure the security and reliability of information proof. In a nutshell, the goal of this protocol is to prove the prover has a secret to the verifier without revealing any information about the secret. There are practical applications that uses zero-knowledge proof to realize transaction anonymity, such as Zcash [25] which is an implementation of the decentralized anonymous payment scheme. It bridges the existing transparent payment scheme used by Bitcoin with a shielded payment scheme secured by zero-knowledge succinct non-interactive arguments of knowledge (zk-SNARKs) to realize transaction anonymity, which can not only make the origin and flow of money completely confidential, but also verify consumption capacity. In this paper, the zero-knowledge proof is validated by Merkle tree structure. The data structure is as Fig. 4. If we want to verify the value of D0 without exposing other content, we can construct Merkel tree to prove that the value of N1, N5, root is provided, if the value of root is consistent with the value provided by the verifier, then we can verify the value of D0. The whole process does not need to provide the value of D0.

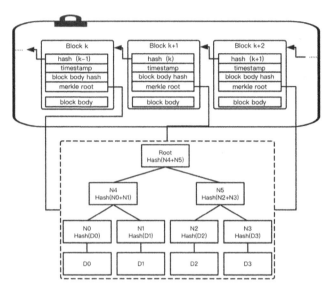

Fig. 4. The Merkel tree data structure

Zero-knowledge proof must satisfy three properties: completeness, soundness and zero-knowledge. The most common computational model is Turing machine. Using P, V and S as the descriptive symbols of Turing machine, where P represents the prover and V represents the verifier. There is a premise that any probabilistic polynomial time verifier V. $View_{\hat{V}}\left[P(x) \leftrightarrow \hat{V}(x,z)\right]$ is a record of the interactions between $P(x)$ and $V(x,z)$, where z is an auxiliary string in the definition plays the role of prior knowledge. There is an interactive proof system with P, V for a language L and satisfy a simulator:

$$\forall x \epsilon L, z \epsilon \{0, 1\}^*, View_{\hat{V}}\left[P(x) \leftrightarrow \hat{V}(x,z)\right] = S(x,z) \tag{3}$$

Here is an example of using zero knowledge proof in our scheme. A prover (user) wants to prove to verifier (TPPs) that he has the right to access the system. Then the following steps are required.

(1) Proofer inputs data information to the trusted third party and chooses validation method;
(2) Proof key and verification key are generated, proof key is provided to proofer and verification key is provided to verifier;

(3) The trusted third party endorses the data information through the digital signature algorithms;

(4) The proofer uses the proof key to generate the proof file;

(5) The verifier uses the verification key to generate the validation contract, deploy the up-link and verify the certification document;

(6) The blockchain return the verified results, which can confirm the validity of the proof file without knowing the specific content.

The process of privacy protection in our scheme is shown as Fig. 5.

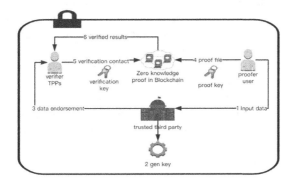

Fig. 5. The process of privacy protection

Zero-knowledge proof is used to solve the privacy protection problem of user information in our scheme, which reduce the cost of trust and avoid privacy disclosure. By generating privacy proof of data information, the validity of some content in digital information is verified without exposing complete data information. Thus, while protecting data privacy, it ensures data information to be validated safely and effectively. Anonymous identity authentication of open banking and information hiding of digital identity can be realized through zero-knowledge proof and users can reach financial agreement without revealing personal information. Moreover, data can be transmitted on the chain in the way of encrypted files, while verifying the authenticity and validity of the data. At the same time, it can realize a verifiable distributed account book without revealing the identity and content of both sides of the transaction. Precisely solve the security verification problem in the process of multiparty data collaboration and sharing under the open banking mode.

5   Results and Evaluation

5.1   System Prototype

The primary purpose of OBBC is to reduce the security risk in the process of open banking data sharing. We developed a software prototype on Hyperledger fabric v1.1 with real-world dataset of bank of china open platform. Hyperledger fabric is an open source project launched by the Linux Foundation in 2015 to promote blockchain digital technology and transaction validation. Due to the characteristics of peer-to-peer network, distributed book-keeping technology is fully shared, transparent and decentralized, so it is very suitable for application in the financial industry. Fabric is more centralized and chains are limited to members of the alliance, but it is relatively easy to achieve higher performance.

The functions of software prototype include user authentication, API query, API writing, API invoke, API test and the record query of publisher and invoke. User authentication includes financial institution authentication and TPPs authentication, which grants different authority to different types of institutions, and authorized financial institutions can write APIs to blockchain of this system; In order to search API information efficiently, API query includes keyword positioning, category positioning, scene positioning and institution positioning for meeting different search needs; if users query API and then submits application for invocation the system automatically generates electronic contracts after successful constraint invocation behavior; users input API test parameters to obtain test results preview and download. We evaluated the feasibility of our scheme by simulating DoS attack on our software prototype. The task information was input by OBBC Client which was developed based on JavaScript. The front end uses Angular Js for page rendering, and the back end uses Node.js to return Json data, which is stored in the database provided by Hyperledger fabric. The homepage of OBBC system prototype is shown in Fig. 6 below.

Fig. 6. The homepage of OBBC system prototype

5.2 Security Analysis

In our design, OBBC solves the problems of data security and privacy protection in the process of open banking data sharing. The following are discussed in detail.

Malicious Writing API. Authenticated banks have the right to write open API information. Private keys are used for data signature before writing, and write requests can be initiated only after verification, thus avoiding malicious writing of API.

API Information Tampering. API information is stored on blockchains through consensus mechanism. In a short time, it is possible to modify API information unless it has more than 51% computing power of the whole network.

Malicious Third-Party Providers (TPPs). Token authentication means that after a financial institution authenticates a user, it generates data (token) indicating the range of data to be accessed to the TPPs and the range of available services, and then transmits the data to the TPPs. It is a method of sending and receiving data between TPPs and data range accessible by TPPs can be controlled.

Privacy Protection. Users can reach financial agreement without revealing personal information through zero-knowledge proof. Providers provide endorsement information and certification documents to verifiers, and then the verification results can be obtained without multiple interactions. (Only the scheme of Privacy protection been proposed, but it has not been implemented in the prototype system currently).

DDoS Attack Resistant. OBBC system requires users to authenticate real identity, which can thwart major DDoS attacks. In addition, users need pay invoking of open API fees for system admin so attackers require money cost to make DDoS attack. Therefore, malicious attackers may pay a huge cost to launch these attacks under the payment mechanism.

5.3 Experimental Verification

To evaluate the utility, security and performance of OBBC, we conducted some sets of experiments to execute test case by Hyperledger caliper, which is a blockchain performance benchmarking framework. We counted the system performance indicators including the success rate, throughput, latency and resource consumption. To build caliper, we first extract the basic dependencies and then boot the caliper project. A single node test is carried out, and the system runs with full threads. The performance test result is shown in Fig. 7 below.

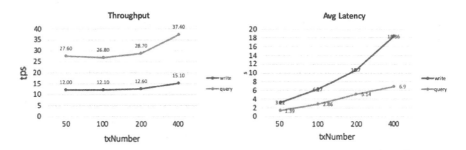

Fig. 7. Performance with varying request rate

5.4 Comparisons and Analysis

Our main contribution is to provide a blockchain-based Data Sharing scheme for open banking system. It should be mentioned that our scheme relies on PBFT-based to achieve the security of open API. Moreover, a lightweight block format has been proposed for the first time to improve the scheme's efficiency compared to the existing blockchain implementations. Table 2 below presents a comparison between different data sharing schemes presented in the literature.

Table 2. Comparison between proposed access control schemes from the literature.

References	Blockchain-Based	Scalability	Privacy protection	Distant-Access
SGC of WSNs [26]	N	Y	N	N
Yue et al. [27]	Y	N	N	Y
Zyskind et al. [28]	Y	N	Y	N
Our proposed OBBC	Y	Y	Y	Y

From the point of view of resource waste, our scheme cancels the mining process and incentive mechanism, and solves the problem of resource waste caused by PoW consensus algorithm. The OB-PBFT algorithm adopted in this paper is more suitable for open banking scenarios, which the reliability of nodes is higher. Although the requirement of fault-tolerant rate is less than 50% of the PoW consensus algorithm, the 3% fault-tolerant rate is enough to meet the scenario requirements. For block time, because PoW needs to calculate random numbers, it is difficult to make block time stable even through adjustment of difficulty coefficient. Uncertainty of block time will lead to branch of blockchain, which is not conducive to the maintenance of blockchain. The consensus algorithm used in this paper can complete the block consistency negotiation and block checking immediately when there is a transaction. Therefore, the trade fair is recorded in the blockchain at the first time, and blocks are generated by a node without branches, which can maintain the data in the blockchain very well.

6 Conclusion and Prospect

In the light of open API consensus and user data privacy protection in the application scenario of open banking data sharing, a blockchain-based open banking data sharing schema is conceptualized. In this schema, PBFT algorithm is proposed as an open API consensus mechanism to prevent the tampering and forgery of open API and avoid the waste of computational resources in workload proof consensus mechanism. In view of the improvement of checkpoint protocol and view switching algorithm in PBFT algorithm, stable checkpoint protocol is used to reduce memory and the use of optimal block timeout monitoring to achieve automatic view switching and reduce the network communication overhead. Moreover, aiming at the problem of user data privacy protection, zero-knowledge proof mechanism and the Merkel tree data structure are proposed to prevent user privacy data leakage. Finally, we implement a software prototype on fabric framework with real-world dataset and the experiment results show the feasibility and usability of our proposed open banking system.

With the development of blockchain technology, new block topology has been innovated continuously, including Directed acyclic graph and Hash Graph [29]. The consensus process can be based on transaction granularity. Each transaction cites the legitimacy of the other two transactions, which block-less consensus can be achieved. It can be a new direction of consensus mechanism in the open banking scenario.

Acknowledgments. This work was supported by Nature Key Research and Development Program of China (2017YFB1400700), the National Natural Science Foundation of China (U1509214), the Central University of Finance and Economics Funds for the First-Class Discipline Construction in 2019.

References

1. http://www.anquan.us/static/bugs/wooyun-2016-0206754.html
2. China Blockchain industry white paper. MIIT (2018). http://www.miit.gov.cn/n114290/n1146402/n1146445/c6180238/part/6180297.pdf
3. Li, M., Weng, J., Yang, A., Lu, W.: CrowdBC: a blockchain based decentralized framework for crowdsourcing. https://eprint.iacr.org/2017/444.pdf
4. Schneider, J.: Blockchain—Putting Theory into Practice. https://t.co/CLJJf0tGp0. Accessed 14 Apr 2017
5. Wang, X.L., Jiang, X.Z., Li, Y.: A model for data access control and sharing based on blockchain. Ruan Jian Xue Bao/J. Softw. **30**(6) (2019). (in Chinese). http://www.jos.org.cn/1000-9825/5742.html
6. Nakamoto, S.: Bitcoin: a peer-to-peer electronic cash system. http://bitcoins.info/bitcoin.pdf. Accessed 10 Apr 2008
7. Jesse, Y.H., Deokyoon, K., Sujin, C., Sooyong, P., Kari, S., Houbing, S.: Where is current research on blockchain technology—a systematic review. PLoS ONE **11**(10), 1–27 (2016)
8. Zyskind, G., Nathan, O., Pentland, A.: Decentralizing privacy: using blockchain to protect personal data. In: Proceedings of IEEE Security and Privacy Workshops, pp. 180–184. IEEE (2015)
9. Zyskind, G., Nathan, O., Pentland, A.: Enigma: decentralized computation platform with guaranteed privacy (2015). https://enigma.co/enigma_full.pdf
10. Jianfeng, L.: Research and application of block chain consensus algorithms based on Byzantine Fault Tolerance Mechanism. Zhengzhou University (2018)
11. Eisenberg, E., Gale, D.: Consensus of subjective probabilities: the Parimutuel method. Ann. Math. Stat. **30**(1), 165–168 (1959)
12. Dwork, C., Naor, M.: Pricing via processing or combatting junk mail. In: Brickell, E.F. (ed.) CRYPTO 1992. LNCS, vol. 740, pp. 139–147. Springer, Heidelberg (1993). https://doi.org/10.1007/3-540-48071-4_10. http://www.springerlink.com/content/l90we8aq0nre2a4n
13. King, S., Nadal, S.: PPCoin: Peer to Peer Crypto-Currency with Proof-of-Stake [OL] (2012). http://ppcoin.org/static/ppcoin-paper.pdf. https://decred.org/research/king2012.pdf
14. BitShares: Delegated proof of stake. http://docs.bitshares.org/bitshares/dpos.html. Accessed 10 Apr 2018
15. Schwartz, D., Youngs, N., Britto, A.: The Ripple protocol consensus algorithm. https://ripple.com/files/ripple_consensus_whitepaper.pdf. Accessed 10 Apr 2018
16. Ongaro, D., Ousterhout, J.: In search of an understandable consensus algorithm. In: Proceedings of the USENIX Annual Technical Conference, pp. 305–319. USENIX ATC, Philadelphia (2014)

17. Castro, M., Liskov, B.: Practical Byzantine fault tolerance. In: Proceedings of the 3rd Symposium on Operating Systems Design and Implementation, pp. 173–186. USENIX Association, New Orleans (1999). http://dl.acm.org/citation.cfm?id=296824
18. Aitamurto, T., Lewis, S.C.: Open innovation in digital journalism: examining the impact of Open APIs at four news organizations. New Media Soc. **15**(2), 314–331 (2013)
19. Financial Data Sharing Series I: Open Banking Initiates Global Financial Change, Cai Kailong (2017)
20. Scott, A., Bolotin, L.: Introducing the open banking standard: helping customers, banks and regulators take banking into a truly 21st-cnetury, connected digital economy (ODI-WP-2016-001) (2016)
21. Zachariadis, M., Ozcan, P.: The API economy and digital transformation in financial services: the case of open banking (2016)
22. Deloitte: How to flourish in an uncertain future: open banking and PSD2, Deloitte (2017)
23. Twenty-Sixth European Conference on Information Systems (ECIS2018), Portsmouth, UK (2018)
24. Petar Maymounkov, D.M.: Kademlia: a peer-to-peer information system based on the XOR metric. In: International Workshop on Peer-to-Peer Systems, vol. 2429, MA, USA, March 2002, pp. 53–65 (2002)
25. Hopwood, D., Bowe, S., Hornby, T., Wilcox, N.: Zcash protocol specification, Zerocoin Electric Coin Company, Technical report, December 2017
26. Wu, F., Pai, H.T., Zhu, X., Hsueh, P.Y., Hu, Y.H.: An adaptable and scalable group access control scheme for managing wireless sensor networks. Telemat. Inform. **30**, 144–157 (2013). [CrossRef]
27. Yue, X., Wang, H., Jin, D., Li, M., Jiang, W.: Healthcare data gateways: found healthcare intelligence on blockchain with novel privacy risk control. J. Med. Syst. **40**, 218 (2016). [PubMed]
28. Zyskind, G., Nathan, O., Pentland, A.S.: Decentralizing privacy: using blockchain to protect personal data. In: Proceedings of the 2015 IEEE Security and Privacy Workshops (SPW 2015), San Jose, CA, USA, 21–22 May 2015, pp. 180–184 (2015)
29. Yong, Y., Xiao-Chun, N., Shuai, Z., Fei-Yue, W.: Blockchain consensus algorithms: the state of the art and future trends. Acta Automatica Sin. **44**(11), 2011–2022 (2018). https://doi.org/10.16383/j.aas.2018.c180268

FutureOTC: An Intelligent Decentralized OTC Option Trading and E-contract Signing System

Qing Zhang[1,2], Jian Gao[1,2], Qiqiang Qin[1,2], Chenyu Wang[1,2], and Keting Yin[3(✉)]

[1] China Financial Futures Exchange, Shanghai, China
{zhangqing, gaojian, qinqq, wangcyl}@cffex.com.cn
[2] Shanghai Financial Futures Information Technology Co., Ltd., Shanghai, China
[3] College of Software Technology, Zhejiang University, Hangzhou, China
yinkt@zju.edu.cn

Abstract. This paper proposes a decentralized, reliable and intelligent system - FutureOTC for China's over-the-counter (OTC) option market based on Consortium Blockchain. Firstly, FutureOTC combines robust Byzantine Fault Tolerance (RBFT) with electronic Identity (EID) and electronic Business License (EBL) to provide solutions for personal and institutional authentication. Secondly, we apply smart contracts to bring OTC option trading more intelligent and reliable, which includes online enquiry, E-contract creation, E-contract signing, reporting and clearing. Last but not the least, we introduce penetrating supervision by setting administrative institution as a node on Consortium Blockchain. Regulators can conduct 7 * 24 h remote supervision based on blockchain address, which reduces institutions' workloads to report daily and ensures the authenticity of OTC option market data.

Keywords: Consortium blockchain · OTC · Authentication · E-contract · Smart contract · Supervision

1 Introduction

OTC option as the part of derivatives market is pivotal to institutional customers who have personalized demands. China's OTC option market is developing in an inspiring speed since 2014 [1]. In 2014, the cumulative initial nominal principal amount was 48.2 billion RMB, with a total number of 3,384 transactions in whole year, accounting for 28.4% of the entire OTC derivate market. In 2017, the cumulative initial nominal principal amount was 501.1 billion RMB, with a total number of 17,647 transactions in whole year, accounting for 66.9% of the entire OTC derivate market. However, behind the breathtaking growth of trading volume, trading risk continues accumulating. Therefore, in 2018, with the stricter policies announced by regulators, OTC option market encounters sharp decline both in the nominal amount and in transaction numbers.

By introducing FutureOTC system based on Consortium Blockchain, this paper aims to solve the problems encountered in current OTC option market. Overall, the main contribution of this paper can be summarized as follows:

© Springer Nature Singapore Pte Ltd. 2020
X. Si et al. (Eds.): CBCC 2019, CCIS 1176, pp. 17–30, 2020.
https://doi.org/10.1007/978-981-15-3278-8_2

- First, we apply Consortium Blockchain into OTC option market, which makes transactions more convenient and reliable.
- Second, we introduce an economical and feasible users authentication mechanism for both personal and institutional participants in OTC option market, which ensures trading behavior legal and compliant.
- Third, the effectiveness of smart contract is maximized which helps on checking users' balance, verifying the signatures and stamps, automatically sending market operations to report library.

The rest of paper is organized as follows. In Sect. 2, we discuss the existing problems in China's current OTC market. Meanwhile, we illustrate the advantages of adopting Consortium Blockchain. In Sect. 3, related works on OTC market in both foreign and domestic is introduced. Proof of concepts (POCs) conducted are also mentioned here. In Sect. 4, we give an overview of our system design, from business design to system architecture and Hyperchain consensus. In Sect. 5, the specific application about FutureOTC is given. We discuss the complete procedures including authentication, transaction process, smart contract and data storage. In Sect. 6, the performance of FutureOTC is illustrated. Finally, we conclude with discussion in Sect. 7.

2   Motivation

Figure 1 shows the development of China's OTC option market from 2015 to 2019. Historically, China's first OTC option was released by a security company on August 19th, 2013. Within six years, we witnessed a rapid development of China's OTC option business. Moreover, we believe the trend will continue based on the following three reasons. First, even though China's OTC option business is keeping a raising trend in recent years, there are still large gaps between the overseas OTC option market and China's OTC option market. Second, the application of the innovative technology such like Consortium Blockchain and smart contract will largely reduce the operation cost of China's OTC option and increase the efficiency of online enquiry and trading which will benefit China's OTC market. Third, comparing the domestic stock market and bond market, the scale of China's OTC option market is still tiny, the market activity is low, and there is large space for growth.

China's OTC option market is dominated by few agencies, which means the risk is also centralized into these agencies. According to the statistics data, commercial banks, securities companies, private equity funds and futures companies are four main brokers in OTC option market who have strong pricing power and risk hedging capabilities. With customer resources in advantage, these agencies can also accumulate large systematic financial risk. And that also makes them manipulate the market easily. Huatai Great Wall Capital, a wholly-owned subsidiary of Huatai Futures, broke its position in OTC option market on July 13th, 2019. After the forced liquidation, the Huatai Futures lost 46.84 million RMB. Tianfeng Futures announced that Tianshen, a wholly-owned subsidiary, traded with Fujian Zhongtuo Company on OTC derivatives and suffered a huge loss of 91.15 million RMB shortly on July 23th, 2019.

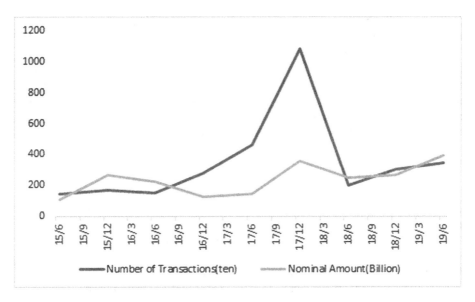

Fig. 1. Development of China's OTC option market

China's OTC option market is not transparent enough, therefore the credit risk is difficult to control. Generally, price brokers can offer the market participants an overview of the whole market since customers have no access to price brokers' electronic bulletin board. In addition, OTC market lacks the guarantee mechanism and margin account system to protect the traders. The counterparties have to bear the risk of trading since there is few ways to learn about each other.

China's OTC option market expands in large scale with little supervise. The development of regulatory regulations and self-regulatory systems is lagging, and the mechanism for handling one-sided default is a blank. On May 31, 2018, Securities Association of China issued "Notice on Further Strengthening the Self-discipline Management of the OTC Options Business of Securities Companies"; on March 20, 2019, the Interim Association issued the "Guidelines for the Pilot Business of Futures Companies' Risk Management Companies". Therefore, the question raised: how do market institutions be self-regulated?

In order to solve the problems listed above, we put forward FutureOTC based on Consortium Blockchain. There are three main advantages for applying FutureOTC into the OTC option market:

First, FutureOTC uses EID to conduct personal identity authentication and EBL to conduct institutional identity authentication. After passing identity confirmation, the users are authorized to access FutureOTC and to trade on FutureOTC.

Second, FutureOTC provides smart contracts for each OTC option. Using FutureOTC, participants ask and bid from anywhere at any time. Smart contracts are in charge of pre-checking and pre-freezing each transaction. Smart contracts allow participants to design personalized options and launch principal agreement and transaction confirmation. Furthermore, smart contract can finish clearing and send settlement instructions automatically without manual operation.

Last but not the least, FutureOTC reforms the way securities supervision and administration institutions involving in the business. Nowadays, participants have to report market operation every day. Regulators collect the information after events happen and cannot guarantee the data integrity and authenticity. With FutureOTC, regulators will get market operation in real time. Once preset condition is triggered, regulators will conduct corresponding measures in case of system financial risk.

3   Related Works

In recent years, many scholars have studied the application of OTC markets from the perspective of technology and policies.

Soonduck [2] suggests for financial institutions to apply and implement Blockchain technology, it is necessary for financial institutions to cooperate together through a blockchain consortium. Molodie [3] finds Blockchain technology has the potential to improve and transform private equity markets at each stage of their lifecycle, from early fundraising to private stock issuance and eventually, OTC trading. Thomas et al. [4] demonstrate certain asset classes and activities are ripe for early Distributed Ledger Technology (DLT) adoption. Among the most promising areas are complex OTC derivatives, such as renewable energy contracts. These markets have a relatively small number of participants, making it easier to reach a consensus on systems and policies. Dr. Robert and Moritz [5] from BearingPoint observe an ongoing development from the actual complex post-trading landscape towards centralized DLT solutions that try to exclude the middleman. They emphasize the role of regulators to have a vital effect on the success of blockchain technology. Felipe [6] suggests in the case of swaps or OTC derivatives where every contract is unique by it, their specific algorithms can be inbuilt into separate smart contracts.

Domestic experts are also concerned about OTC option development. Su and Zhao [7] find the concentrated ratio of OTC options is about 84%. Affected by this, securities companies with business qualifications may form a certain industry monopoly, and may adopt unified actions through agreements to intervene and manipulate market prices, which will disrupt the financial market order while damaging the interests of investors. Lei [8] suggests some core principles including respecting the rules of OTC options trading, preventing market risks and violations, establishing a market maker system etc. Xing [9] believes Blockchain is to be practiced in the issuance and trading of OTC market. These will bring about changes in existing regulatory requirements, and supervision should also develop in parallel with technological development. Qian etc. [10] propose an intelligent structured chain which combines traditional OTC transactions with enhanced Blockchain. The system integrates the scattered OTC market into a network to simplify traditional OTC processing processes, improve its efficiency and reduce trading risk. Li Zhu etc. [11] use Blockchain to transfer trust relationship from traditional financial institutions to the automatically executed smart contracts' procedure, which weakens the intermediary and channel functions of traditional financial institutions.

Exchanges are also taking actions. The Korea Exchange conducted the Korea Start-up Market (KSM) project and adopted Blockchain in 2017, who was globally the second exchange for applying the blockchain technology to the capital market following the US Nasdaq. In addition, ASX is also developing a new system to replace existing stock clearing and settlement system using the blockchain-led technology. China Securities Depository and Clearing Corporation Limited (CSDC) developed Financial Investment Support Platform for Institutions (FISP) in 2017. CSDC planned to provide electronic information circulation and management services for institutional investors' OTC investment registration and settlement business. CSI Inter-Agency Quotation System Company (CIQS) also provides trading place and facilities for OTC derivatives. However, both FSIP and platform from CIQS are centralized trading systems which might impede the widely spread among OTC option investors.

Based on our works, to make a better OTC option market, we concentrate on solving the existing inconvenience and inefficiency of OTC option market by proposing a Consortium Blockchain based solution.

4 System Design Overview

4.1 Business Process

Here is the life cycle of an OTC option, as shown in Fig. 2. Suppose a nature or a legal person has passed through authentication and earned the qualified investor certification. During business operation, he need to handle the risk produced by the price raising on raw materials. However, there is few matching products found on the exchange.

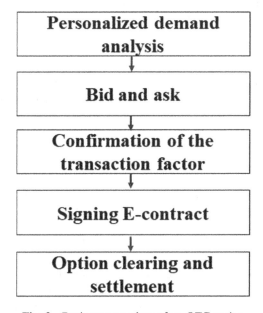

Fig. 2. Business procedure of an OTC option

Therefore, a customized OTC option product is designed according to his personalized demands. Next, option bid and ask happens on inter-institutional market. After several rounds of bargaining, the counterparties reach consensus on the price. Ideally, they will fulfill the principal Agreement. After that, the buyer and the seller must confirm detail transaction factors and other additional notes before signing the e-contract. The buyer and the seller sign on the contract. Finally, the buyer decides whether or when to execute the option contract and the option comes to clearing and settlement.

4.2 System Architecture

The system architecture of FutureOTC is divided into four layers, as shown in Fig. 3.

(1) *First Layer: Blockchain Service Layer.* Obviously, the first layer is the foundation of FutureOTC. Our work is based on Consortium Blockchain: Hyperchain. Hyperchain is independently developed by Hangzhou Qulian Technology Co., Ltd. Once authenticated, the Consortium Blockchain automatically creates Blockchain accounts for users. The public key will be kept on Consortium Blockchain while the private key is encrypted and stored locally. The consensus algorithm is capable of allow 1/3 nodes' failure on Consortium Blockchain. It is called robust Byzantine Fault Tolerance, which will be discussed later. Smart Contracts play an important role in FutureOTC. Users can preset rules and call smart contracts though Blockchain interfaces. Smart contracts are like intelligent functions on distributed ledgers. Blockchain-based applications can call these intelligent functions to complete transactions and manipulate data, such as store data on Consortium Blockchain or pre-check the counterparty's balance.

(2) *Second Layer: Business Service Layer.* This layer is the core to FutureOTC. We implement our business logic and general service here. It consists of four services: general service, e-contract service, trading service and supervisor service. The general service is to provide access for users. Users must register first and wait to be approved. After conducting personal identity authentication or institutional identity authentication, the passed ones will get both a legal FutureOTC account and a Blockchain account. The FutureOTC account is used to conduct business manipulate business behaviors while the Blockchain account is for access control of the Consortium Blockchain. E-contract service is as described to offer e-contracts signing and archiving. FutureOTC also offers interface to inquiry users' history and unsigned e-contract. A template E-contract is provided for convenience. The trading service is the most important part. Participants acquire the market data to make final decisions. Once opportunities found, they click to strike. Transactions are pre-checked here and the counterparty's balance is checked by calling smart contract. Only transactions satisfied are in the queue waiting for a strike. After finishing the bilateral contract, the clearing is done on real time. Another significant part is supervisor service. This module allows supervisors to handle all market operations on FutureOTC. The Supervision work is done remotely 7 * 24 h. More importantly, if supervisors pre-set indexes to monitor the OTC market. Once the system financial risk comes closer to certain threshold, the supervisors get the first-hand information. They have more time to conduct strong

and decisive measures to quell risk events, such as banning on some participants or raising the requirement of trading balance etc.

(3) *Third Layer: Interface Layer.* This layer is easily confused with interfaces to call smart contracts on Consortium Blockchain. It provides a way to interact with external service such as sending instructions to banks, checking balance, sending transaction details and keeping the private key etc.

(4) *Fourth Layer: External service Layer.* This layer is for external services. We would not put everything on Consortium Blockchain, which is not necessary and stupid. Some Services may not require real time response. Some services is not provided on Consortium Blockchain. Then it is wise to put them on this layer.

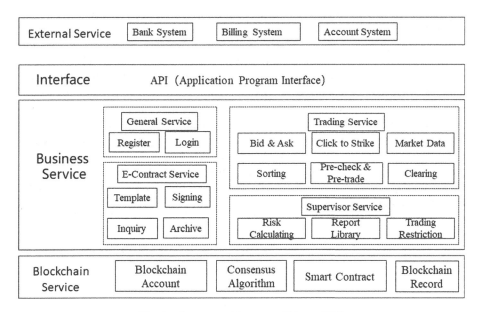

Fig. 3. System architecture of FutureOTC

4.3 Hyperchain Consensus

As mentioned in Sect. 4.2, the consensus algorithm is robust Byzantine Fault Tolerance, as shown in Fig. 4. RBFT reduces the traffic of the broadcast strategically by forwarding to Primary instead of broadcasting to the full-network. The nodes on Consortium Blockchain are divided into Primary node and Replica nodes. The Primary node is in charge of validating a batch of transactions while the Replica nodes can only validate and sort the transactions after the Primary node. There is one and only one Primary node any time on Consortium Blockchain. Once a consensus procedure achieved, the data and status of Primary node and Replica nodes synchronize data with each other. If the Primary node is out of service, the Consortium Blockchain automatically elects a new Primary node.

Suppose there are 3f + 1 nodes on Consortium Blockchain, where f stands for the number of failure or attacked nodes. RBFT consensus procedure is divided into 6 stages. In Transaction stage, A client sends received transaction via its connected node. In Batch stage, suppose Replica node 3 receives the transaction request and then forwards the transaction to Primary node. Primary node 1 receives the transaction. Once the transaction confirmed legal and compliance, it is put in the batching list of the Primary node. Primary node 1 computes the results of batching transactions and its hash value. In Pre-Prepare Stage, Primary node 1 broadcasts transactions, results, and hash value to full-network. In Prepare Stage, all Replicas receive the transactions sent by Primary node 1. They start to compute the results based on its ledger and check the hash value with that of the Primary node 1. If the hash values are the same, Replica node agrees with the Primary node 1 and send agreement message. Otherwise, Replica node does not send agreement message. In Commit stage, if Replica node receives 2f agreement messages that means a consensus status is reached. Replica node runs the transactions on its virtual machine. Otherwise, all nodes remain in the previous consensus status. In Write Back stage, if all Replica nodes receives 2f + 1 Commit messages, it means achieving a successful consensus process. All Replica nodes including Primary node will write the result into its ledger.

By adopting RBFT, Hyperchain reduces the burden of full-network broadcast. First, after receiving a new transaction, instead of computing itself and broadcasting the results, the Replica node forwards it to Primary node first and that reduces the bandwidth consumption. Second, the illegal transactions is removed immediately once the Primary finishes the validation which make sure illegal transactions do not consume the full-network computing power.

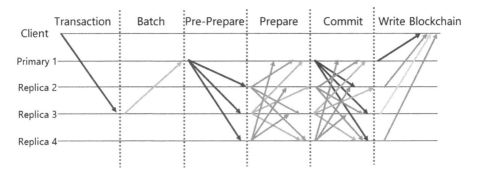

Fig. 4. Robust Byzantine fault tolerance algorithm

According to experiments, RBFT help Consortium Blockchain achieve a performance of 10000 transactions per second and with an average transaction delay of 300 ms.

5 The Specific Program

5.1 Authentication

In financial trading, authentication is extremely important. According to the law, service providers are in charge of adopting reliable technical or management measures to identify online investors because of the counterfeiting of identity. We come up with a way to solve the problem in identifying both personal and institutional users using Electronic Identity (EID) and Electronic Business License (EBL), as shown in Fig. 5.

EID is rooted in the citizenship number. The Ministry of Public Security generates EID based on cryptographic algorithms for Chinese Citizens. The uniqueness of EID to stand for digital identity is guaranteed.

EBL is a paperless electronic license. It records the registration items of the market subject in unified layout and format. EBL is signed by the market supervision and management department according to law.

Both the Ministry of Public Security and State Administration for Market Regulation can join Consortium Blockchain. If a personal user or an institutional user wants to become a customer in FutureOTC. He or she must goes to the Ministry of Public Security or State Administration for Market Regulation to apply for a valid EID or EBL. After that, they turn in the information Consortium Blockchain needed to contract with the Ministry of Public Security and State Administration for Market Regulation. Every time they log in or conduct critical behavior, they should identify themselves on Consortium Blockchain.

By introducing EID and EBL, we successfully identify users without Authentication Authority (CA) at low price for the verification of EID and EBL is free. More importantly, we are upward compatible with traditional CA system when necessary.

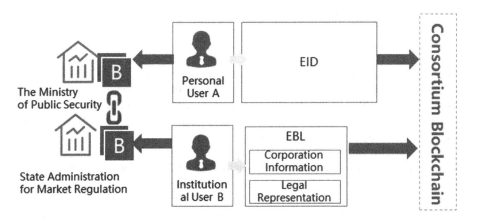

Fig. 5. Personal user authentication and institutional user authentication

5.2   Transaction Procedure

After passing users authentication, users are allocated accounts on Consortium Blockchain and be allowed to trade on FutureOTC. The transaction procedure is as shown in Fig. 6. Both the seller and the buyer connect to Consortium Blockchain via their client connected to specified node. Suppose Seller 1 is intend to issuance an option like this: he wants to sell an option at the price of 1000000.00 RMB to cover the risk of his business. The order is broadcasted on the full-network. Buyer 1 renews the market data and receives the broadcast. He is happy to catch the opportunity to take the risk and get the royalties. He clicks to strike. The transaction is sent to Primary node from one Replica node. The transaction is processed as we talked about in Sect. 4.3. Suppose the transaction is legal and compliant, the seller and the buyer sign an E-contract. Finally, the E-contract is reported to the supervisors and be stored on report library.

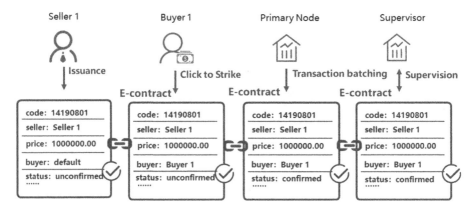

Fig. 6. An OTC option transaction procedure

5.3   E-contract Management

To confirm a transaction, an E-contract is necessary for both counterparties. The rights and obligations are listed on an E-contract. The status of an E-Contract is divided into seven statuses, i.e. Start, Template, Unconfirmed, Confirmed, Modified, Dismissed and End. They together form a full lifecycle for an E-contract. Through the states transitions of an E-contract, a transaction is completed (Fig. 7).

Start stands for the beginning of an E-contract. If a buyer or a seller finds a trading opportunity, he will click to launch a transaction. Then the E-contract turns from Start to Template. On Template status, the E-contract is filled with parameters getting from smart contract, such as price, time and counterparties. After that, the E-contract is signed by the seller or the buyer to confirm the behavior to take the risk and get the premium. After checking the parameters, the seller or the buyer signs the E-contract if he agrees with it. Then the E-contract turns from Template to Unconfirmed. The E-contract is sent to the counterparty and FutureOTC system starts counting down. If the counterparty finishes signing the E-contract within 10 min, the E-contract turns to Confirmed. Otherwise, if the counterparty fails to sign it in time or deny the E-contract,

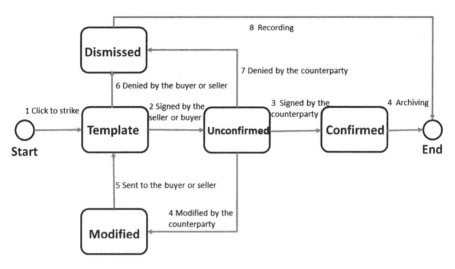

Fig. 7. E-contract state transition process

it turns to Dismiss. If the counterparty wishes to modify the E-contract, the E-contract turns to Modified. The Modified E-contract is sent to the other sponsor again. If the buyer or the seller agrees with its modification, it turns to Unconfirmed after signing on it. Otherwise, if the Modified E-contract fails to sign within 10 min or he is not agree with its modification, the E-contract turns to Dismissed. E-contract in Dismissed or Confirmed status is archived to End. The life cycle of an E-contract ends.

5.4   Smart Contracts

Smart contract plays an important role on FutureOTC. To meet the rule and compliance of OTC market, we do not use tokens or coins on FutureOTC. Users' balance data is acquired from external systems though it will increase the responding time. The result is stored on local database to reduce the response time for enquiring next time. To fully validate and prove the concept of smart contracts, we design four scenes to validate its execution characteristics.

(1) When a buyer or a seller raises an order, smart contract checks the balance to see if the order is legal. If the balance is enough, smart contract sends an instruction to lock part of the balance. Otherwise, smart contract sends a message to terminate the transaction.

(2) If a buyer of a seller decides to click to strike, smart contract does the similar things with that of procedure 1. If the counterparty has enough money, the transaction moves on to E-contract signing part. Otherwise, a signal is sent to terminate click to strike.

(3) If one party tries to sign on the contract, smart contract validates the EID of EBL to see whether it is qualified. Besides, smart contract checks whether the signature or the stamp is on the E-contract before sending it out.

(4) If a transaction comes to the end, smart contract makes sure the result is wrote to local database and sent to the supervisors' report library (Fig. 8).

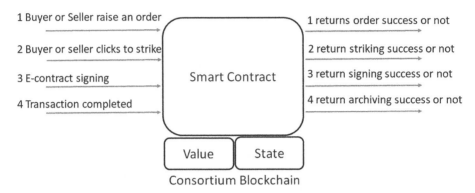

Fig. 8. Inputs and outputs of smart contract

Using smart contract, the risk of transactions is under control and the report library is updated real on time. All things are done without man's interpretation and efficiently.

5.5   Data Structure and Storage

On Consortium Blockchain, data blocks link with each other in time sequence. Generally, a data block consists of Public Data and Private Data, as shown in Fig. 9. Public Data has Order ID, Father Block, and Transaction Hash. Private Data is hash of a set of

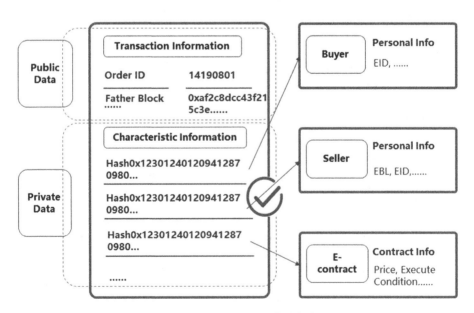

Fig. 9. Data structure of a block

privacy data, i.e. EID, EBL and E-contract. In this way, once the data is on Chain, outsiders can only see an abstract of a transaction. Its details remains confidential to others while the hash is on Consortium Blockchain. Transaction Details are stored on local database and sent to report library.

Data is heterogeneously stored on FutureOTC. Data in hash format is stored on Consortium Blockchain while data on transaction details is stored locally and sent to report library. Smart contract helps send transaction details to the supervisors automatically.

6 Experiment and Evaluation

In this section, our purpose is to test the efficiency and responding time of FutureOTC. The experiment uses 5 servers, with a total of 4 nodes on Consortium Blockchain. Another one acts as an application server. All servers are unified in configuration, which have 8 core, 16G memory and 500G hard drive. We use Hyperchain 1.6.15 and MySQL 14.14. The experiments conducted are in two perspectives: transaction per second and the latency. The result is shown in Fig. 10. FutureOTC completes 100 to 200 transaction per second and its corresponding latency is around 600 to 1000 ms. Considering the low frequency of the OTC option trading, we think FutureOTC can meet the daily needs. Because the total transaction amount is less than 5000 in one month. Besides, Users get a response from FutureOTC within one second and the responding speed of FutureOTC is acceptable.

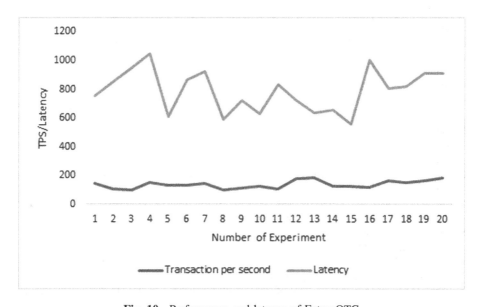

Fig. 10. Performance and latency of FutureOTC

7 Conclusion and Future Work

In this paper, we present FutureOTC - a decentralized and intelligent system for China's OTC market. FutureOTC takes advantage of EID and EBL to solve the problem of authentication in low cost. At the meantime, we put up a state transition process for handling E-contracts. In addition, we use smart contracts to automatically judge transaction conditions and send instructions. By using heterogeneous storage method, we successfully isolate public data with private data on Consortium Blockchain. Hash of a transaction is public on Consortium Blockchain while details remain in report library and user's local database. This helps supervisors get market operations at first hand and on real time to evaluate market risk dynamically.

Never the less, there are still some problems. We have encountered with the problem of storing files on Consortium Blockchain. The storage and query efficiency of files is quite low. We have to use structured and unstructured data instead of an encrypted file. Besides, the performance of FutureOTC is not as good as expected. Our performance is one-fiftieth of its best TPS. We believe there is much space to make progress.

To solve the problems above in the future, we may considering moving services to external system or to the middleware. And we will be working on optimizing smart contract to make it faster and more intelligent.

References

1. Jian, C.: Development Status, Core and Application of OTC Options, April 2018. http://www.ewww.com.cn
2. Soonduck, Y.: Blockchain based financial case analysis and its implications. Asia Pac. J. Innov. Entrep. **11**(3), 312–321 (2017)
3. Molodie, L.: The Blockchain Revolution: New Opportunities in Equity Markets (2016). https://dspace.mit.edu
4. Thomas, O., et al.: Blockchain in Financial Markets: How to Gain an Edge (2017). http://www.bain.com
5. Robert, B., Moritz, P.: OTC-Derivatives and Distributed Ledger Technology: A scenario on how blockchain could disrupt the prevailing post-trading landscape (2018). https://www.bearingpoint.com
6. Felipe, C.: Blockchain Technology: Between High Hopes and Challenging Implications (2018). https://works.bepress.com
7. Su, Z.H., Zhao, L.: Analysis and Suggestions on the Development Status of OTC Derivatives Market in China (2018). http://www.sse.com.cn
8. Lei, X.B.: The nature of options trading and the core of legal regulation. Futures Financ. Deriv. **104**, 34–40 (2018)
9. Xing, M.: Research on the Application and Supervision of Blockchain Technology in the Securities Field (2018). http://www.sse.com.cn
10. Qian, Q.M., et al.: Application of intelligent blockchain in the OTC market. China Securities, vol. 5, pp. 19–26 (2019)
11. Zhu, L., Yu, H., et al.: Research on high-performance consortium blockchain technology. J. Softw. **30**(6), 1577–1593 (2019)

One-Stop Efficient PKI Authentication Service Model Based on Blockchain

Tao Feng[(✉)], Wuyang Chen[(✉)], Di Zhang, and Chunyan Liu

Lanzhou University of Technology, Lanzhou 730050, China
fengt@lut.cn, 820680184@qq.com

Abstract. Public Key Infrastructure (PKI) technology is a widely used identity authentication technology. This paper uses blockchain technology to improve it and implements decentralized PKI authentication, which resolves the issues in the traditional PKI such as single point of failure and certificate transparency. However, most of the current research uses the method of traversing the blockchain to query the certificate (identity, public key) to realize identity authentication, which is inefficient. And as the size of blockchain continues to grow, storage overhead is growing. In this paper, we combine the blockchain and the dynamic accumulator to construct a blockchain PKI model that can batch update certificates, which improves the efficiency of identity authentication. The model can effectively add, revoke and update user certificates. Meanwhile, this paper builds a one-stop PKI authentication service model based on blockchain, Through the certificate blockchain, we can provide one-stop user authentication service to third-party service providers. Finally, we verify the security and effectiveness of the scheme.

Keywords: Blockchain · Dynamic accumulator · PKI · One-stop identity authentication

1 Introduction

PKI is a universal security infrastructure that provides information security services based on public key cryptography, so that users can communicate and make e-commerce transactions through a series of trust relationships based on certificates when they do not know each other's identity. As the foundation and core of current network security, PKI is the basic guarantee for e-commerce security development. To ensure the secure transmission of information, an effective PKI system must be secure and transparent. However, faced with the biggest problem that the CAs are not trusted, traditional centralized PKI in a distributed environment results in an untrustworthy problem of the identity of the entity. A CA that is attacked or maliciously issues certificate will bring significant security risks to the information system. The hacker can achieve a man-in-the-middle attack by attacking a trusted CA to perform malicious operations, such as issuing a user's certificate containing false information. The user cannot verify the process of issuing a certificate by CAs, and there is a certificate transparency issue. In addition, the centralized CA management architecture will lead to

X. Si et al. (Eds.): CBCC 2019, CCIS 1176, pp. 31–47, 2020.
https://doi.org/10.1007/978-981-15-3278-8_3

single point of failure [1]. As a new type of distributed technology that cannot be tampered with, blockchain brings new ideas to the implementation of decentralized PKI.

At present, the blockchain-based PKI uses the blockchain to store information such as identity and public key. In the process of implementing identity authentication, the method of traversing the blockchain is generally used to look up the certificate, and then check whether the public key belongs to its declared identity. Finally, verifying the digital signature to determine whether the other party holds the matching private key by sending a challenge information. However, the block-chain is a public chain that can only be added. Its characteristics ensure that the amount of data will continue to grow. In recent years, the blockchain has exceeded 100 Gb in volume and will continue to grow in the future. By then, the method of traversing the blockchain will be more inefficient, and the time required for identity authentication will be difficult to meet the actual needs. At the same time, such a large amount of data cannot be stored for carriers such as mobile phones. The dynamic accumulator maps a collection containing multiple elements to an accumulated value and provides a smaller witness to prove that a given element does belong to the set. Its introduction can resolve the issue that member verification is inefficient in the process of identity authentication.

In this paper, we improve the traditional PKI model by using dynamic accumulator and blockchain, and propose a PKI authentication service model based on blockchain. First, we build an interaction model between users, miners, and supervisory nodes. The miner is responsible for the distribution and management of the certificate, at the same time, provides authorization tickets to third-party service providers. The supervisory node reviews the transaction submitted by the user and ensures the consistency of the block transaction with miners through the consensus mechanism. It resolves the problem of single point of failure and certificate transparency in the traditional PKI. Secondly, in view of the shortage of certificate management methods, this paper proposes a certificate management method that can batch update and revoke certificates based on dynamic accumulators, which improves the efficiency of identity authentication. Thirdly, this paper builds a one-stop PKI authentication service model based on blockchain to ensure that users can access the third-party services by registering the certificate simply in the certificate blockchain. Finally, we analyze the security of the scheme in detail, and the results show that the scheme can resist the enemy forgery attack and Sybil attack. In terms of efficiency, the space complexity of storage overhead is $O(1)$.

The rest of the paper is organized as follows: In Sect. 2, we introduce the relevant research of blockchain-based PKI systems. In Sect. 3 we introduce the supporting techniques of this scheme. In Sect. 4, we describe the system model, security model and threat model. The specific construction of the program is discussed in detailed in Sect. 5. A security analysis and efficiency analysis for the scheme are described in Sect. 6. In Sect. 7 we compare the relevant scheme. Section 8 draws a conclusion of our scheme.

2 Related Work

An important application of blockchain in the direction of identity authentication is to build a distributed public PKI based on blockchain [2]. PKI can be established based on public general ledger, which can eliminate the trust center CA of PKI and realize real distributed PKI construction.

In 2014, MIT scholar Conner proposed the first distributed PKI solution based on blockchain which called Certcoin [3, 4]. The core idea is to record the user certificate through the public general ledger, and associate the user identity with the certificate public key in a public manner to realize the decentralized PKI construction. Any user can query the certificate issuance process and resolve the issue of certificate transparency and CA single point of failure. Certcoin implements the registration, update and revocation of certificates by publishing users and their public keys in the form of blockchain transactions. The normal operation of the PKI is guaranteed by the attributes of the blockchain that cannot be tampered with. The Merkle root only records the hash value of the transaction, and users do not need to download all blockchain transaction data to complete the verification of the certificate. However, on the one hand, Certcoin cannot prevent the illegal occupancy of legitimate users like other schemes. On the other hand, the scheme completes the user's certificate revocation by retaining the certificate blacklist and periodically recalculating the accumulator from zero, which will increase the computational overhead.

Authcoin is a decentralized PKI scheme proposed by Benjamin [5]. To reduce illegal occupancy and Sybil attack, Authcoin emphasizes the actual binding of the user when registering the public key by adding a complex challenge response step that makes it resilient to Sybil attack. However, as the number of interactive communication steps increases, so does the performance cost. This scheme does not take into account the credibility of the person performing the operations during the verification and authentication process.

BIX protocol is more flexible for cyber-attack and doesn't cause single point of failure [6]. The BIX protocol is designed to distribute the role of CAs and preserve security features. In fact, the BIX protocol is designed with a blockchain-like structure, with a decentralized structure replacing CAs, which implements distributed certificate distribution. The certificate is a block in the blockchain, an effective user can attach their certificates to the blockchain by proper interaction protocol. Then Longo et al. proposed improvements to the BIX protocol and security proof. The formalized analysis shows the PKI system based on BIX protocol is more suitable for large-scale network attacks than the standard PKI protocol based on CA [7]. However, the protocol is still incomplete and there are no steps to revoke and update certificates.

Matsumoto et al. proposed a timely and automatic response PKI framework IKP (instant karma PKI) [8]. Based on the Ethereum platform, IKP uses the smart contract and consensus mechanism to stimulate the CA center to issue certificates correctly. It introduces detector to give reward to report illegal certificates, and imposes financial penalties on CAs that issue illegal certificates. In addition, the detector also needs to pay for the report. If the reported certificate is indeed an illegal certificate, the detector will receive a corresponding reward which can effectively prevent the detector from reporting all certificates to defraud the reward. However, the problem is that a malicious user may maliciously register a fake identity for execution fraud.

BKI is a blockchain-based PKI [9]. It uses a tunable number of CAs to issue certificates, but it is not extendable. In addition, BKI requires all clients to contact third parties (blockchain-based log maintainers) during certificate verification, which can cause latency and privacy issues. Syta et al. proposed an efficient method for joint signature of statements issued by CA using multiple signatures [10]. Each certificate requires a certain number of witnesses to sign together in order to be accepted by others. Therefore, even if an attacker compromises a certain privilege, all malicious statements need to be made public before being used for the attack. But CoSi needs to be coordinated in the cosign protocol and relies on direct communication between witnesses. In addition, the security of CoSi is still limited by its weakest link, because witnesses only approve statements issued by CA, without full domain verification, and the attacker can still exploit the vulnerability. Based on base on BKI and Cosi, Dykcik et al. propose an automated public key infrastructure relying on smart contracts called BlockPKI [11], in which CAs use multi-signature to sign and verify certificates. BlockPKI uses the smart contract to realize the automated certificate creation and the automated domain verification, and it encourages the CAs to participate in the authentication and obtain the reward.

Qin et al. proposed a distributed certificate scheme called Cecoin [12]. Cecoin treats certificates as currency processing and records them on the blockchain to eliminate single points of failure. Miners can verify the validity of a certificate against a set of rules to ensure consistency of ownership and allow identity to bind multiple public key certificates. At the same time, based on the Merkle Patricia tree, this paper describes the distributed management of certificates, including efficient retrieval and verification of certificates, and fast operations, also supports the transaction of certificates. However, this solution does not consider the correspondence between nodes and identities. One identity can correspond to several certificates, which will lead to the risk of being attacked by Sybil. At the same time, for the average user, it cannot withstand the huge storage overhead brought by the distributed certificate library.

3   Preliminary Knowledge

3.1   Cryptographic Accumulator

Benaloh et al. first proposed the use of a cryptographic accumulator as a decentralized digital signature alternative in 1993 [13]. It is a constant size representation of a set of elements. When an element is added to the cryptographic accumulator, a witness is generated that can be used to prove that the added element has been accumulated.

Definition 1. The cryptographic accumulator scheme consists of the following four polynomial time algorithms:

KeyGen(k, M): A probabilistic algorithm for instantiating a scheme. Enter the security parameter 1^k and the upper bound M on the number of accumulated elements, returning an accumulator key $\mathcal{P} = (PK, SK)$ where PK is the public key and SK is the private key.

AccVal$(L, \mathcal{P})$: A probabilistic algorithm for calculating the cumulative value. Enter a set of elements $L = \{c_1, \ldots, c_m\}(1 \leq m \leq M)$ based on set C and parameters $\mathcal{P}$, returning an accumulated value v and auxiliary information Aux that can be used by other algorithms.

WitGen$(a_c, Aux, \mathcal{P})$: A probabilistic algorithm that generates a witness for an element. Enter auxiliary information Aux, parameters $\mathcal{P}$, and elements $c_i\{i = 1, \ldots, m\}$, and if the element c_i is indeed in the collection L, return a corresponding witness W_i.

Verify(c_i, W_i, v, PK): A deterministic algorithm that checks if a given element is in the accumulated value v. Input c_i, W_i, v, and accumulator public key PK, verify whether c_i is accumulated in v according to W_i, then output Yes or No.

Applying a password accumulator to authentication not only enables efficient authentication, but also ensures security. However, when a general password accumulator adds or deletes an element, it needs to recalculate the current accumulated value and the respective witnesses. The accumulator cannot operate efficiently to cope with the actual application requirements when the element set dynamically changes. How to ensure that the accumulated value and the witness of each element can be updated and revoked efficiently when the set of elements changes. Thus, Camenisch and Lysyanskaya proposed the concept of a dynamic accumulator [14]. The dynamic accumulator accumulates a set of input values into a value such that the input values can prove themselves in the accumulated value, while allowing the operator to dynamically add or delete a value such that the cost of adding or deleting is independent of the number of members being added. In 2008, Peishun Wang et al. summarized the formal definition of the accumulator and proposed a new dynamic accumulator [15]. The dynamic accumulator adds adding, deleting and updating operations on the four algorithms of the original accumulator scheme.

Definition 2: A dynamic accumulator consists of the following seven polynomial time algorithms:

KeyGen, AccVal, WitGen and Verify are consistent with the algorithm in Definition 1.

Add$(L^+, Aux, v, \mathcal{P})$: A probability algorithm for adding new elements to the accumulated value. Enter a set of new elements $L^+ = \{c_1^+, \ldots, c_k^+\}(L^+ \subset C, 1 \leq k \leq M - m)$ that are to be added, the auxiliary information Aux, the accumulated values v and the parameters $\mathcal{P}$, return the new accumulated value v' corresponding to the set $L^+ \cup L$, the witness $W_1^+, \ldots, W_k^+$ of the newly added element $\{c_1^+, \ldots, c_k^+\}$ and the new auxiliary information Aux' for future updates.

Delete$(L^-, Aux, v, \mathcal{P})$: A probability algorithm for deleting certain elements. Enter a set of elements $L^-\{c_1^-, \ldots, c_k^-\}$ $(L^- \subset L, 1 \leq k < m)$ that are to be deleted, auxiliary information Aux, the accumulated values v and the parameters $\mathcal{P}$, and output a new accumulated value v' corresponding to the set $L \backslash L^-$, and the new auxiliary information Aux' being used in future update operations.

UpdWit(W_i, Aux, pk): Deterministic algorithm for updating the witness of element which has been added to v'. Enter the witness W_i, the auxiliary information Aux, and the accumulator public key pk, return an updated witness W_i'.

3.2   Complexity Assumption

Let $n = pq$, p, q are different odd prime numbers, so the elements in the multiplicative group Z_n^* which contains $\phi(n) = (p-1)(q-1)$ elements are all positive integers smaller than n and mutually prime with n. $\phi(n)$ is the Euler function and $\phi(n^2) = n\phi(n)$. Carmichael number $\lambda(n) = lcm(p-1, q-1)$, $\lambda(n^2) = lcm((p-1)p, (q-1)q)$. There are three difficult assumptions described as below.

Strong RSA Assumption: Given the security parameters n and random numbers $y \in Z_n^*$, there is no polynomial time algorithm to find s and x make $y \equiv x^s \pmod{n}$.

CSR Assumption: Given security parameters n, integers $s \in Z_{n^2}^* (s > 2)$ and random numbers $y \in Z_{n^2}^*$, there is no polynomial time algorithm to find out $x \in Z_n$ and make $y \equiv x^s \pmod{n^2}$.

es-RSA Assumption: Given the security parameters n and random numbers $y \in Z_{n^2}^*$, there is no polynomial time algorithm to find s and $x \in Z_n$ make $y \equiv x^s \pmod{n^2}$, where $n^2 > s > 2$.

Lemma 1: If the CSR hypothesis and the strong RSA assumption are true, the es-RSA assumption is true.

4   System Model

Conner Fromknecht proposed in Certcoin that there are two ways to deploy a password accumulator in a blockchain [3]. One is that each user node maintains its own password accumulator, and the other is that the entire blockchain maintains one Cryptographic accumulator. Since the general cryptographic accumulator accumulates the number of elements subject to the threshold, it is not sufficient to maintain only one accumulator in the blockchain, especially as the number of users in the blockchain increases. Therefore, this paper adopts the method of grouping users. Each user group jointly maintains a password accumulator. Since this paper uses the dynamic accumulator proposed by [15], its own function of batch dynamic update members can be a very good solution to the problem of not being able to effectively test new members (values) in [3]. Compared with the global accumulator and the solution for accumulator information attached to each block proposed in [3], our solution is relatively simple, and the required storage space is small, which effectively saves computational overhead and improves verification efficiency.

The system model of the proposed scheme is shown in the Fig. 1. The whole system includes five participating entities: user, miner node, supervisory node, certificate blockchain and third-party service provider.

- User: Submit the identity and its own public key to the supervisory node for investigation in the registration phase. After joining the system, apply to the miner node or query the blockchain to obtain its own witness for future identity authentication.
- Miner node: Initialize the system, generate the system parameter, accumulate the initial participating user information and output the initial accumulated value and the witness corresponding to each user. Select certificate transactions signed by the

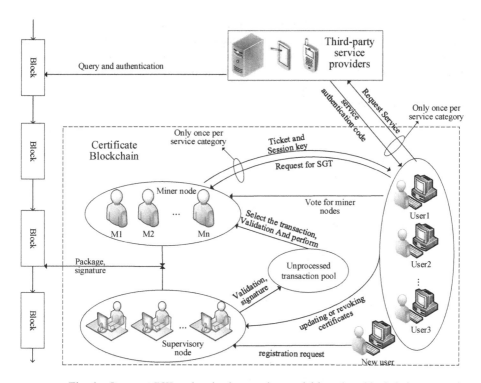

Fig. 1. One-stop PKI authentication service model based on blockchain

supervisory node and execute the corresponding algorithm, then package the corresponding information into blocks for broadcast to the network. Provides the user with a Server-Granting Ticket (SGT). Receives the authorization request sent by the user, verifies and returns session key $K_{c,V}$ and the SGT $Ticket_V$ for the user to use. The miner node was initially 21.

- Supervisory node: It is composed of 11 institutions (such as government agencies, core enterprise nodes, etc.), which are responsible for receiving user certificate registration, update or revocation requests, and questioning the transaction initiator. After verification, sign the transaction and sent it to the Pool for further processing.
- Certificate blockchain: After the miner node broadcasts new block information, the supervisory node and other miner nodes respectively verify the block, and after the consensus is reached, the block is mined.
- Third-party service providers: Provide third-party applications or services to users. Receive user service requests, verify and provide related services. Third-party service providers itself have completed the authentication in the certificate blockchain, that is, each service *ID* has a corresponding witness.

When A proves identity to B, since the nodes in the blockchain are divided into full nodes and light nodes, the efficiency of identity verification is different corresponding to the different node states of B. If B is a full node, you must query all the locally stored information on the chain, that is, traverse the entire blockchain. The authentication efficiency decreases as the blockchain size increases. If B is a light node, the local area is not stored. Blockchain, unable to authenticate, can only request queries from all nodes, which will traverse the blockchain again. The introduction of a dynamic cryptographic accumulator can alleviate the problem of reducing authentication efficiency due to the increase in blockchain size. The authentication procedure of introducing of the dynamic accumulator is improved as follows:

1. A sends to B (c_A, W_A, pk_A, v_A), where $c_A = h(id_A, AD_A)$, h is a hash function, AD_A is a hash of the network address which uses the unidirectionality of the hash function to guarantee One-to-one correspondence between c_A, id_A and AD_A, at the same time, it can ensure that the private information is not stolen. It is called that witness W_A belongs to user c_A.
2. B compares the accumulated value v with v_A which query from the blockchain, if they are consistent, then B runs the algorithm Verify(c_A, W_A, v, PK) to verify Whether the user's identity and witness are legal.
3. B sends a random challenge string ch to A, A signs $\sigma = sig(sk_A, ch)$ for the information containing the string.
4. B uses pk_A to verify the digital signature, if Verify$(pk_A, \sigma, ch) = 1$, it proves that A holds the private key sk_A, that means A has identity $c_A(id_A, AD_A)$.

4.1   Threat Model

This article assumes that communication is secure, it means the private keys of participating entities and systems are not compromised. This makes the supervisory nodes in the proposed scheme completely credible; most miners are honest but curious, will participate in block production and certificate registration, revocation and update according to the rules, but may steal users when participating. Identity privacy information. For the miner node M1 that is partially faulty or evil, when it does not produce the block or even falsify the false certificate according to the regulations, the right of the production block is handed over to the next miner node M2; some users are malicious and may initiate false transactions and malicious preemption registration, even forgery of identity and witness.

4.2   Security Model

In this paper, we define the security model of this scheme by the Chosen Element Attack security game which is described as follows:

Setup: The challenger $\mathcal{B}$ executes the initialization algorithm, and the adversary $\mathcal{A}$ adaptively selects a set of elements $L^* \in C$ to send to the challenger who calculates their accumulated value and witness return to the adversary.

Query: The adversary $\mathcal{A}$ chooses the element to be added or the element to be deleted and sends it to the challenger $\mathcal{B}$. The challenger returns the witness of the added element after adding or deleting, the new accumulated value, and the auxiliary information of the updated witness. The adversary calculates the witness after each element is updated.

Challenge: After performing several inquiries, the adversary $\mathcal{A}$ selects a set of elements $L \in C$ to send to the challenger $\mathcal{B}$, and the challenger returns the corresponding accumulated value and witness. The adversary gives an element c_i and its corresponding witness W_i, then sent them to the challenger who verifies whether the element and its corresponding witness are legal, that is mean, whether the element has been accumulated in the accumulator.

If the polynomial time adversary $\mathcal{A}$ forges a legitimate element c_i and witness W_i with a non-negligible advantage, the witness W_i can prove that the element is included in the set corresponding to the accumulated value, which means that the adversary can forge a legal certificate, and the adversary wins this game.

5 Specific Construction

In this part, we present the specific algorithm structure and concrete implementation of the blockchain-based PKI authentication service model.

1. *Initialization:* First, a node group elects miner nodes according to the consensus mechanism such as DPOS, and the miner node M1 with the highest weight creates a security parameter n of length k-bit and an empty set A_u. Let $C = Z_{n^2}^* \backslash \{1\}$, $T' = \{3, \cdots, n^2\}$, set the initial participating member list $L = \{c_1, \ldots, c_m\}$, the number of members m $1 \le m \le M$, then proceed with the following steps:

   - Adaptability choose $\sigma \in Z_{n^2}$, calculate $\beta = \sigma\lambda \mod \phi(n^2)$, $\beta \in T'$. Uniform random choose $\gamma \xleftarrow{R} Z_{\phi(n^2)}$, $\gamma \notin (\beta, \sigma)$, remember the dynamic accumulator key $\mathcal{P} = (PK, SK)$, where $PK = (n, \beta)$ $SK = (\sigma, \lambda, \gamma)$.
   - Choose $c_{m+1} \xleftarrow{R} C$, calculates

$$x_i = F(c_i^{\gamma\sigma^{-1}} \mod n^2) \mod n \ (i = 1, \cdots, m+1),$$

$$v = \sigma \sum_{i=1}^{m+1} x_i \mod n,$$

$$y_i = c_i^{\gamma\beta^{-1}} \mod n^2 \ (i = 1, \cdots, m+1),$$

$$a_c = \prod_{i=1}^{m+1} y_i \mod n^2$$

(1)

   Output initial v_0, auxiliary information a_c and $A_l = (y_1, \cdots, y_m)$. P.S. $F(x) = (x-1)/n$.
   - Package v_0, a_c, A_l and other related parameters into block and broadcast to network. If block is verified by other miners and supervisory nodes, mining blocks will be successful. Otherwise mining right takes turns to the next miner node M2. The initialization is completed.

2. *Certificate generation:* After the system is initialized, the accumulated users can calculate their own witnesses according to the information disclosed on the blockchain, or they can initiate an application to the miner node, and the miner node signs the corresponding witness. The specific steps are as follows:

Query to get existing auxiliary information a_c, A_l parameters $\mathcal{P}$, and randomly select a collection $T = (t_1, \cdots, t_m) \subset T' \backslash \{\beta, \gamma\}$ and calculated:

$$w_i = a_c y_i^{\frac{-t_i}{\gamma}} \bmod n^2 \quad (i = 1, \cdots, m) \tag{2}$$

$W_i = (w_i, t_i)$ is the witness for the user c_i. Think of the $(c_i = h(id_i, AD_i), W_i, pk_i, v_i)$ quad as the user's public key certificate.

3. *Verify:* Give c_i, W_i, v and PK, check if $\{c_i, w_i\} \subset C$, $t_i \in T'$ and $F(w_i^\beta c_i^{t_i} \bmod n^2) \equiv v \pmod{n}$, if true, output Yes which proved the user c_i has indeed been accumulated in v, otherwise output No.

4. *New user certificate registration:* The new user c_i^+ submits encrypted identity information c_i, id_i, AD_i, and public key pk_i to the supervisory node, initiates a registration transaction request, the supervisory node checks $c_A = h(id_A, AD_A)$ and initiates an acknowledgment to the network address. If supervisory node receives the acknowledgment, that is, the verification transaction can be legal. Then supervisory node signs and puts the transaction into the unprocessed transaction pool. The miner node selects some new user certificate registration transactions from the pool, which is recorded as the set $L^+ = \{c_1^+, \ldots, c_k^+\}$ to be added. Then select $c_{k+1} \overset{R}{\leftarrow} C$ and $T^+ = \{t_1^+, \ldots, t_k^+\} \overset{R}{\leftarrow} T' \backslash \{T \cup \{\beta, \gamma\}\}$, calculate:

$$
\begin{aligned}
x_i^+ &= F((c_i^+)^{\gamma\sigma^{-1}} \bmod n^2) \bmod n \quad (i = 1, \cdots, k+1), \\
v' &= v + \sigma \sum_{i=1}^{k+1} x_i^+ \bmod n, \\
y_i^+ &= (c_i^+)^{\gamma\beta^{-1}} \bmod n^2 \quad (i = 1, \cdots, k+1), \\
a_u &= \prod_{i=1}^{k+1} y_i^+ \bmod n^2, \\
w_i^+ &= a_u a_c (y_i^+)^{\frac{-t_i^+}{\gamma}} \bmod n^2 \quad (i = 1, \cdots, k+1)
\end{aligned}
\tag{3}
$$

Let $T = T \cup T^+$, $A_u = A_u \cup \{a_u\}$, $a_c = a_c a_u \bmod n^2$, then get new accumulated values v', new auxiliary information a_u, a_c and new witnesses $W_i^+ = (w_i^+, t_i^+)$ of user c_i^+. Being similar to the initialization, the miner node packages the corresponding information and broadcasts, and other miners add the new block to the blockchain. In addition, the recommended value is in the actual application.

5. *User certificate revocation:* The pre-revoked user c_i^- presents his own witness $W_i = (w_i, t_i)$ and signature σ to the supervisory node, initiates an identity revocation

request, and also counts the signature into the unprocessed transaction pool. The miner node selects some user identity revocation transactions from the unprocessed transaction pools, which is recorded as the set $L^-\{c_1^-,\ldots,c_k^-\}$ $(L^- \subset L, 1 \le k < m)$ to be revoked. For a user identity revocation transaction, the supervisory node first verifies the signature σ to verify that the witness actually belongs to the user, and then proceeds to step 3 to verify that the user identity has been accumulated.

If yes, select $c_{k+1}^- \xleftarrow{R} C$ and calculate:

$$x_i^- = F((c_i^-)^{\gamma\sigma^{-1}} \bmod n^2) \bmod n \quad (i = 1, \cdots, k+1),$$

$$v' = v - \sigma \sum_{i=1}^{k} x_i^- + \sigma x_{k+1}^- \bmod n$$

$$y_i^- = (c_i^-)^{\gamma\beta^{-1}} \bmod n^2 \quad (i = 1, \cdots, k+1),$$ (4)

$$a_u = y_{k+1}^- \prod_{i=1}^{k} (y_i^-)^{-1} \bmod n^2$$

Let $a_c = a_c a_u \bmod n^2$, $A_u = A_u \cup \{a_u\}$ then get the new accumulated value v', the new auxiliary information a_c and a_u. Then, being similar to the initialization, the miner node packages and broadcasts the corresponding information. Other miners and supervisory nodes verify and add the new block to the blockchain, and the certificate revocation transaction is recorded on the chain. The witness $W_i = (w_i, t_i)$ expires, that is, the user certificate has expired.

6. *Certificate update:* There are two ways to update a certificate. The first is to update the witness only. User presents his own witness and signature to the supervisory node, initiates a certificate update transaction request, which is verified into the unprocessed transaction pool. The miner node selects some user certificate update transactions from the pool, which is recorded as the set $L'\{c_1,\ldots,c_k\}(L' \subset L, 1 \le k < m)$ to be updated. Then it calculates $w_i' = w_i a_u \bmod n^2$ and the user's update witness is $W_i' = (w_i', t_i)$. t_i is generated when the user is added to the accumulator, it remains the same, and only changes with witness update and other transactions. Therefore, t_i can also be used as an alternative identifier in the accumulator.

It should be noted that each certificate has a corresponding time stamp and accumulator related information. Whenever a miner performs a certificate transaction, the parameters a_u are updated once and are credited to the collection A_u. When a user initiates a certificate update transaction, the miner needs to query the user's for finding the elements $a_{u_i} (i = 1 \cdots k)$ in the collection A_u from last certificate update or registration to this time, k is the number of times for a_u changes between the last certificate update and this transaction. Calculate $a_u = a_{u_1} \cdots a_{u_k} \bmod n^2$, $w_i' = w_i a_u \bmod n^2$, then the user's new witness is $W_i' = (w_i', t_i)$. In this way, the user certificate update is independent of the change of the accumulated value.

The second way is to update the witness and key. The user submits c_i, $W_i = (w_i, t_i)$, pk_i, pk_i', AD_i and v_i, where pk_i' is the new public key. When the user issues a request transaction to update the key, the supervisory node first performs a third step to verify that the user is registered and verifies the consistency of the network address with the user. Then find the current certificate of the user and verify that pk and pk_i are consistent. This is to prevent the adversary from maliciously updating the user certificate with the old public key that the user has previously leaked. After the verification, the miner updates the user's witness, then packages the user's new public key and other information into block and broadcastes. Other nodes verify the block and add it to blockchain.

7. *User-service authentication exchange:* The specific description is shown in Table 1. The user c sends c, id_V of the service and the witness W_c to the miners for Server-Granting Ticket, and the miner returns the session key $K_{c,V}$ and SGT $Ticket_V$. Then user c sends $Ticket_V$ and $Authenticator_c$ to the third-party service provider V, and the server provider gives corresponding respond after verification. If mutual authentication is required, a reply message should be sent to c according to message (4) by V. Obviously, the message is encrypted by $K_{c,V}$, which guarantees that the message is only generated by V, and confirms the source of the message by verifying W_V.

$Authenticator_c$ is a legal authentication ticket generated by the user which ensures that the owner of the ticket is the same as the owner when the SGT generated. $Authenticator_c$ can only be used once and has a very short lifetime. Miner queries blockchain for pk_c according to id_c and W_c to make decryption of the authentication ticket. The session key $K_{c,V}$ is issued by the miner to ensure secure exchange of information between the user and the third-party service provider. AD_c is network address that used to prevent the ticket from being used on wrong workstations. *Lifetime* is used to prevent the ticket from using after it expires; TS is a timestamp for the ticket.

Table 1. User-service authentication exchange

Object	The message format
(1) $c \rightarrow$ Miner	$c\|\|W_c\|\|id_V\|\|Authenticator_c$
(2) Miner $\rightarrow c$	$c\|\|Ticket_V\|\|E(pk_c, [K_{c,V}\|\|id_V\|\|TS_2])$
	$Ticket_V = E(pk_V, [K_{c,V}\|\|id_c\|\|AD_c\|\|TS_2\|\|Lifetime])$
	$Authenticator_c = E(sk_c, [AD_c\|\|TS_1])$
(3) $c \rightarrow V$	$c\|\|W_c\|\|Ticket_V\|\|Authenticator_c$
(4) $V \rightarrow c$	$E(K_{c,V}, [W_V\|\|TS_3 + 1])$
	$Ticket_V = E(pk_V, [K_{c,V}\|\|id_c\|\|AD_c\|\|TS_2\|\|Lifetime])$
	$Authenticator_c = E(sk_c, [AD_c\|\|TS_3])$

6 Security Analysis

According to the attack form summarized in the threat model, if the user issues a false transaction, the miner node can detect whether the transaction is legal when packing the block. When the enemy maliciously seizes the identity of others for registration, he must submit $c = h(id, AD)$ and pk_c, and the supervisory node initiates an acknowledgment to the network address. If the network address is false, no agreement can be reached between c, id and AD, no malicious preemption is formed. If true, the preempted user will receive a confirmation message, then he can refuse to register and the transaction is invalid. In order to achieve the preemption registration, the adversary must ensure that the preempted user cannot receive the confirmation message and reply to the supervisory node with the correct network address, so that the certificate ownership belongs to the preempted user, as long as he logs in, the certificate can be found, and the preempted user can revise the certificate at any time.

Theorem 1. Based on the es-RSA assumption, this scheme can resist Chosen Element Attack.

Proof. Assume that a polynomial time adversary $\mathcal{A}$ wins a CEA game with a non-negligible advantage in a defined security model, which means that for input (n, β), the adversary $\mathcal{A}$ gets l elements $L^* : \{c_1, \cdots, c_l\} \subset C$, $\{W_1, \cdots, W_l\}$ and corresponding accumulated values v, he can find element $c' \in C \backslash \{c_1, \cdots, c_l\}$ and corresponding $W' = (w', t')$ make $F(w'^\beta c'^{t'} \bmod n^2) \equiv v (\bmod n)$ with a non-negligible advantage. This paper constructs the following simulator $\mathcal{B}$ to break the es-RSA hypothesis with a non-negligible advantage.

Initialization. $\mathcal{B}$ runs the initialization algorithm and gets the relevant system parameters, the accumulated values v and witnesses of l elements $L^* : \{c_1, \cdots, c_l\} \subset C$, the adversary request, and $\mathcal{A}$ requests $L^* : \{c_1, \cdots, c_l\} \subset C$, v and $\{W_1, \cdots, W_l\}$ from $\mathcal{B}$.

Query 1. The adversary $\mathcal{A}$ selects the set of elements $L^\pm (L^\pm \subset C)$ to be added or deleted and sends them to $\mathcal{B}$. $\mathcal{B}$ runs the corresponding algorithm to complete the addition or revocation of the user certificate, and gets the new accumulated value v', the new auxiliary information a_c, a_u and the corresponding witness $W_i^\pm = (w_i^\pm, t_i^\pm)$. Return to the adversary.

Query 2. The adversary $\mathcal{A}$ selects a set $L'(L' \subset L^*)$ of updated users to send to the $\mathcal{B}$. .. runs the algorithm to update the user certificate and returns the update witness $W_i' = (w_i', t_i)$ corresponding to the relevant user.

Challenge: After performing Query 1 and Query 2 several times, the adversary $\mathcal{A}$ selects $L : \{c_1, \cdots, c_m\} \subset C$ queries $\mathcal{B}$ for corresponding v and $\{W_1, \cdots, W_m\}$, then forges element $c'(c' \in C \backslash L)$ and its corresponding witness $W' = (w', t')$ and sends them to $\mathcal{B}$. $\mathcal{B}$ runs the algorithm and verifies if the element c' has been accumulated in v. If the algorithm *Verify* outputs Yes with a non-negligible advantage, which means $\mathcal{B}$ can break the es-RSA assumption with a non-negligible advantage.

$\mathcal{B}$ calculates v and $\{W_1, \cdots, W_m\}$ corresponding to $L : \{c_1, \cdots, c_m\}$ and therefore exist $F(w_i^\beta c_i^{t_i} \bmod n^2) \equiv v(\bmod n)$, $(i = 1, \cdots, m)$, which means that:

$$\exists k \in Z, \frac{w_i^\beta c_i^{t_i} \bmod n^2 - 1}{n} = kn + v \tag{5}$$

Therefore,

$$w_i^\beta c_i^{t_i} \equiv (vn + 1)(\bmod n^2) \tag{6}$$

Also, we have

$$w_i^\beta \equiv (vn + 1)c_i^{-t_i}(\bmod n^2), c_i^{t_i} \equiv (vn + 1)w_i^{-\beta}(\bmod n^2) \tag{7}$$

So there are m triplets (c_i, w_i, t_i), c_i, w_i and t_i can be calculated from Eqs. (6) and (7).

Since v is calculated by adding a random element each time an element is added or revoked, and t_i is the randomly selected, the probability distributions of v, w_i, t_i and a_u are consistent, so Query 1, 2 does not help $\mathcal{A}$ forging. If $\mathcal{B}$ breaks the es-RSA hypothesis with a non-negligible advantage, he can get a different triplet (c', w', t') make (6) true with a non-negligible advantage. At this time, we have:

$$w'^\beta \equiv (vn + 1)c'^{-t'}(\bmod n^2) \Rightarrow w'^\beta \equiv \left((vn + 1)^{-\frac{1}{t'}}c'\right)^{-t'}(\bmod n^2) \tag{8}$$

If $y = w'^\beta$, $x = (vn + 1)^{-\frac{1}{t'}}c'$, $s = -t'$, that is $y \equiv x^s(\bmod n^2)$.

Obviously, if the adversary $\mathcal{A}$ can forge a triple (c', w', t'), it can resolve Eq. (8), which is equivalent to solving $y \equiv x^s(\bmod n^2)$. This means that the es-RSA assumption is broken. This contradicts with Lemma 1. So, it can be concluded that no enemy can win the security game with obvious advantages. The scheme can defend against CEA. According to the previous security model, our scheme can prevent adversary from forging witnesses and identities.

Theorem 2. The scheme can resist Sybil attack.

Proof. Sybil attack refers to the creation of multiple account identities in one malicious node. The adversary $\mathcal{A}$ can control most of the network with few nodes to achieve refusal to deal, fork, double payment and so on. In this paper, the user's network address and the user's identity are bound, and the joining of the new node needs to be authenticated by the supervisory node, so that $\mathcal{A}$ cannot create multiple identities in one node, so the scheme can resist Sybil attack.

7 Analysis and Comparison

7.1 Efficiency Analysis

The overhead of this scheme is mainly divided into storage overhead and computational overhead, and communication overhead is not considered. For storage overhead, the user node only needs to store its own witness and the accumulated value can realize the identity verification. The miner node must retain the certificate data (c_i, W_i, pk_i, v) of the entire node group and maintain the relevant information of the accumulator (auxiliary information a_u, a_c, A_l etc.). Supervisory node is only responsible for identity information and transaction auditing, no need to store relevant information. Since the magnitude of the witness and the accumulated value are small and constant, that is, the size of the dynamic accumulator is small, the full node and the light node can complete the corresponding identity authentication at any time only by updating regularly, and the space complexity of the corresponding storage overhead is $O(1)$, which improves the efficiency of certification.

The computation overhead mainly includes requests for registration, deletion, and update of certificates. Let Md be the cost of modular operation, E be the cost of exponential operation. For a group with m initial member, the calculation cost of the scheme mainly includes:

Compute initial key: Md; Generate initial parameters: $2(m+1)E + (3m+5)Md$; Generation of each certificate: $E + Md$. Verification a certificate: $2E + 3Md$. k Certificate registration: $(3k+2)E + (4k+6)Md$. k Certificate revocation: $2(k+1)E + (3k+6)Md$. Update a certificate: $2Md$.

7.2 Scheme Comparison

The comparison between this paper and related PKI schemes is shown in Table 2. Certcoin proposed in [3] builds a PKI model based on blockchain, and uses the offline key to protect the online key. At the same time, the certificate is efficiently managed by means of RSA accumulator and distributed hash table. Aucoin is a decentralized PKI scheme [5]. The scheme uses a flexible challenge response mechanism for verification and authentication when issuing a public key, thereby reducing illegal occupancy and Sybil attack. The IKP scheme proposed in [8] uses smart contracts to reward detectors that report illegal certificates, impose financial penalties on CAs that issue illegal certificates, and to motivate CAs that work correctly to ensure proper certification. Cercoin in [12] proposed a set of rules based on the Bitcoin system to verify the validity of the certificate and the consistency of ownership, and to provide a method of identity assignment. At the same time, the scheme improves the Merkle Patricia tree to achieve efficient management of certificates, including efficient retrieval and verification of certificates.

Table 2. Comparison of this article and other PKI schemes

Scheme	CAs	Certcoin [3]	Aucoin [5]	IKP [8]	Cercoin [12]	Our scheme
Update	√	√	×	×	√	√
Revocation	√	√	×	×	√	√
Multiple certificates	√	×	√	√	√	√
Single point of failure	×	√	×	√	√	√
Resist Sybil attack	–	√	√	×	×	√
Preemptive registration	×	×	√	×	√	√
Certificate transparency	×	√	√	√	√	√
Batch update	–	×	–	–	–	√
Resist replay attack	×	×	√	√	×	√

8 Conclusion

This paper proposes a one-stop efficient PKI authentication service model based on blockchain. Firstly, we divide the node group into five different participating entities: user, miner node, supervisory node, certificate blockchain and third-party service providers, and propose a new blockchain based PKI model that resolves the single point of failure problem and can resist Sybil attack. In addition, this paper uses the witness generated by the dynamic accumulator to replace the role of certificates in traditional PKI, and proposes new user certificate management (registration, revocation and update) algorithms based on the dynamic accumulator, which improves efficiency of authentication. This paper also builds an authentication interaction model between the certificate blockchain and the third-party service providers. This model can provide a one-stop authentication service for users and third-party service providers, which will facilitate the deployment of PKI on blockchain. Finally, Security and efficiency analyses show that our scheme can effectively resist the Chosen Element Attacking, and improve the identity verification efficiency.

However, there still exists improvement spaces in our scheme. Because this article uses the network address to ensure the identity authentication, once the user's network address is changed, he must carry out the corresponding revoke and add a new certificate, this will bring inconvenience to users and improve the system overhead. In addition, the dynamic accumulator used in this paper exists much modular arithmetic, which brings high computational overhead. We will improve the dynamic accumulator to increase the calculation efficiency in future work, and further improve the model to avoid frequent certificate revocation and adding transactions in some cases.

Acknowledgment. This work is supported by the National Science Foundation of China (No. 61462060, No. 61762060).

References

1. Lin, J.Q., Jing, J.W., Zhang, Q.L.: Recent advances in PKI technologies. J. Cryptol. Res. **27** (1), 487–496 (2015)
2. Yuan, Y., Wang, F.Y.: Blockchain: the state of the art and future trends. Acta Automatica Sinica **42**, 481–494 (2016)
3. Fromknecht, C., Velicanu, D., Yakoubov, S.: CertCoin: a NameCoin based decentralized authentication system 6.857 class project. Unpublished class project (2014)
4. Fromknecht, C., Velicanu, D., Yakoubov, S.: A decentralized public key infrastructure with identity retention. IACR Cryptol. ePrint Arch. **2014**, 803 (2014)
5. Leiding, B., Cap, C.H., Mundt, T., Rashidibajgan, S.: Authcoin: validation and authentication in decentralized networks. arXiv preprint arXiv:1609.04955 (2016)
6. Muftic, S.: Bix certificates: cryptographic tokens for anonymous transactions based on certificates public ledger. Ledger **1**, 19–37 (2016)
7. Longo, R., Pintore, F., Rinaldo, G., Sala, M.: On the security of the blockchain BIX protocol and certificates. In: 2017 9th International Conference on Cyber Conflict (CyCon), pp. 1–16. IEEE (2017)
8. Matsumoto, S., Reischuk, R., M.: IKP: turning a PKI around with decentralized automated incentives. In: 2017 IEEE Symposium on Security and Privacy (SP), pp. 410–426. IEEE (2017)
9. Wan, Z., Guan, Z., Zhuo, F., Xian, H.: BKI: towards accountable and decentralized public-key infrastructure with blockchain. In: Lin, X., Ghorbani, A., Ren, K., Zhu, S., Zhang, A. (eds.) SecureComm 2017. LNICST, vol. 238, pp. 644–658. Springer, Cham (2018). https://doi.org/10.1007/978-3-319-78813-5_33
10. Syta, E., Tamas, I., Visher, D.: Keeping authorities "honest or bust" with decentralized witness cosigning. In: 2016 IEEE Symposium on Security and Privacy (SP), pp. 526–545. IEEE (2016)
11. Dykcik, L., Chuat, L., Szalachowski, P., Perrig, A.: BlockPKI: an automated, resilient, and transparent public-key infrastructure. In: 2018 IEEE International Conference on Data Mining Workshops (ICDMW), pp. 105–114. IEEE (2018)
12. Qin, B., Huang, J., Wang, Q., Luo, X., Liang, B., Shi, W.: Cecoin: a decentralized PKI mitigating MitM attacks. Future Gener. Comput. Syst. (2017)
13. Benaloh, J., de Mare, M.: One-way accumulators: a decentralized alternative to digital signatures. In: Helleseth, T. (ed.) EUROCRYPT 1993. LNCS, vol. 765, pp. 274–285. Springer, Heidelberg (1994). https://doi.org/10.1007/3-540-48285-7_24
14. Camenisch, J., Lysyanskaya, A.: Dynamic accumulators and application to efficient revocation of anonymous credentials. In: Yung, M. (ed.) CRYPTO 2002. LNCS, vol. 2442, pp. 61–76. Springer, Heidelberg (2002). https://doi.org/10.1007/3-540-45708-9_5
15. Wang, P., Wang, H., Pieprzyk, J.: A new dynamic accumulator for batch updates. In: Qing, S., Imai, H., Wang, G. (eds.) ICICS 2007. LNCS, vol. 4861, pp. 98–112. Springer, Heidelberg (2007). https://doi.org/10.1007/978-3-540-77048-0_8

Distributed Electronic Data Storage and Proof System Based on Blockchain

Jitao Wang, Guozi Sun$^{(\boxtimes)}$, Yu Gu, and Kun Liu

School of Computer Science, Nanjing University of Posts and Telecommunications,
Nanjing, China
joten_wang@qq.com, sun@njupt.edu.cn, 243477384@qq.com, liukun_it@163.com

Abstract. In the context of the Internet, whether it is daily business or social networking, the penetration of electronic data is ubiquitous. Internet companies, financial institutions, government agencies and many other fields, more and more documents, notices, contracts, transaction vouchers, technology and trade secrets are stored in the form of electronic data. However, the existing traditional electronic data storage and proof systems are often encountered with third-party trust crisis and potential data security risks. To cope with these challenges, a distributed electronic data storage and proof system is designed, making use of the core features of the blockchain's decentralization and non-tampering to effectively solve the tampering and security problems of electronic data storage and proof. The system encodes and fragments information using Reed-Solomon code. And this system provides users with data uploading, downloading, querying, comparing and authorizing services. By using the system interaction, smart contracts are compiled to anchor key data information on the main chain, ensuring the non-tampering of electronic data. In the meantime, the access rights of different users to electronic data are restricted accordingly. Finally, based on an improved RFM model, the distributed storage nodes are determined to achieve load balancing of storage nodes. It also increases the high availability of the system.

Keywords: Blockchain · Smart contract · Decentralization · Distributed storage · Electronic data · Load balancing

1 Introduction

In the past few years, blockchain technology has gained tremendous growth, mainly attributed to the success of Bitcoin cryptocurrency. A blockchain (also known as a distributed ledger) is essentially an additive database maintained by a set of nodes that are not fully trusted by each other. Since the blockchain is kept running in the decentralized network, it provides a constant source of power for the transaction, verification, and interconnection of the blockchain. However, with the continuous development of application scenarios, the design

© Springer Nature Singapore Pte Ltd. 2020
X. Si et al. (Eds.): CBCC 2019, CCIS 1176, pp. 48–67, 2020.
https://doi.org/10.1007/978-981-15-3278-8_4

of Bitcoin has the problems with lack of Turing complete, lack of account preservation, excessive resource consumption and limited efficiency. Bitcoin has not been applied in many blockchain scenarios, so in this case, a multi-layered, cryptographic-based open source technology agreement Ethereum comes into being. It integrates different functional modules through the overall design and is a comprehensive platform for creating and decentralized applications [1–3].

Electronic data is the product of modern technology, which requires us to store it and prevent from tampering. Electronic data storage and proof is a system structure that is easy to browse, easy to prove, easy to identify, and easy to save. First, it stores the data well according to the data type and has a good guarantee for the credibility and integrity of the data [4]. The storage and proof of electronic data is convenient for storing and verifying, which also provides effective data sharing securely. Blockchain technology can provide a complete security encryption technology and user authentication system [5,6].

At present, there are several problems in the electronic deposit certificate that need to be solve [7,8]:

(1) The degree of automation in the process of depositing certificates is not high.
(2) The risk of electronic data storage and proof is large.
(3) The legal processing procedure of third-party organizations is cumbersome.
(4) The security of electronic data is limited.
(5) There is lack of trust between the two organizations.

In this paper, we present a secure, scalable electronic data storage and proof system. We use data and user mapping to ensure efficient access control to the electronic data pool. We design a blockchain-based data storage and proof scheme that allows data users/owners to access electronic data from an electronic repository after authentication. The data storage mainly performs fragment redundancy algorithm and distributed storage to ensure data security, and the system introduces a user point mechanism to ensure system load balancing. The verification and subsequent services are enclosed within the system, written to the block, and become part of the blockchain.

2   Related Work

In this section, an overview of the systematic research related to blockchains is presented, with an emphasis on the application of blockchain technology. The application of blockchain technology in real life scenarios involves medical, insurance, copyright protection, and the Internet of Things.

Qi et al. briefly solve the access control management problem in medical data sharing system in their research. It mainly designed a blockchain-based data sharing scheme, allowing data users/owners to visit the electronic medical records from shared repositories after identity authentication and encryption key authentication. Sifah et al. propose a blockchain-based shared medical data solution, with a focus on providing data access control, source, and audit, and sharing medical data among cloud service providers [9].

There is also consideration in security, cloud storage and other aspects: Liang et al. propose a decentralized and trusted cloud data origin architecture using blockchain technology. Blockchain-based data sources can provide tamper-proof records, transparency of data in the cloud, and enhanced privacy and usability of source-based data [10]. An Binh Tran et al. propose a browser-based tool for managing and deploying user registrations and calling smart contracts on the blockchain.

In the application research of electronic data storage and proof based on blockchain, Li et al. study how to combine business with blockchain technology and propose a method to optimize current data storage from the application scenarios of electronic data storage to provide effective services for users. Li et al. explore the collection meaning of electronic evidence in cybercrime in the collection and preservation analysis of cybercrime, analyze the particularity of electronic evidence collection in cybercrime, and propose the method of collecting and preserving electronic evidence [11].

The form of electronic data is confusing, and the data format cannot be effectively unified, which brings extra work during data storage process. There is a big data security risk in the electronic data storage in that the centralized storage method may cause the data to be tampered with and lost, making the whole system not completely credible. Secondly, the electronic data has a long waiting time for obtaining the verification result, and the obtained result is sluggish, so that the user cannot obtain the result in time. The corresponding information cannot be given in time, and the system efficiency is limited [10, 12]. Therefore, this paper is devoted to solving various problems encountered in electronic data, and proposes a research based on blockchain technology to solve the problem of electronic data storage and proof. The main contributions of this paper are as follows:

(1) This paper proposes a system that combines electronic data storage with blockchain technology. The storage and proof of electronic data is used to store and verify various types of data. The blockchain technology is used to fix and save the acquired electronic data [13].
(2) This paper applies the distributed storage method of electronic data and performs redundant fragmentation on data to ensure the security of data storage. We introduce the credit system in the system, according to the user uploading the storage and proof and providing the storage method to integrate the data changes, maintaining the load balance of the system, ensuring the security and stability of the system [14].

3   Technology Architecture

The design of the system adopts the idea of "high cohesion and low coupling". The main functions of the whole system have four layers. From top to bottom, it is the business layer, the logic layer, the intelligent contract layer, and the blockchain layer [15–17], as shown in Fig. 1.

(1) Application layer: The application layer mainly includes the front-end UI, the display layer and the business layer in Fig. 1, and the front-end UI provides a visualized web interface for the user access system. It receives the request submitted by the user, performs simple pre-processing, and sends the request to the logic layer for core calculation. After the calculation is completed, the data information is received from the logical layer, and is intuitively fed back to the user through the web interface [18, 19]. The user can be a customer who needs to maintain data, or a third party that needs to download data for notarization.

(2) Logical layer: It is the implementation layer of the core functions of the system. According to the six interfaces provided by the application layer, the logic layer respectively gives the implementation method of the corresponding functional modules [20]. Among them, the TCP-based Socket multi-threaded concurrent module is the framework foundation for the entire system to run smoothly. The system uses this module to achieve reliable transmission of data between different nodes. Based on the above basic framework, the system introduces the coding and decoding of Reed-Solomon codes, and node selection module used in the implementation of file uploading and downloading modules and introduces the user node performance test module to determine its advantages and disadvantages. It introduces the Hash comparison module to determine whether the file has been maliciously tampered with. Finally, it introduces user registration and point module to complete the management of user information.

(3) Smart contract layer: The smart contracts deployed on the Ethereum platform. As a bridge between the logical layer and the blockchain layer, the smart contract layer anchors the calculation results of the logical layer (such as the electronic data and its fragmentation fingerprint information, the user node's point information, etc.) to the blockchain layer storage area. In the process of writing smart contracts, the system defines several structures (such as File, Record, User, etc.) to store key information of electronic data in the form of customized data. This method significantly improves the efficiency of electronic data query and enhances the readability of electronic data [21, 22].

(4) Blockchain layer: As a decentralized database of the system, the data information generated by the logic layer is stored. The network layer undertakes to verify the transaction information, generate new blocks, and maintain the stable operation of the blockchain network. The data layer stores all the key information uploaded by the entire system [23].

In this paper, based on the new idea of block chain, the distributed storage records of electronic data are placed on the block chain, and combined with redundant slice algorithm, time stamp, hash algorithm, Reed-Solomon code, fuzzy analytic hierarchy process, ideal base point, improved RFM model and smart contract, the distributed storage system based on block chain is set up and built.

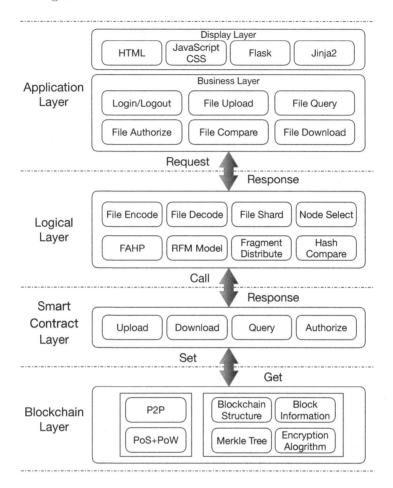

Fig. 1. System function architecture diagram

The system mainly adopts the data redundancy fragmentation technology, which divides electronic data into n information slices and M redundant pieces, and then carries out distributed storage of data slices to ensure the security of data information, collect the host server of the system, combine fuzzy analytic hierarchy process and ideal base points to test the network comprehensive performance parameters of the system storage host to ensure load balancing of system information storage.

Firstly, it uses the P2P network technology to implement the centralization of the system, which is based on the decentralization characters of smart contracts. Secondly, it uses the hash algorithm to ensure the integrity of the data. Finally, the consensus algorithm is used to ensure the consistency of the data between the nodes.

In this way, a decentralized and verifiable distributed storage system is designed. Based on the system, the smart contracts can automatically realize the transaction processing and saving mechanism of the electronic data storage and proof under the participation of the two or more parties, and the third party institutions such as the public security law [24–26].

3.1   Blockchain Technology

A blockchain is a transaction database shared by all nodes that participate in the network based on a transaction protocol. The blockchain contains every transaction that has been executed in the system. Based on this, people can find information about any address at any time. If the blockchain is used as a state machine, each transaction is an attempt to change the state, and each time the consensus generated block is the participant confirms the result of the state change caused by the transaction in the block [14, 27].

In implementation, it is first assumed that there is a distributed data record book, which can be added and cannot be deleted. The basic structure of the bottom of the account is a linear linked list, which is also the source of its name "block chain". The linked list is composed of a series of blocks. The successor blocks record the hash (pre hash) of the leading block [28]. New data to be added must be put in a new block. And whether the block and transactions in this block are legitimate can be quickly checked by calculating the hash value. Any maintenance node can propose a new legal block. However, a consensus mechanism must be adopted to reach agreement on the final selected block.

3.2   Reed-Solomon Code

Reed-Solomon code is a linear coding method defined on the domain. The coding method generates k source data to generate l coded data, which is consistent with the FEC coding idea. In our system, the Reed-Solomon code is used to implement the FEC coding transformation of the packet layer [29].

When the user uploads electronic data, the system will first segment the electronic data. The fragmentation is mainly dependent on coding in Reed-Solomon code. Users need to provide two important parameters, the number of information fragments and the number of redundant fragments. Based on the above two parameters and the size of the files to be uploaded, the system adjusts the appropriate size of the encoding buffer to complete the fragmentation of the files [30].

Suppose the message length is d, there are n information data blocks, m redundant parity blocks.

(1) Divide the message D by word length $= 8$, and fill the missing part with 0 to get the data matrix. Get the data matrix $D = (D_1, D_2, ..., D_n)'$.

(2) Generating an encoding matrix.

$$B = \begin{pmatrix} 1 & 0 & 0 & \cdots & 0 \\ 0 & 1 & 0 & \cdots & 0 \\ \vdots & \vdots & \vdots & & \vdots \\ 0 & 0 & 0 & \cdots & 1 \\ B_{11} & B_{12} & B_{13} & \cdots & B_{1n} \\ B_{21} & B_{22} & B_{23} & \cdots & B_{2n} \\ \vdots & \vdots & \vdots & & \vdots \\ B_{n1} & B_{n2} & B_{n3} & \cdots & B_{nn} \end{pmatrix}$$

(3) The matrix is multiplied by the coding matrix B and the data matrix D to obtain an encoded data matrix E.

$$\begin{pmatrix} 1 & 0 & 0 & \cdots & 0 \\ 0 & 1 & 0 & \cdots & 0 \\ \vdots & \vdots & \vdots & & \vdots \\ 0 & 0 & 0 & \cdots & 1 \\ B_{11} & B_{12} & B_{13} & \cdots & B_{1n} \\ B_{21} & B_{22} & B_{23} & \cdots & B_{2n} \\ \vdots & \vdots & \vdots & & \vdots \\ B_{m1} & B_{m2} & B_{m3} & \cdots & B_{mn} \end{pmatrix} \cdot \begin{pmatrix} D_1 \\ D_2 \\ \vdots \\ D_n \end{pmatrix} = \begin{pmatrix} D_1 \\ \vdots \\ D_n \\ C_1 \\ \vdots \\ C_m \end{pmatrix}$$

(4) Decoding process: delete the row corresponding to the missing piece of data from the coded slice and the coding matrix (assuming D_1 and C_2 are lost).

$$\begin{pmatrix} 0 & 1 & 0 & \cdots & 0 \\ 0 & 0 & 1 & \cdots & 0 \\ \vdots & \vdots & \vdots & & \vdots \\ 0 & 0 & 0 & \cdots & 1 \\ B_{11} & B_{12} & B_{13} & \cdots & B_{1n} \\ B_{31} & B_{32} & B_{33} & \cdots & B_{3n} \\ \vdots & \vdots & \vdots & & \vdots \\ B_{m1} & B_{m2} & B_{m3} & \cdots & B_{mn} \end{pmatrix} \cdot \begin{pmatrix} D_1 \\ D_2 \\ \vdots \\ D_n \end{pmatrix} = \begin{pmatrix} D_2 \\ \vdots \\ D_n \\ C_1 \\ C_3 \\ \vdots \\ C_m \end{pmatrix}$$

(5) Calculate the invertible matrix of B'.

$$(B')^{-1} \cdot B' \cdot D = (B')^{-1} \cdot E'$$

(6) Calculate the original message D, complete the encoding.

$$D = (B')^{-1} \cdot E'$$

3.3   Improved RFM Model

This paper uses the improved RFM model to score the storage nodes and use this score to achieve load balancing of distributed storage [31]. First, the storage node is specified to store an information slice for the first time to obtain 20 points. The gain obtained by storing one piece of information each time later is calculated by the following formula:

$$r_i = \begin{cases} \frac{20b_i}{B}, & b_i \neq 0 \\ 20, & b_i = 0 \end{cases}$$

where b_i indicates the number of storage slices of the storage node; B indicates the total number of storage slices of all storage nodes.

R indicator: The ratio of the last time the storage node stores the file to the total running time of the system.

$$R = \frac{t_1 - t_0}{T}$$

where t_1 indicates the time at which the storage node stores the current slice; t_2 indicates the time of the last slice storage; T indicates the total running time of the system.

F indicator: the average ratio of storage revenue per storage node to the system's specified revenue.

$$F = \frac{c}{aS}$$

where c indicates the total revenue of the storage node; a indicates the storage node storage fragment number; S indicates the revenue of the first specified storage of one slice (20 points)

M indicator: the storage node's storage revenue level of the points in all storage nodes of the system.

$$M = \frac{1}{\sqrt{2\pi}\sigma} exp[-\frac{(c_i - \mu)^2}{2\sigma^2}]$$

where c_i indicates the total revenue of the storage node; n indicates the number of storage nodes; $\mu = \frac{1}{n}\sum_{i=1}^{n} c_i$ indicates the mean of the number of revenues of all storage nodes; $\sigma = \frac{1}{n}\sqrt{\sum_{i=1}^{n} (c_i - \mu)^2}$ indicates the standard deviation of the revenue of all storage nodes;

This paper Uses FAHP to analyze the weights of R, F and M, the corresponding weights are as follows:

$$\overrightarrow{w} = [0.2296, 0.3459, 0.4245]$$

When performing storage node selection, calculate the RFM model score for each node using the following formula:

$$Score = \overrightarrow{w} \cdot \overrightarrow{m}$$

where $\vec{m}$ indicates the current R, F and M index value vector of the storage node.

In order to enable the storage node to implement load balancing of information slice storage, when the score is larger, the probability of being selected should be lowered, so the reciprocal is used to represent the final score.

$$Score_{final} = \frac{1}{Score}$$

3.4   Multi-target Node Decision Model

As an electronic data storage and proof system, the system relies on multiple user nodes to complete the storage and proof of electronic data. This process involves the selection of multi-user nodes, and we design how to select several of the best current nodes of the system and cooperate with the distributed storage work. Figure 2 shows the main design process of user node performance evaluation.

According to Ethereum, it relies on the computational power of each node to keep it running. In this system, it relies mainly on the storage power of each node. Therefore, it evaluates the performance of the user node from both network performance and storage level. More specifically, the network performance affects the transmission speed of the electronic data fragmentation, and the storage level affects the storage reliability of the electronic data fragmentation.

The parameter weight of the network performance is calculated by the fuzzy analytic hierarchy process (FAHP) [32] to calculate the weight of the bandwidth, network delay and packet loss rate, and the network performance is obtained. Then, the ranking of the user nodes is mainly calculated by the Three-base point method (TOPSIS) [33, 34] to calculate the Euclidean distance between the ideal base point and the ideal superior base point and the inverse ideal base point, and the integrated distance is used to rank the nodes. (Before the storage node sorting operation, this paper has normalized the network performance, storage performance and RFM score.).

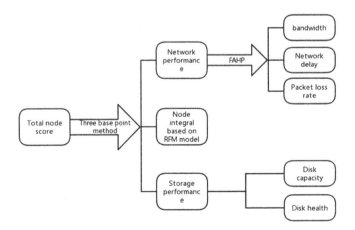

Fig. 2. Node evaluation framework

(1) Calculate the ideal superior base point and the inverse ideal optimal base point.

Assume that the maximum network performance is $s_1^\triangle$, the maximum storage performance is $s_2^\triangle$, and the maximum RFM score is $s_3^\triangle$ for all storage nodes.(n indicates the number of storage nodes; $k = 1$, 2, 3)

$$s_k^\triangle = \max\{s_{k_1}, s_{k_2}, \ldots, s_{k_n}\}$$

Assume that the minimum network performance is $s_1^\triangledown$, the minimum storage performance is $s_2^\triangledown$, and the minimum RFM score is $s_3^\triangledown$ for all storage nodes.

$$s_k^\triangledown = \min\{s_{k_1}, s_{k_2}, \ldots, s_{k_n}\}$$

(2) Calculate the distance between each point and the ideal superior base point and the inverse ideal base point.

In the m-dimensional space, it is not difficult to find that the excellent base points appear in the form of points. Using the Euclidean distance calculation method, we can calculate the distance $(d_i^\triangle)$ between the excellent base point of the network performance, storage performance, the RFM score and the ideal superior base point, and the distance $(d_i^\triangledown)$ from the inverse ideal optimal base point. $(i = 1$, 2, ..., $n)$

$$d_i^\triangle = \sqrt{\sum_{k=1}^{3} (z_{k_i} - s_k^\triangle)^2}$$

$$d_i^\triangledown = \sqrt{\sum_{k=1}^{3} (z_{k_i} - s_k^\triangledown)^2}$$

(3) Calculating the integrated distance.

By measuring the gap between the current plan and the optimal and worst case ideals, the pros and cons of the current programs are judged. According to the principle of minimum distance, the scheme corresponding to the point with the smallest integrated distance is selected as the optimal scheme.

$$\min\{d_i = \frac{d_i^\triangle}{d_i^\triangle + d_i^\triangledown}\}$$

4   System Design

We develop data sharing mechanism for data sharing based on block chaining to ensure data security and provenance. The detailed flow chart of the storage and proof system, as shown in Fig. 3, is divided into 6 main steps.

As shown in Fig. 3, the block chain storage system consists mainly of the proof user node, the storage user node and the smart contract, in which the node A can either be a proof user node or a storage user node. The system carries out a storage procedure as follows:

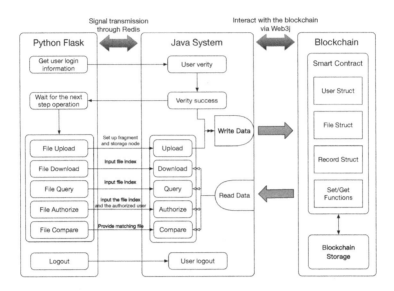

Fig. 3. Detailed flow chart of system

(1) After the user login system, the contract class member gets the user information and obtains the performance information of other nodes through the user node and obtains the value for the later data slice storage performance host computing.

(2) Files uploaded by users need to be stored in documents, and the key information of files is stored in the contract class file to form corresponding mapping relationship between data and users.

(3) The redundant fragment algorithm is used to slice the uploaded electronic data and select several optimal performance nodes according to the performance information of the nodes, which can be used to store each piece of data.

(4) According to the selected nodes, the system distributes data to different nodes, and returns the key information to the smart contract, including the IP address of the data storage, the absolute path of the data storage and the hash value of the data fragment in the record object.

(5) When the user needs to download or query the electronic data, the system puts forward the authorization request and establishes the corresponding mapping relation between the user information and the data needed to be accessed, then the user can carry on the related operation.

(6) After the user has access to the authority, it reads the relevant information of the electronic data from the contract. The system finds the location of the electronic data storage according to the storage information, downloads the electronic data and reduces the data and compares the hash value of the file to verify the integrity of the electronic data.

The main process of this system is to upload, save, view, download, compare, and authorize electronic data files. The process is introduced as follow.

4.1   System Upload Function

First, the user logs in to the system. When the user requests an electronic data upload operation, the system calculates the number of points m spent on the upload according to the number of electronic data fragments, and then calls the contract point function to obtain the current number of point c of the user. The system performs the judgment of the number of point.

After the judgment, it provides the upload function to the user, and updates the point information corresponding to the user on the blockchain. If the judgment is not passed, the user is informed that he/she does not have enough points.

4.2   System Data Preservation Function

First, the system uses Reed-Solomon code to divide the electronic data into redundant data and obtains n data sheets and m redundant slices. The system uses iperf to obtain the performance parameters of the system storage host, mainly including throughput, delay, and bandwidth, and calculates the network performance by calculating three parameters based on fuzzy analytic hierarchy process.

At the same time, the system uses smart to get the hard disk capacity and hard disk health of the storage host. The network performance score and disk storage capacity are used as parameters, and the ideal base point method is used to calculate the comprehensive distance of the performance of the storage host and sort it to obtain the optimal performance hosts.

The system randomly distributes the fragments of the electronic data to the selected hosts, fixes them into the storage area of the blockchain through the consensus algorithm of the blockchain, and writes the fragmentation information into the blockchain.

4.3   System Data Query Function

The user can use the electronic data query function at any time to obtain the stored information with the file. According to the need for electronic data storage and proof, the data is only visible to uploaders by default. When users need to view the electronic data of other users, they need to obtain the authorization of the corresponding user. When the user makes a query request, the system interacts with the contract, determines the user authority and judges whether the file belongs to the user node.

After the success, the index number corresponding to the data file and the index number of the fragment storage location are read. Then, it is determined whether the file index is smaller than the number of user files, and the absolute index bit of the file is obtained. The information (IP address and stored absolute path) is stored in the blockchain and the electronic data is found through the information.

4.4   System Data Download Function

When the user submits the download request to the system, the automatic downloading and decoding of the file is realized after locating the corresponding data information in the block chain storage area and finding the location of the data storage. This is similar to data query function. Data files that users can download must be uploaded by themselves or authorized by others to ensure users' privacy and security.

4.5   System Data Comparison Function

After getting the data returned, the system calls the SHA-1, SHA-256 and MD5 hash algorithms respectively, and compares the hash values of each slice to the hash value stored in the smart contract. If the hash value is equal, it means that the file has not been tampered with. When the hash value of part of the system is not equal to the storage in the contract, if the number of unequal fragments is less than the number of redundant pieces of the system data, the system can still restore the source file.

4.6   System Data Authorization Function

Due to the needs of the system, the user's personal privacy needs to be protected, so the default user's electronic data is their personal information file. Users need to authorize others, so that other users can have access to the authorized documents and electronic data. In authorization, the user's public key is input, that is, user account and the serial number of the authorized file. The system will write the authorized file information to the blockchain, then the authorization ends.

4.7   The Distributed Storage Architecture Diagram of File Fragmentation

The biggest advantage of distributed system is that it enhances the fault tolerance and balances the different elements of the same type in the entire system [26,35]. We run the system program on several servers and use Nginx server to achieve load balancing. When users access files through domain names, the Nginx server receives HTTP requests from the interconnected files. It will select the appropriate system server according to the server connection situation and forward the HTTP requests from the users to the selected system server.

Since each system server can communicate with each other, when file distribution is performed, the fragments are distributed to each system server according to the distribution policy. And each system server carries a geth client, which connects to the same private chain through IPC files. The multi-node private chain architecture ensures that file information generated by the system is stored in the same chain, as shown in Fig. 4.

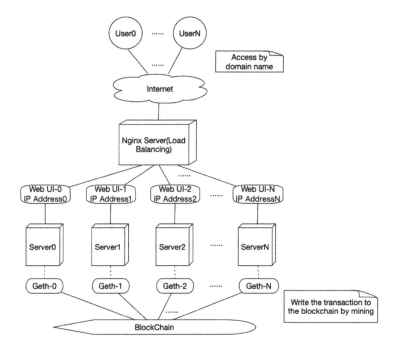

Fig. 4. The distributed storage architecture diagram

This section introduces the implementation of the electronic storage and proof system based on blockchain intelligent contract, and describes the data uploading, preserving, querying, downloading, verifying, authorizing and the interaction with the system. Among them, the intelligent contract part is the underlying data storage method to support the system. File uploading, fragmentation, storage, downloading, and verification are the main functional points of the system.

5   System Function Test and Evaluation

Before providing a systematic test evaluation, we summarize these capabilities of the system:

(1) The system provides real-time auditing of all data accesses in the storage application. We use electronic data files as data units, audit all operations on the data objects, and record using blockchains. In this way, all electronic data access situations can be collected and monitored.

(2) For each piece of electronic data, we upload the data to the blockchain network. By doing so, we create an unchangeable file data fingerprint, and the system has secure and permanent record keeping and tamper-proof timestamps. Any changes to system data are detected by verifying blockchain data comparisons.

(3) Users can view data services while protecting their privacy. User access records are anonymous in the blockchain network. The data source is unable to query the user account. Anonymous saving is reflected in two aspects: on the one hand, because the user ID is hashed randomly, the user identity is not connected to the source data. On the other hand, non-connectivity between each user is also achieved, especially for uploading user protection of authorized data.

5.1   The Analysis of System File Upload Performance

Keep the number of fragments unchanged, change the file size.
Before performing performance tests, we make some files of specified size. To analyze the impact of file size on upload performance more easily, it is necessary to keep the number of fragments unchanged. The number of fragments in this experiment is set to 5. According to the file size increasing order, the file encoding and fragmentation in the uploading process, the storage server selection time, the fragment distribution time, and the total upload time are counted, which is shown in Table 1.

Table 1. File upload duration (5 slices)

	1.2 Mb	2.4 Mb	12.4 Mb	59.0 Mb	108 Mb	190 Mb
File encoding and fragmenting duration(s)	3.584	3.706	4.189	6.852	10.302	19.538
Server selection duration(s)	0.490	0.439	0.424	0.417	0.416	0.438
Fragment distribution duration(s)	10.631	10.516	10.596	10.935	11.427	11.904
Total duration(s)	14.705	14.661	15.209	18.204	22.145	31.880

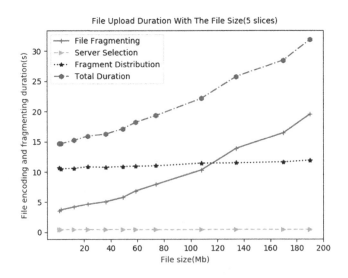

Fig. 5. File upload duration with the file sizes

Based on the data obtained, the line graph more directly shows the trend of the cost of the file during the various stages of the upload process, as shown in Fig. 5. It can be easily seen from the figure that the file size has a great influence on the time of file encoding and fragmentation, whereas it has little effect on the time and fragment distribution of the storage server selection. Therefore, it can be concluded that the file encoding fragmentation time increases with the file size, which lead the total upload time to increase.

Keep the file size unchanged, change the number of fragments.

By fixing the file size to 19.8 Mb and changing the number of fragments, we obtain the statistics in Table 2.

Table 2. File upload duration (File size is 19.8 Mb)

	3	6	9	15	24	30
File encoding and fragmenting duration(s)	4.153	4.174	4.447	4.264	4.668	4.724
Server selection duration(s)	0.455	0.453	0.405	0.437	0.408	0.405
Fragment distribution duration(s)	6.685	12.687	18.775	30.736	49.619	61.315
Total duration(s)	11.293	17.314	23.627	35.437	54.695	66.444

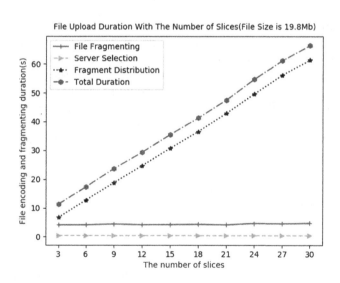

Fig. 6. File upload duration with the number of slices

Similarly, we show the trend of change as a line chart in Fig. 6. It can be easily seen from the figure that the number of fragments has a great influence on the time of fragment distribution, which exhibits a linear variation characteristic. However, it has little effect on the duration of storage server selection and file encoding. Therefore, it can be concluded that the time of fragment distribution increases with the number of fragments, so that the total upload time increases.

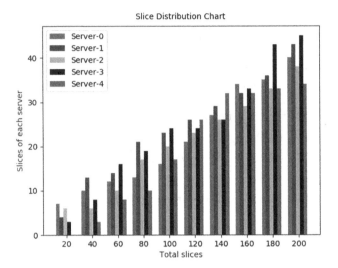

Fig. 7. Slice distribution

5.2   The Balance Test of File Distribution Strategy

For the distribution of file fragmentation, we combine the integration model and server performance to comprehensively evaluate the storage server situation, and select the corresponding server to receive file fragmentation by comprehensive evaluation score. In theory, as the total number of slices in the system increases, the number of slices on each storage server should be similar. It would be unexpected if some server utilization is too low. To verify our expectation, we prepare 5 cloud servers for deployment, constantly change the number of total slices in the system. We count the number of slices owned by each storage server and plot it as a composite bar chart shown in Fig. 7.

As is directly depicted by the graph, the fragment distribution meets our expectations comparatively, which further verifies that the fragment distribution strategy is reasonable.

6   Conclusion

We mainly record the electronic data storage in a decentralized storage and proof system on the blockchain based on the non-tampering feature of the it. First, we introduce the research background and significance of electronic data storage and proof. Then we draw relevant solutions according to its existing problems. Subsequently, we investigate the status of research and development in the world and use it to develop our system. Secondly, we introduce the main functional architecture of the system, the theoretical knowledge involved in the system, and explain the related technologies in the architecture. Then the system total process is analyzed, and the detailed requirements analysis of the main functional modules of the system is carried out, while the key points involved in the system improvement function are clarified. On this basis, we use the latest blockchain technology and distributed storage technology to design and implement a blockchain-based electronic data storage and proof system, which is illustrated by the system graphics module.

With the emerging technology of blockchain, we anchor the key "digital fingerprint" of electronic data in the storage area of blockchain, and combine technologies such as intelligent contract, distributed storage, fault-tolerant coding, and multi-attribute decision making. We realize the electronic data storage and proof system based on blockchain. The system ensures the authenticity, integrity, and uniqueness of electronic data by making use of the core features of the block chain's decentralization and non-tampering. At the same time, the system fully considers the fault-tolerant requirements of the distributed storage system and uses the Reed-Solomon code to protect the electronic data redundantly, which reduces the problems caused by the failure of a single server or the transmission channel. In addition, the system has also developed a point system for users to ensure that the system can attract more users to join, and thus improve the reliability of this storage and proof system.

Currently, we have developed a simple blockchain-based electronic data storage and proof system. The interaction between the hosts of the system is only carried out in the local area network. In the future, the system is further optimized to realize the electronic data storage in the WAN. The formula algorithm used in the blockchain of this paper is proof of workload. The execution time of this algorithm is long, and there is a waste of system resources. The current consensus mechanism algorithm can be optimized later. In the process of communication between the client and the server in the system, the plain text communication method is adopted, which has potential security risks, and symmetric encryption can be used later to improve security.

References

1. Liao, D.Y., Wang, X.: Design of a blockchain-based lottery system for smart cities applications (2017)
2. Shae, Z., Tsai, J.J.P.: On the design of a blockchain platform for clinical trial and precision medicine. In: IEEE International Conference on Distributed Computing Systems (2017)
3. Xu, R., Lu, Z., Zhao, H., Yun, P.: Design of network media's digital rights management scheme based on blockchain technology. In: IEEE International Symposium on Autonomous Decentralized System (2017)
4. Yue, X.: Healthcare data gateways: found healthcare intelligence on blockchain with novel privacy risk control. J. Med. Syst. **40**(10), 218 (2016)
5. Ouaddah, A., Elkalam, A.A., Ouahman, A.A.: Towards a novel privacy-preserving access control model based on blockchain technology in IoT. In: Rocha, Á., Serrhini, M., Felgueiras, C. (eds.) Europe and MENA Cooperation Advances in Information and Communication Technologies. Advances in Intelligent Systems and Computing, vol. 520, pp. 523–533. Springer, Cham (2017). https://doi.org/10.1007/978-3-319-46568-5_53

6. Zyskind, G., Nathan, O., Pentland, A.S.: Decentralizing privacy: using blockchain to protect personal data. In: IEEE Security & Privacy Workshops (2015)
7. Cheng, J.C., Lee, N.Y., Chi, C., Chen, Y.H.: Blockchain and smart contract for digital certificate. In: 2018 IEEE International Conference on Applied System Invention (ICASI) (2018)
8. Pilkington, M.: Blockchain Technology: Principles and Applications. Social Science Electronic Publishing, Rochester (2015)
9. Qi, X., Sifah, E.B., Asamoah, K.O., Gao, J., Guizani, M.: MeDShare: trust-less medical data sharing among cloud service providers via blockchain. IEEE Access 5(99), 14757–14767 (2017)
10. Liang, X., Shetty, S., Tosh, D., Kamhoua, C., Kwiat, K., Njilla, L.: ProvChain: a blockchain-based data provenance architecture in cloud environment with enhanced privacy and availability. In: 2017 17th IEEE/ACM International Symposium on Cluster, Cloud and Grid Computing (CCGRID) (2017)
11. Schwerha, J.J.: Cybercrime: legal standards governing the collection of digital evidence. Inf. Syst. Front. 6(2), 133–151 (2004)
12. Hardjono, T., Smith, N., Pentland, A.S.: Anonymous Identities for Permissioned Blockchains (2016)
13. Wu, F., Pai, H.T., Zhu, X., Hsueh, P.Y., Hu, Y.H.: An adaptable and scalable group access control scheme for managing wireless sensor networks. Telematics Inf. 30(2), 144–157 (2013)
14. Dinh, T.T.A., et al.: BLOCKBENCH: A Framework for Analyzing Private Blockchains (2017)
15. Cachin, C., Vukolić, M.: Blockchain Consensus Protocols in the Wild (2017)
16. Kakavand, H., Nicolette, K.D.S., Chilton, B.: The Blockchain Revolution: An Analysis of Regulation and Technology Related to Distributed Ledger Technologies. Social Science Electronic Publishing (2016)
17. Kuo, T.T., Kim, H.E., Ohno-Machado, L.: Blockchain distributed ledger technologies for biomedical and health care applications. J. Am. Med. Inf. Assoc. 24(6), 1211–1220 (2017)
18. Stanciu, A.: Blockchain based distributed control system for edge computing. In: International Conference on Control Systems & Computer Science (2017)
19. Dorri, A., Steger, M., Kanhere, S.S., Jurdak, R.: BlockChain: a distributed solution to automotive security and privacy. IEEE Commun. Mag. 55(12), 119–125 (2017)
20. Herlihy, M.: Blockchains and the future of distributed computing. In: ACM Symposium on Principles of Distributed Computing (2017)
21. Christidis, K., Devetsikiotis, M.: Blockchains and smart contracts for the Internet of Things. IEEE Access 4, 2292–2303 (2016)
22. Cong, L.W., He, Z.: Blockchain Disruption and Smart Contracts. Social Science Electronic Publishing, Rochester (2018)
23. Xu, X., et al.: A taxonomy of blockchain-based systems for architecture design. In: IEEE International Conference on Software Architecture (2017)
24. Peters, G.W., Panayi, E.: Understanding modern banking ledgers through blockchain technologies: future of transaction processing and smart contracts on the internet of money. In: Tasca, P., Aste, T., Pelizzon, L., Perony, N. (eds.) Banking Beyond Banks and Money. NEW, pp. 239–278. Springer, Cham (2016). https://doi.org/10.1007/978-3-319-42448-4_13
25. Sharples, M., Domingue, J.: The blockchain and kudos: a distributed system for educational record, reputation and reward. In: Verbert, K., Sharples, M., Klobučar, T. (eds.) EC-TEL 2016. LNCS, vol. 9891, pp. 490–496. Springer, Cham (2016). https://doi.org/10.1007/978-3-319-45153-4_48

26. Shi, E., Shi, E.: FruitChains: a fair blockchain. In: ACM Symposium on Principles of Distributed Computing (2017)
27. Suzuki, S., Murai, J.: Blockchain as an audit-able communication channel. In: Computer Software & Applications Conference (2017)
28. Khalil, R., Gervais, A.: Revive: rebalancing off-blockchain payment networks. In: ACM SIGSAC Conference on Computer & Communications Security (2017)
29. Huo, Y., El-Hajjar, M., Maunder, R.G., Hanzo, L.: Layered wireless video relying on minimum-distortion inter-layer FEC coding. IEEE Trans. Multimed. **16**(3), 697–710 (2014)
30. Glaser, F.: Pervasive Decentralisation of Digital Infrastructures: A Framework for Blockchain Enabled System and Use Case Analysis. Social Science Electronic Publishing, Rochester (2017)
31. Dudhia, A.: The reference forward model (RFM). J. Quant. Spectrosc. Radiat. Transf. **186**, 243–253 (2017)
32. Sadovykh, A., Hein, C., Morin, B., Mohagheghi, P., Berre, A.J.: An MAGDM based on constrained FAHP and FTOPSIS and its application to supplier selection. Math. Comput. Model. **54**(11), 2802–2815 (2011)
33. Shih, H.S., Shyur, H.J., Lee, E.S.: An extension of TOPSIS for group decision making. Math. Comput. Model. **45**(7), 801–813 (2007)
34. Yu, Z., Wen, J.: The IoT electric business model: using blockchain technology for the Internet of Things. Peer Peer Networking Appl. **10**(4), 983–994 (2017)
35. Aniello, L., Baldoni, R., Gaetani, E., Lombardi, F., Margheri, A., Sassone, V.: A prototype evaluation of a tamper-resistant high performance blockchain-based transaction log for a distributed database (2017)

Bye Audit! A Novel Blockchain-Based Automated Data Processing Scheme for Bank Audit Confirmation

Xiaoyan Chu[1,3], Tao Jiang[1,3], Xiaohu Li[2,3], and Xiaowei Ding[2,3(✉)]

[1] School of Business, Nanjing University,
163 Xianlin Road, Nanjing 210023, China
[2] School of Information Management, Nanjing University,
163 Xianlin Road, Nanjing 210023, China
dingxiaowei@nju.edu.cn
[3] Inclusive & Rural Financial Technology Innovation Research Center,
Nanjing University, 163 Xianlin Road, Nanjing 210023, China

Abstract. An audit confirmation letter is an inquiry that an auditor sends to a third party to verify the contents of accounting records of the entity that is being audited. Traditional process for delivering the paper confirmation is unnecessarily inefficient, relying much on manual processes and other outdated technologies, making it also vulnerable to fraudulent activities. In this paper, we adopt blockchain technology to address the low-efficiency and fraud risk in conventional bank confirmation process. Our solution involves two processes: Authorization Process and Data Acquisition Process. We integrate smart contract into these processes for automated authorization and automated data acquisition. We implemented our solution based on the open source FISCO-BCOS platform and used simulation of auditing process to prove its feasibility. Our evaluation benchmarks include latency and storage efficiency. The result shows that our system can support long-term stable operation.

Keywords: Blockchain · Audit confirmation · Automated authorization · Automated data acquisition · FISCO BCOS

1 Introduction

An audit confirmation letter is an inquiry that the auditor sends to a third party to verify the contents of the audited entity's accounting records. Based on the respondents, it falls into the following categories: bank confirmation, corporate confirmation, attorney confirmation, and other confirmation. ISA (International Standard on Auditing) 240 "Auditors and Fraud" indicates that the auditor may design confirmation requests to obtain additional corroborative information as a response to address the assessed risks of material misstatement due to fraud at the assertion level.

We focus on bank confirmation letters. Among those respondents, banks deal with a huge number of letters every year. Yet both banks and auditors have encountered many problems in actual implementation of bank confirmation process. The traditional bank confirmation process is shown in Fig. 1. First, the CPA fills out the inquiry letter

© Springer Nature Singapore Pte Ltd. 2020
X. Si et al. (Eds.): CBCC 2019, CCIS 1176, pp. 68–82, 2020.
https://doi.org/10.1007/978-981-15-3278-8_5

and submits to the bank by mail or personal delivery after the customer seals it; then, the bank staff checks the items and contents listed in the inquiry letter, which mainly consist of bank deposits, loans, the investor (shareholder) capital contributions and guarantees, and other commitments such as letters of credit, letters of guarantee of the audited entrepreneur; finally, after signing and stamping on it, the bank directly sends the letter with verification results to the CPA.

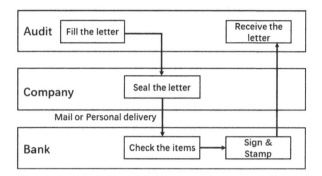

Fig. 1. Traditional bank confirmation process

As can be seen from the above process, the current bank confirmation process is mainly based on manual processing and other outdated technologies, which is carried out around the circulation, processing and control of paper documents. This process involves three participating parties: companies, banks and CPAs. Each party acts accordingly in the three-party game based on its own interests and incentives.

As a result, processing audit confirmations may become unnecessarily inefficient. Here are some of the major problems in this bank confirmation process:

1. The cumbersome and unstandardized control process of the letter leads to low efficiency in the auditing. Before issuing the letters, the CPAs need to collect the addresses of the banks and identify the authenticity of the address and the recipient information. Different banks have different requirements for letters. Auditors tend to spend a large amount of time in getting in touch with bank to meet the requirements of different banking departments. Some banks may even require auditors to bring letters onsite and present the costumers' letters of introduction and the auditors' ID certificates on the spot, which causes auditors to waste a lot of time on compliance of these requirements.

2. The bank's cumbersome verification process results in long period for confirmation response. After being delivered to the bank by mail or personal delivery, the confirmation usually needs to be circulated among multiple departments before all the information can be verified and confirmed, because the acquisition of the data needs the authorization of multiple departments. It may take as long as 1–3 weeks for a normal confirmation to be collected back after being sent out to a domestic bank. This poses a challenge to short-term auditing programs which typically require the authorized confirmations to be collected back as audit evidence in a fairly short

period of time. And the long response time greatly affects the audit completion schedule. If the bank does not respond within the specified time, auditors need to execute alternative procedures, requiring CPAs to manually check the bank slips, invoices and voucher records of selected significant transactions.

3. The fraudulent collusion between the auditees and the bank staff may invalidate the confirmations, leading to the loss of authenticity and reliability of the confirmations. Moreover, paper letters are easy to counterfeit, e.g. thru using just simple fake stamps.

4. The loss of the confirmations during the mailing process can cause unnecessary costs to the CPAs. Such unfortunate incidents occurred before, not infrequently, which has brought cost burdens and waste of human resources to the unfortunate accounting firms.

To deal with the above-mentioned problems, an electronic confirmation platform is ought to be established in order to achieve the confirmation procedure in a more automated and secure manner. The intrinsic property of the blockchain can help tackle these problems well: public and private key distributions can help banks confirm the identities of auditors and companies to avoid fraud. Smart Contracts can help auditors and banks automatically fill out the requests and feedbacks, eliminating the possibility of counterfeiting in the whole process, and thus establishing an efficient, trustworthy and immutable confirmation platform.

In this paper, we adopt blockchain technology to address the low efficiency, error-proneness and the lack of trust in the manual processing in traditional bank confirmation processes. More specifically, we developed two processes: (1) Authentication Process, where we designed a SDK to interact with blockchain to obtain audit identity authorization information stored in the Smart Contract, (2) Acquisition Process, where we designed a SQL plug-in to verify the permissions and retrieve data from the database. Our contribution lies in that we are the first to present a blockchain implementation in authorization and data acquisition during the audit confirmation process. We evaluate the feasibility of our approach in terms of latency, storage efficiency and anti-fraud performance. To this end, we randomly generated 11 companies, 1 bank, 7 auditing firms, and 1 administrator to simulate the operation pipelines. A total of more than 1,000 deposit and loan data were generated and 100,000 process simulations were performed.

The paper proceeds with a discussion of the related work and the blockchain technology in Sect. 2. Section 3 presents the details of our approach. In Sect. 4 we interpret the implementation of the new blockchain based bank conformation process. Section 5 evaluates our approach based on simulation, and Sect. 6 concludes.

2 Background

2.1 Blockchain

The blockchain is an entirely new approach that consists of non-destructive and immutable decentralized shared ledgers [1]. The blockchain uses distributed consensus mechanisms to generate, verify, process, and update data. It uses a cryptographic chained block structure to validate and store data, and uses automatic scripting code (Smart Contracts) to program and manipulate data [2]. It is an innovative approach that provides us with secure, transparent, anonymous, decentralized, low-cost, and reliable data or asset transactions [3, 4].

The Smart Contract is one of the core components of the blockchain. Smart Contracts use computer language instead of legal provisions to record transactions [5] and can be seen as programs that automatically execute on the blockchain. Smart Contracts support active or passive processing of data, the acceptance, storage, and delivery of an asset, as well as the control and management of smart assets on blockchains [6]. Smart Contracts have two main advantages. One is the digitization, as long as the assets need to be or could be digitalized on blockchains. The other is the programmability. Real-world functionalities can be programmed through Smart Contracts on blockchains, which facilitates and widens the usage of blockchains [7]. Owing to their special features, Smart Contracts can be used to bridge the lower layer data chains and the upper layer services and applications [5] and accounting and auditing system can be built on top of blockchains and Smart Contracts.

The public and private keys are one of the other core components of the blockchain. Blockchains use asymmetric cryptography to encrypt and sign data. This ensures high data security and privacy [8].

Several articles propose the concept of blockchain related access control systems with Smart Contracts. In Zyskind et al. the authors built a personal data management platform in pursuit of privacy with the combination of blockchain and off-chain data storage [9]. However, the control is limited for not addressing the general problem of access control systems at large. Furthermore, more researches tackle these problems, among which Shafagh et al. used the blockchain simply for access control for IoT data stored elsewhere [10], Cruz et al. presented a Role Based access control system which uses smart contracts and blockchain technology as infrastructures to represent the trust and endorsement relationship essential to realize a challenge-response authentication protocol that verifies users ownership of roles [11]. Our work involves role based access control system using blockchain and smart contract to manage the identity authorization.

In recent years the benefits and irreplaceable role of the blockchain have been increasingly recognized. Blockchains possess the following five features: (1) Decentralization. Blockchains do not rely on central intervention to store or to update data to avoid creating central dependencies on third-party organizations or other facilities. (2) Openness [12]. It is open to anybody to request blockchain data and develop related applications. (3) Independence [13]. Based on agreements and protocols, all nodes can automatically and securely verify and exchange data within the system, without any intervention. (4) Security. Security is a complex issue that is affected by internal and external factors. Theoretically, people can forge or alter the data in the blockchain system [14], only if they control at least 51% of the consensus nodes, which is usually too expensive for them, economically speaking. (5) Anonymity [5, 15]. Unless it is legally required, people do not have to disclose or to verify the identity or the related information of each node. Some of above-described features satisfy the needs of the auditing industry.

2.2 Blockchain Applications in Auditing

Blockchain applications in auditing have been previously discussed by a limited number of scholarly works. Firstly, the blockchain is conducive to advancement of auditing.

Casey and Vigna refer to the blockchain as a 'truth machine' that contains all the necessary tools to establish unprecedented levels of trust and transparency [16]. Due to its distributed and decentralized nature, the blockchain eliminates institutional intermediation from accounting and auditing, making it a peer-to-peer domain [17]. The blockchain provides distributed data security, transparency and immutability [18]. According to several scholars, the above features could significantly improve accounting and auditing practice and could force auditors and accountants to make a substantial shift towards more transparent behavior [19, 20]. Researches in this area concentrated on two areas, namely the continuous auditing and the Smart Contract [21].

Continuous auditing means transactions are validated almost instantaneously instead of at the end of reporting periods [19, 22]. Therefore, the blockchain can help save time and reduce the risk of human error [23]. However, given storage costs, 'real-time auditing' is more of an idea than a practical solution. Recent studies have shown that organizations currently employing blockchains record only certain transactions (related with accounts receivable and accounts payable accounts) on blockchains.

Other articles discussed 'Smart Contract' applied in auditing. Blockchains can carry not only transactional data in real time but can also encode human actions into executable code. Rozario and Vasarhelyi propose that external auditors utilize smart contracts [24] (see also Rozario and Thomas [25]). Automating the transaction reconciliation procedure makes auditing work more time-efficient and transparent. However, smart contracts are not 'smart' enough to address all the auditing procedure.

In our research, we work on smart contracts applied in the process of confirmation, in the form of access control system in auditing domain which involves less complicated judgements and can be easily executed by computer scripts.

2.3   Current Solution

In response to the above-mentioned inefficiencies in the current audit process, people from all over the world have proposed several solutions to tackle the challenges. One typical success story is the electronic audit confirmation platform Confirmation.com in the United States.

As early as 2000, Confirmation.com was founded to replace the traditional paper letter process. Confirmation.com is a privately-created third-party platform that provides an online solution that automates audit verification and credit inquiry processes, enabling banks to increase efficiency and reduce risk while complying with regulatory standards. Confirmation.com helps nearly a million and a half clients across 160 countries confirm more than $1 trillion in financial transactions every year. Globally Confirmation.com has more than 16,000 accounting firms and 200,000 accountants as its users.

To illustrate its commitments to effective operational controls and best practices in privacy and security, Confirmation.com undergoes all three Service Organization Control (SOC) examinations annually, and it has received an ISO 27001 certification, TRUSTe Privacy Policy certification, and EU Privacy Shield certification for its services.

Even though with such stringent security inspections and scrutiny, Confirmation. com can only ensure the data privacy and confidentiality. What it cannot ensure are the data authenticity and identity verification.

First, data authenticity and validity. According to the official website, the Confirmation.com according to the official website, Confirmation.com only provides an intermediary platform, which cannot guarantee the authenticity of the letter, the authenticity of the transaction, and the correctness of the data received by the other party. It has no control over the quality, accuracy, timeliness or legality of the requests and the responses, or the truth or accuracy of the requests and responses.

Second, ID authenticity and validity. Confirmation.com uses many techniques to identify its users when they register on website. However, because user verification on the Internet is difficult, Confirmation.com cannot and does not confirm each user's purported identity. Thus, it has established a user-initiated communication system to help users identify whom they are dealing with. It encourages users to communicate directly with other individual parties through the tools available on its website.

To draw an analogy, Confirmation.com is similar to a telephone line, providing a communication channel between the issuing side and the receiving side of the letter, but it does not guarantee the person who is talking under Tom's name is truly that Tom in real life, nor can it guarantee the authenticity and validity of the contents of the call.

Compared to Confirmation.com, our blockchain-based Automated Data Processing scheme automatically acquires data from the bank database through smart contracts, ensuring the authenticity of the data. It also verifies the true identities of the participating entities through the distribution of public and private keys.

One other strand of the current solutions is the centralized processing at the auditee and accounting firms' side. At present, the major accounting firms have begun to set up their own departments of audit service centers, where the inefficient and heavy-duty works of auditing letters are in-sourced to such in-source centers. For example, KPMG has set up the KPMG Delivery Center (KDC) to transfer the highly repetitive and pipeline works to KDCs internally to improve the work efficiency and productivity of the main offices; KDCs are generally located in second-tier cities with lower taxes and labor costs to complete these highly repetitive and pipeline tasks. However, this does not solve the fundamental problem. Although the main office work efficiency and productivity has increased by 10%, these works have been handed over to KDC staff with less qualifications, for whom the chance of job promotion is almost zero.

From the perspective of work efficiency and productivity, in-sourcing the letters to KDCs has spawned other issues. For example, because of the need to meet the batch processing requirements of the delivery center, the project team has to spend a lot of time filling out the templates and sending them to the delivery center, rendering the KDCs to be not much helpful. In many cases, it is actually even faster for the project team to issue the letters and send out by itself. In addition, due to the fact that the person filling in the letters are not the same as the person sending out the letters, information updates are often asymmetric, which disrupts the progress of audit.

The third strand of the current solutions lies at the receiving side – the banks. Of course, banks have taken similar centralization measures to reduce the workload. Major banks in Australia, the United Kingdom, the United States, Hong Kong and other countries and regions have set up centralized confirmation letter processing centers, which obtain permissions from customer companies, and handle the inquiries requested by accounting firms or other third parties directly.

Our system is similar to the above process, where we establish an online electronic bank confirmation process platform on top of blockchain architecture.

3 Blockchain-Based Bank Confirmation Process Platform

3.1 Overview of Our Approach

Our system combines blockchain and traditional database. The underlying data storage of the system is handled by the traditional SQL database and the blockchain. The blockchain layer is responsible for the storage and execution of the core authorization logic and the storage and verification of the core authorization data. The traditional SQL database stores the enterprises and business flow data in the bank.

An overview of our approach is shown in Fig. 2. We use blockchain to facilitate two process - Authorization Process and Acquisition Process. The Authorization Process is carried out on the chain, and the Acquisition Process is carried out off the chain. The Software Development Kit (SDK) acts as a bridge between the user and the system to fulfill data interaction between those on the chain and those off the chain, deploying the auditor identity and authorization information stored in the smart contract. SQL plug-in is to verify the permissions and retrieve data from the SQL database. The details of these two processes and the interface layer will be illustrated in Sects. 3.2, 3.3 and 3.4.

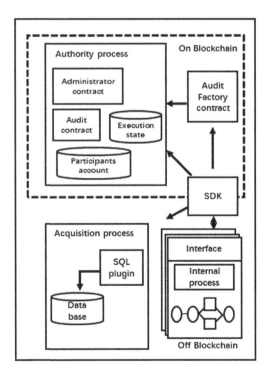

Fig. 2. Blockchain-based bank confirmation system

3.2 Authorization Process

The Authorization Process enables banks and audited companies to verify the identities of the auditors, thereby allowing auditors to obtain authorization and corresponding rights of data acquisition.

This process is implemented on the blockchain. We deploy a chain of alliances, including three types of nodes: banks, auditors, and companies. Only authenticated organizations can log in to the nodes to ensure information confidentiality, authentication, completeness and non-repudiation.

We employ the FISCO-BCOS framework as our blockchain runtime environment. FISCO-BCOS is a low-level blockchain architecture which customizes the Ethereum framework to suit the application scenarios of the alliance chain. It is deeply customized product with secureness and controllability, very suitable for the financial industry and is open source.

Specifically, we designed the following smart contracts to execute the identity authentication of all participating parties.

Audit Factory Contract: the Audit Factory contract is the entry contract for the entire certificate authentication contract system, providing the necessary contract entry. Basically all functions must start with the Audit Factory.

Audit Contract: the Audit contract stores specific audit permission information, and updates, adds, deletes, and maintains these rights information. The off-chain system restricts the accesses to audit data by querying the audit permissions stored in this contract.

Administrator Contract: the Administrator contract is used to store administrator information in the contract system, including: God administrators, bank administrators, enterprise administrators, etc., to provide permissions for the call of other contracts in the contract system.

3.3 Acquisition Process

Due to the high storage cost of blockchain, data needs to be stored off-chain, e.g. in banks and other data carriers. Acquisition Process enables auditors to acquire the corresponding data from the database according to the permissions they have obtained. Moreover, the SQL plug-in is needed for verifying the permissions and retrieving the corresponding data from the database.

The traditional SQL database in a bank mainly stores the business flow data of the bank. In the actual implementation process, the main problem we encountered was how to design our system such that it cooperates with a variety of bank data storage methods and storage structures, while ensuring the privacy in the bank. To solve this problem, we introduced a universal query interface in our system. Based on this interface, we developed specific data query plug-ins for various data storage structures and data storage methods to improve data security and usability.

In the overall structure, the data query plug-ins can also be spliced and combined with each other to form data access interfaces with hierarchical structure, which is convenient for coupling data accesses across multiple departments in the same bank, facilitating aggregation and summarization of data, and facilitating analysis and integration of audit data on the front desks.

A typical Acquisition Process is shown in Fig. 3. After receiving the audit application, the system automatically verifies the authorization information. And after verifying the authorization of the company and the bank, the system extracts the data from the database through the plug-ins, and then automatically deprives off the permissions. It then fills the data into the confirmation templates, generates and returns the complete forms to the auditor.

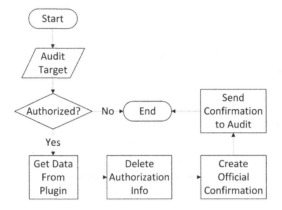

Fig. 3. Acquisition process flow diagram

3.4 The Interface Layer

As a bridge between the on-chain and the off-chain, the SDK plays an important role in the entire automated confirmation letter system. The SDK unifies the data on the chain and the data off-chain to jointly fulfill the confirmation work. The off-chain service obtains the necessary service functionalities by calling the SDK to obtain the data on-chain as well as the program interface provided by the contracts on-chain.

4   Executing the Blockchain-Based Bank Confirmation Process

4.1 The Auditor, Bank, and Auditee Registers to Obtain the Private Keys

When the auditor, bank, and company submit to the platform the necessary identity authentication information, such as a business license, the platform automatically grants private key addresses, which can be bound to a fixed IP address and mobile phone number to ensure the consistency between identity on-chain and identity off-chain (Fig. 4).

The public-private keys are a key pair generated strictly according to the RSA asymmetric encryption algorithm, which assumes functionalities such as identity verification and message signature in the blockchain system.

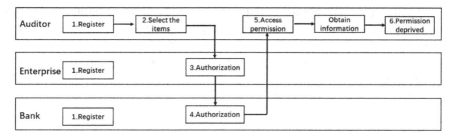

Fig. 4. Blockchain-based bank confirmation process

4.2   The Auditor Submits Inquiries and Obtain the Authentication

The auditor can submit inquiries to the banks and companies who have joined the alliance chain, through the on-chain messaging protocol AMOP provided by FISCO-BCOS.

The on-chain messaging protocol AMOP system aims to provide a secure and efficient message channel for the alliance chain. Each organization on the alliance chain can use AMOP for communication as long as the blockchain node is deployed, whether it is a consensus node or an observation node.

4.3   Auditee Node Authorization

Before the auditor obtains the specific audit data, it needs to obtain the unanimous authorization of the auditee and the data source bank. The auditee authorization process is shown in Fig. 5:

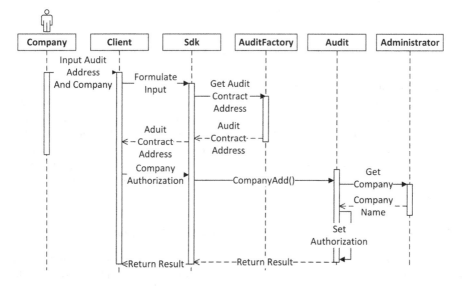

Fig. 5. Auditee authorization process

The auditee first enters the authorized auditor's chain address in the client-end GUI of our platform. After retrieving the specific address of the auditor's license contract through SDK, the client-end software invokes the auditee authorization interface of the specific license contract through SDK. The authorization contract will first use the administrator contract to obtain the caller's identity, and then record and return the authorization results according to the input permission rights information.

4.4   Bank Node Authorization

Before the auditor obtains the specific audit data, it needs to obtain the unanimous authorization of the auditee and the data source bank. The bank authorization process is as Fig. 6:

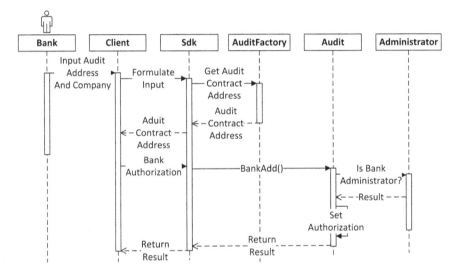

Fig. 6. Bank authorization process

The bank first enters the authorized auditor's chain address, auditee and specific permissions in the client-end GUI of our platform. After retrieving the specific address of the auditor's license contract through SDK, the client-end software invokes the bank authorization interface of the specific authorization contract through SDK. The authorization contract will first use the administrator contract to verify whether the identity of the caller is legitimate. If the identity of the caller is legitimate, the audit authorization is recorded according to the input permission rights information, and the authorization results are returned.

4.5   The Auditor Obtains the Requested Auditee Information

After obtaining the authorization both from the auditee and the bank, the auditor can then obtain the business flow information of the corresponding auditee stored in the bank databases. The data acquisition process is as Fig. 7:

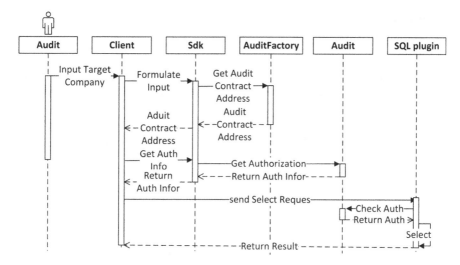

Fig. 7. Data acquisition process

The auditor queries the business flow data of the auditee through the query interface provided by our platform. The query interface first verifies the authentication of the auditor through the blockchain. If the bank's authorization is consistent with the auditee's authorization and both are valid, the requested data can then be obtained thru query interface provided by the bank and the confirmation template can be generated.

4.6 The Retrieved Information Is Returned to the Auditor and a Fixed Format Letter Is Automatically Generated

After the data query is completed, the system will automatically generate the electronic version of the standard letter in PDF format according to the fixed standard document template and seal it with the official stamp of the bank. The platform will then send the letter to the auditor online. The auditor can download the PDF file or opt to receive a paper copy of the document.

4.7 Deprivation off Audit Permission

After the above process is completed, the system will deprive the auditor off the query permissions used in the above process. For example, if both the bank and the auditee have granted the auditor deposit and loan enquiry permissions, and the auditor only obtains the deposit information, the system will only deprive the auditor off the deposit inquiry permission rights, and the loan inquiry permission rights granted by the bank and the auditee will be retained.

5 Evaluation

5.1 Latency

In our evaluation, we randomly generated 11 companies, 1 bank, 7 auditing firms, and one administrator to simulate the typical workflows on our confirmation platform, with a total of more than 1,000 deposit and loan data.

We randomly selected auditing queries from the auditing firm and the auditee, and queried 100,000 times. According to the typical workflow of bank authorization -> auditee authorization -> data query -> authorization destruction, we measure the time elapsed starting from the bank authorization and ending at the returning of queried results. During our tests, the server load was stable and no data errors or server failures were caused by large traffic data. In all 100,000 tests, the shortest processing time was 1.5437 s. The longest processing time was 1.7835 s. And all 100,000 tests take about 1 day, 20 h, 41 min, 27.3848 s.

The processing time of an offline manual inquiry letter is about 4 h and the mailing of the inquiry letter takes 6–8 days. Through our platform, the processing time can be greatly shortened to less than 10 min (submitting application takes about 5 min, multi-party authorization takes about 2 s, and generating and downloading reply letter takes about 3 min), with the mailing time shortened to 0. On average, each confirmation letter saves about 220 min of processing time and 6–8 days of mailing time, which is a 95% of total time reduction. Currently, the number of confirmation letters that banks need to process is several million each year. The application of the system can save banks and auditors about 18,333,000 h per year. The exact numbers are very difficult to calculate precisely, but the scale of time saving and productivity boosting is huge.

5.2 Storage Efficiency

In the actual tests, we also measured the consumption of storage space. The Audit Factory contract occupies approximately 534 bytes, the Audit License contract occupies approximately 686 bytes, and the Administrator contract occupies approximately 297 bytes. A single authorization and deprivation authorization transaction takes up approximately 127 bytes. From the above data, it can be calculated that in 20 auditing firms, 10,000 auditing queries consume about 3.634 GB of space, which does not occupy a lot of space and can support long-term stable operation of the system. In the current market, the price of a 6 TB enterprise-class hard disk is about 1,300 RMB. If only calculating the consumption of block data storage, the 6 TB hard disk can store about 16,000,000 audit authorization information, meeting at least one year of audit business needs.

5.3 Anti-fraud

Compared to the information on blockchain, paper materials can be easily forged. While based on the blockchain, we can track and trace the full audit process because the information of all links is stored in the chain and is immutable. The blockchain authenticates the user's identity through public and private keys and is automatically executed through smart contracts, thereby improving process efficiency while ensuring material authenticity.

6 Conclusion

In this paper we present our novel blockchain-based automated data processing scheme in the area of bank audit confirmation. Our main contribution is the application of blockchain technology to the process of auditing to automate the authorization of many participating parties, to build a secure, reliable and immutable system using access control tools and to unburden the audits from the cumbersome auditing confirmation procedure, while conforming to the standards of auditing. Our system has feasibility thanks to the relatively small time and storage costs. Our future direction of research is to optimize the system for performance and scalability. Most importantly, we will take into account the regulatory supervision and integrate financial regulators into the system and extend the system to provide traceable evidence for regulatory inspections.

In fact, our automated auditing system can do a lot more than what we have presented here. We will find that the three roles involved in the entire audit process - banks, auditees, auditors - can be abstracted into three types of data roles: data store, data owner, and data consumer. Our system provides privacy management for data owners, rights management for data storage, and data acquisition services for data consumers. Therefore, our system can actually be seen as a third-party platform for privacy preserving and rights managed data sharing.

References

1. Narayanan, A., Bonneau, J., Felten, E., Miller, A., Goldfeder, S.: Bitcoin and Cryptocurrency Technologies: A Comprehensive Introduction. Princeton University Press, Princeton (2016)
2. Wright, A., De Filippi, P.: Decentralized blockchain technology and the rise of lex cryptographia. (2015). SSRN 2580664
3. Crosby, M., Pattanayak, P., Verma, S., Kalyanaraman, V.: Blockchain technology: beyond bitcoin. Appl. Innov. 2(6–10), 71 (2016)
4. Iansiti, M., Lakhani, K.R.: The truth about blockchain. Harvard Bus. Rev. 95(1), 118–127 (2017)
5. Christidis, K., Devetsikiotis, M.: Blockchains and smart contracts for the internet of things. IEEE Access 4, 2292–2303 (2016)
6. Luu, L., Chu, D.H., Olickel, H., Saxena, P., Hobor, A.: Making smart contracts smarter. In: Proceedings of the 2016 ACM SIGSAC Conference on Computer and Communications Security, pp. 254–269. ACM, October 2016
7. Delmolino, K., Arnett, M., Kosba, A., Miller, A., Shi, E.: Step by step towards creating a safe smart contract: lessons and insights from a cryptocurrency lab. In: Clark, J., Meiklejohn, S., Ryan, P.Y.A., Wallach, D., Brenner, M., Rohloff, K. (eds.) FC 2016. LNCS, vol. 9604, pp. 79–94. Springer, Heidelberg (2016). https://doi.org/10.1007/978-3-662-53357-4_6

8. Atzei, N., Bartoletti, M., Cimoli, T.: A survey of attacks on Ethereum smart contracts (SoK). In: Maffei, M., Ryan, M. (eds.) POST 2017. LNCS, vol. 10204, pp. 164–186. Springer, Heidelberg (2017). https://doi.org/10.1007/978-3-662-54455-6_8

9. Zyskind, G., Nathan, O.: Decentralizing privacy: using blockchain to protect personal data. In: 2015 IEEE Security and Privacy Workshops, pp. 180–184. IEEE, May 2015

10. Shafagh, H., Burkhalter, L., Hithnawi, A., Duquennoy, S.: Towards blockchain-based auditable storage and sharing of IoT data. In: Proceedings of the 2017 on Cloud Computing Security Workshop, pp. 45–50. ACM, November 2017

11. Cruz, J.P., Kaji, Y., Yanai, N.: RBAC-SC: role-based access control using smart contract. IEEE Access **6**, 12240–12251 (2018)

12. Lin, I.C., Liao, T.C.: A survey of blockchain security issues and challenges. Int. J. Network Secur. **19**(5), 653–659 (2017)

13. Conoscenti, M., Vetro, A., De Martin, J.C.: Blockchain for the Internet of Things: a systematic literature review. In: 2016 IEEE/ACS 13th International Conference of Computer Systems and Applications (AICCSA), pp. 1–6. IEEE, November 2016

14. Karame, G.O., Androulaki, E., Capkun, S.: Double-spending fast payments in bitcoin. In: Proceedings of the 2012 ACM Conference on Computer and Communications Security, pp. 906–917. ACM, October 2012

15. Reid, F., Harrigan, M.: An analysis of anonymity in the bitcoin system. In: Altshuler, Y., Elovici, Y., Cremers, A., Aharony, N., Pentland, A. (eds.) Security and Privacy in Social Networks, pp. 197–223. Springer, New York (2013). https://doi.org/10.1007/978-1-4614-4139-7_10

16. Casey, M.J., Vigna, P.: The Truth Machine: The Blockchain and the Future of Everything. St. Martin's Press, New York (2018)

17. Atzori, M.: Blockchain technology and decentralized governance: is the state still necessary? J. Governance Regul. **6**(1) (2017)

18. Piazza, F.S.: Bitcoin and the blockchain as possible corporate governance tools: strengths and weaknesses. Penn State J. Law Int. Aff. **5**(2), 262 (2017)

19. Rooney, H., Aiken, B., Rooney, M.: Q&A is internal audit ready for blockchain? Technol. Innov. Manag. Rev. **7**(10), 41–44 (2017)

20. Yermack, D.: Corporate governance and blockchains. Rev. Finance **21**(1), 7–31 (2017)

21. Schmitz, J., Leoni, G.: Accounting and auditing at the time of blockchain technology: a research agenda. Aust. Acc. Rev. (2019)

22. Wang, Y., Kogan, A.: Designing confidentiality-preserving blockchain-based transaction processing systems. Int. J. Acc. Inf. Syst. **30**, 1–18 (2018)

23. Kokina, J., Mancha, R., Pachamanova, D.: Blockchain: emergent industry adoption and implications for accounting. J. Emerg. Technol. Acc. **14**(2), 91–100 (2017)

24. Rozario, A.M., Vasarhelyi, M.A.: Auditing with smart contracts. Int. J. Digital Acc. Res. **18** (2018)

25. Rozario, A., Thomas, C.: Reshaping the audit with blockchain and artificial intelligence: an external auditor blockchain for close to real-time audit reporting. Rutgers University Working Paper (2017)

A New Approach to Prevent Reentrant Attack in Solidity Smart Contracts

Chunyan Dong[1(✉)], Yuanhong Li[2], and Liang Tan[1,3]

[1] College of Computer Science, Sichuan Normal University,
Chengdu 610101, Sichuan, China
460635825@qq.com
[2] Sichuan Institute of Science and Technology Information,
Chengdu 610016, Sichuan, China
[3] Institute of Computing Technology, Chinese Academy of Sciences,
Beijing 100190, China

Abstract. Currently, Solidity is a high-level language for smart contracts that need to run on Ethereum virtual machines, it is being promoted with the widespread use of Ethereum. However, the Solidity has a feature of fallback function, makes it easier for attackers to use fallback function to launch reentrant attack, which may cause huge economic losses about the user. Therefore, a new method based on Solidity and Condition-Orientated programming is proposed to prevent reentrant attack. This method separates conditional branches and major logical state changes, encapsulates the separated conditional branches into multiple modifiers and defines a global state variable, packages the state of the state variable in the modifier, and finally uses the modifier as a precondition for the transfer function in the smart contract. When an attacker reenters the transfer function in the smart contract, the reentrant attack can be prevented by controlling state variable. The experimental results show that this method not only makes the logic of the contract code more reasonable, but also effective.

Keywords: Blockchain · Smart contract · Solidity · Reentrant attack

1 Introduction

In recent years, Blockchain [1, 2] is developing rapidly, and received key attention from the government departments, financial institutions, and technology companies [3]. Simultaneously, blockchain enters the 2.0 era represented by Ethereum [5, 6] from the 1.0 era represented by Bitcoin [4]. Based on the Ethereum platform, the smart contract [7–12] born on ethereum is a highlight of the blockchain. Essentially, smart contract is a piece of code that runs in blockchain, it's a pre-written piece of code, identifies and judges data information obtained from outside. When the conditions preset by the program are met, the system is automatically triggered to execute the corresponding contract terms, thereby completing the transfer of the transaction and the smart asset [11].

At present, Large-Scale Decentralized Applications [13] (DApps) based on smart contracts are also widely used in financial and supply chain systems [14, 15]. For example, the blockchain project GSENetwork is applied in the field of digital financial

© Springer Nature Singapore Pte Ltd. 2020
X. Si et al. (Eds.): CBCC 2019, CCIS 1176, pp. 83–103, 2020.
https://doi.org/10.1007/978-981-15-3278-8_6

inclusion to solve the problem of "centralization" in the development of digital financial inclusion. Apart from this, Jingdong applies blockchain smart contract technology to anti-counterfeiting traceability in supply chain scenarios, and consumers can see the full traceability and supervision process of important commodities on the mobile or PC side. The reason why smart contract can get the attention of domestic and foreign financial institutions and central banks is mainly because it has the following technical advantages. On the one hand, it implements programmable currency and programmable financial functions; On the other hand, it can guarantee the automatic execution of transactions without the mutual trust between the two parties, which improves the level of automatic transactions and reduces the cost of financial transactions and contract execution [14, 15]. But at the same time, due to it involves the financial transactions and amount transfer business between major financial enterprises and institutions, and cannot be interfered by human, its own security has also aroused wide concern and discussion from all walks of life in the society. In particular, the high-level language Solidity [16–18] for writing smart contracts has become the focus of smart contract security.

Solidity is an object-oriented high-level language that runs on the Ethereum Virtual Machine [19] (EVM). It is also the common language recommended by the official website for writing smart contracts. With the widespread use of the Ethereum platform, the Solidity is gradually being promoted [20]. As a high-level programming language, Solidity's language mechanism is also flawed. Since the Solidity has the function of the fallback, once the executed program code involves the Ethereum transaction, the receiver's program must be accompanied by a fallback function and the function is called [21]. It is easy for contract attackers to exploit the vulnerability of fallback function to write arbitrary malicious code in fallback function, implement the infinite loop of transfer function, and launch reentrant attack [21, 23]. The so-called reentrant attack means that there are two smart contracts, contract A and contract B respectively. When contract B calls the transfer function of the contract A, all transactions between the two contracts and the transfer of Ether will be controlled by contract B. This may result in contract B entering contract A multiple times before the end of the transaction. In addition, smart contracts have the characteristics of immutability. Once deployed on the blockchain, they can't be modified even if there are errors, which will bring huge economic losses to users. Unless smart contracts start a self-destructive program and end its life cycle. Currently, the DAO event, the world's largest smart contract vulnerability event, exploited the vulnerability of reentrant attacks, causing users to lose nearly $60 million [21].

To prevent reentrant attacks, this paper proposes a solution that uses the condition-orientated programming design pattern and based on the Solidity to combine the modifiers and state variables to prevent reentrant attacks. The scheme separates the conditional branches and the main logic state change, encapsulates the separated conditional branches into multiple modifiers and defines a global state variable, encapsulates and judges the state of the state variable in the modifier. The experimental results show that this scheme can solve reentrant vulnerabilities through Solidity, preventing malicious traders that using reentrant attack vulnerabilities to conduct malicious transactions effectively, guaranteeing the security of transactions in smart contracts, and making the contract code logic more reasonable and clearer.

2   Related Work

Two problems that cause reentrant attacks are mainly due to the Solidity mechanism [24]. The first problem is that the Solidity has fallback function. In Fig. 1, the function in contract B is called the fallback function. The fallback function is a function in the Solidity that does not have function name, parameter, and return value. It is called in the following two cases: (1) None of the other functions match the given function identifier (2) The contract receives the Ether [16]. Therefore, contract B can take advantage of the second feature of the fallback function. Once the contract receives the Ether, it will trigger its own fallback function. If the fallback function of contract B has malicious code, it will cause the transfer function of contract A to be called repeatedly until the balance of contract A is 0 Ether. The second problem is the transfer method call.value(). In smart contracts, there are three ways to send Ether to implement the transfer function: transfer(), send(), and call.value() [16]. The first two methods will specify the upper limit of the 2300 gas value. If the Gas consumed by the code execution is greater than 2300 gas, the program will stop executing and roll back all the states. Gas [25, 26] refers to the cost of executing smart contract. If the transaction is executed step by step according to the rules of the smart contract, each command will generate certain consumption. This consumption is calculated by using Gas as a unit. call.value() differs from the other two methods in that not only it sends the specified number of Ether, but also has no Gas limit. Once the contract is transferred through this method, the executed code is given to all available Gas in the account until Gas is given out. Transactions initiated in this way can lead to reentrant attacks to a large extent.

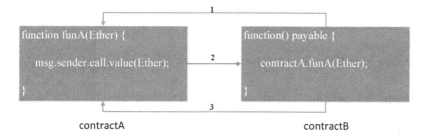

Fig. 1. The process of the reentrant attack

At present, for the reentrant attacks in smart contract, relevant experts and research scholars have proposed two kinds of solutions. One is to design a smarter smart contract language to avoid this attack. In the literature [27], Michael et al. proposed a new object-oriented language—Obsidian. This version is immune to reentrant calls because the external code [28] is invoked in a safe state: the payouts only occur on entering the state, not on calling a named function, and no unsafe functions are available in that state, and further restricting the execution of transfer from the state perspective. But the language is still in the prototype stage, not put into practical use, and Obsidian is a new language, which requires a lot of testing and has a long cycle. The other is to propose a solution in combination with the Solidity [29]. For example, use the transfer() or send() function when sending Ether. As mentioned in the previous article, they have a 2300 gas limit, making it insufficient to call another contract or execute more code. Up to a point, this will prevent the occurrence of reentrant attacks, but it may also cause some normal functions to be disabled because of insufficient Gas [29]. Another way is to ensure that all the logic that changes the state variables occurs before the transfer statement, update the state variables firstly, and then transfer the Ether after the conditions are met. This can prevent the reentrant attack effectively, but the code is not structured and clear. Furthermore, this is not convenient to reuse.

To sum up, whether it is to design a new smart contract programming language to avoid reentrant attacks, or to propose relevant solutions based on the Solidity, all have their own shortcomings and deficiencies. To this end, this paper will present a different solution based on the Solidity. The experimental results of this method show that it can effectively suppress reentrant attack without too much cost, which greatly reduces the time cost compared with the proposed new language. In addition, this paper adopts COP design pattern and adds function modifier to solve the problem that the previous method is not highly structured and inconvenient to reuse.

3 Solidity Smart Contract Against Reentrant Attack

In this section, we will introduce design and realization of the solidity smart contract against reentrant attack.

3.1 Design of Solidity Smart Contract Against Reentrant Attack

COP Design for Solidity. Condition-Orientated Programming [22] (COP) is subdomain of contract-orientated programming, and sits as a hybrid approach between functional and imperative programming. The idea of this design pattern is to separate the preconditions and the main logic code to ensure that there are no potential errors and to avoid overwriting the conditional logic. This design pattern makes the condition fragment be properly documented and standardized, and ensure the security of contract. COP is not specific to any language. However, it is particularly suitable for solidity because of its modifiers and events. In order to prevent reentrant attack on Solidity smart contracts, we designed the COP structure of solidity smart contract. As shown in Fig. 2.

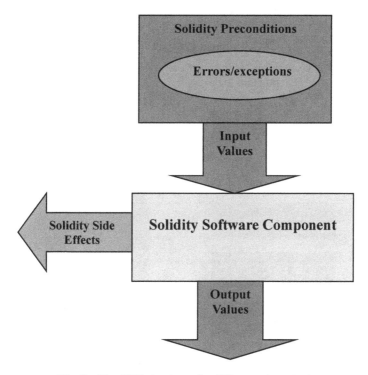

Fig. 2. The COP structure of solidity smart contract

As can be seen from Fig. 2, before entering the formal Solidity Software Component, we extract all the conditional branches and process them through the modifier in the prerequisites (Solidity Preconditions). If the condition is satisfied, it will enter the program from the Input Values to the Output Values; if the condition is not satisfied, enter Errors/exception handling mode. Different exception handling has different Solidity Side Effects.

Structure Design for Solidity. Figure 3 shows the basic structure of general smart contract, which we can understand it as an Ethereum bank.

The structure consists of five methods: constructor, the function of the constructor in solidity smart contract is the same as the constructor in other languages, mainly used to initialize the object when creating the object (create a contract object in Solidity); withDraw, in this function, we can use transfer(), send() or call.value() to transfer money. However, in order to present reentrant attack, we use call.value() to transfer Ether. Other contracts can call this function to transfer the Ether to their account through external call; receiveEther, update the user's account balance when the user deposits Ether into the contract. Corresponding to the ledger structure in Fig. 3, each user has account balance in the bank (contract); showAccount, which is used to display the amount of ether currency remaining in the current contract; fallback, a function

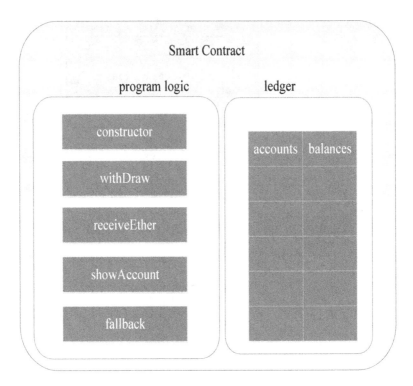

Fig. 3. Basic structure of general smart contract

without function name in contract is fallback function. When a contract wants to receive Ether, the contract must have fallback function, but you don't have to write logical code in fallback function.

Based on the COP design pattern structure of solidity designed in the previous section, we designed solidity smart contract structure against reentrant attack. As shown in Fig. 4.

As can be seen from Fig. 4, this smart contract structure is based on Fig. 3, adding the following elements: Firstly, the global state variable of the Boolean type. This state variable has two states, True and False. When the state variable is False, it indicates that the transfer transaction has not been performed before and the transaction will be conducted; When the state variable is True, it means that the transfer transaction has been executed and the transaction is no longer performed. Secondly, since this experiment is based on the COP mode and involves multiple layers of conditions, we extract all the conditional branches in the main logic function withDraw, encapsulate the conditional branches into modifiers noReentrancy and atLeast, and redefine a function callValue. noReentrancy modifies the main logic function withDraw, controls the number of external calls, prevents reentrant attacks; atLeast modifies callValue, judges the balance of the user, if there is balance, then transfer. Finally, call callValue in withDraw to complete the actual transaction.

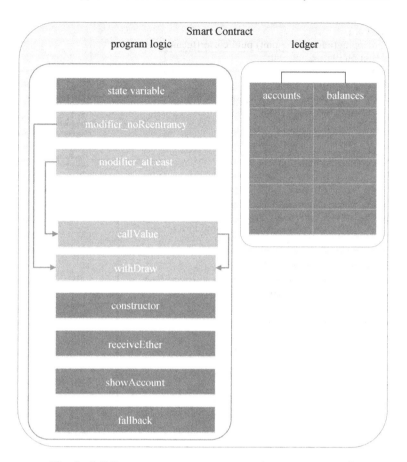

Fig. 4. Solidity smart contract structure against reentrant attack

3.2   Realization of Solidity Smart Contract Against Reentrant Attack

According to the design of Sect. 3.1, we implemented a COP template for smart contract (contract A) against reentrant attacks, as shown in Fig. 5.

As can be seen from Fig. 5, this contract template is based on the general smart contract structure and adds the anti-reentrant attack smart contract scheme proposed in this paper, which is the specific implementation of Fig. 4. The specific changes are as follows: 1. Line 4, define a state variable reenTrancylock and set its state to False 2. Line 5–10, define the modifier noReentrancy to determine the state of the state variable reenTrancylock. If reenTrancylock is false, it means that no transfer has been made before, so the reenTrancylock is set to true and the transfer function is executed, the "_" on line 8 represents that executes the function modified by the modifier; If reenTrancylock is true, it means that the transfer has been executed before, so stop the program

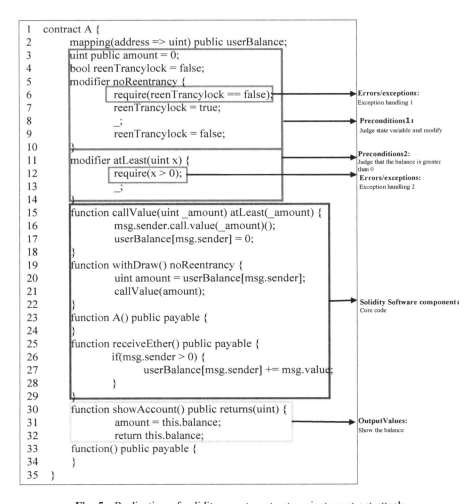

Fig. 5. Realization of solidity smart contract against reentrant attack

execution and throw an exception 3. Line 11–14, define the modifier atLeast to determine whether a user has stored Ether in the contract. If the user stores the Ether, the transfer is allowed to execute; Otherwise, the execution is rejected and an exception is thrown 4. Line 15, modifier atLeast modifies callValue; Line 19, modifier noReentrancy modifies withDraw. Two functions are combined to complete the transfer function. The part corresponding to the COP includes Solidity Preconditions, Errors/exception, Solidity Software Component, and Output Values. Input Values need to be initiated on the user side, and the Side Effect is reflected in the results.

4 Experiments and Comparative Analysis

4.1 Experimental Environment

We list the basic configuration information of the hardware platform and software platform in the experiment in Table 1. The software platform uses Remix, a browser-based integrated development environment that can be used to write, deploy, and run smart contracts, as well as an integrated debugger and test environment (testing the blockchain network). Link Remix: https://remix.Ethereum.org/

Table 1. Experimental environment configuration information

Hardware platform	Software platform
CPU: Intel(R) Core(TM) i5-4200U CPU @1.60 GHz System version: Windows10 Enterprise Memory: 12.0 GB Disk: 400 GB	IDE: Remix online

4.2 Experimental Process

In order to verify the feasibility and effectiveness of the smart contract for preventing reentrant attacks proposed in this paper, and compare it with the existing smart contract scheme for preventing reentrant attacks, we will carry out four experiments. Specific experiments are as follows:

Case 1: Reentrant attack process of traditional smart contracts [30]. The purpose of this experiment is to demonstrate the reentrant attack of smart contract. The specific steps are: First, start the Remix compiler and select the compiler version 0.4.24; Then, write the contract A and contract B used in this experiment. As shown in Figs. 6 and 7, contract A is a general smart contract's structure, corresponding to Fig. 3, contract B is a malicious contract that will launch a reentrant attack; Third, deploy contract A and contract B, contract A comes with 10 Ether, contract B comes with 1 Ether; Fourth, call contract B's sendMoney() method. Contract B deposits its own 1 Ether into contract A. Currently, the contract A balance is 11 Ether, and the contract B balance is 0 Ether; Finally, call contract B's reentry() method, contract B initiates reentrant attack.

The specific experimental results of Case 1 are shown in Figs. 8, 9, 10 and 11. Figure 8 shows contract B launches reentrant attack; Fig. 9 shows that after contract B launches reentrant attack, the balance of contract A is 0 Ether; Fig. 10 shows that after contract B launches reentrant attack, the balance of contract B is 11 Ether; Fig. 11 shows that the fallback function in contract B is called 11 times in total. The above results show that contract B launched reentrant attack successfully and transferred all the balances in contract A to its own account.

```
1    contract A {
2            mapping(address => uint) public userBalance;
3            uint public amount = 0;
4            function A() public payable {
5            }
6            function withDraw() {
7                    uint amount = userBalance[msg.sender];
8                    if(amount > 0) {
9                        msg.sender.call.value(amount)();
10                       userBalance[msg.sender] = 0;
11                   }
12           }
13           function receiveEther() public payable {
14                   if(msg.value > 0) {
15                           userBalance[msg.sender] += msg.value;
16                   }
17           }
18           function showAccount() public returns(uint) {
19                   amount = this.balance;
20                   return this.balance;
21           }
22           function() public payable {
22           }
23   }
```

Reentrant attack occurs here

Fig. 6. Contract A is used in case 1

Case 2: The Transfer() or Send() method for preventing reentrant attacks. The purpose of this experiment is to demonstrate the reentrant attack of smart contracts inhibited by traditional methods: Transfer() or Send(). Since the principles of Transfer() and Send() are the same, this experiment only takes Transfer() as an example. According to literature [15], this method is also adopted in most cases. Contract A of Fig. 6 and contract B of Fig. 7 still used in this experiment, but to modify the contract A as follows: Change msg.sender.call.value(amount)() on line 9 to msg.sender.transfer (amount) or msg.sender.send(amount). As shown in the Fig. 12. The specific experimental steps are the same as Case 1.

```
1    contract B {
2          uint public amount = 0;
3          uint public test = 0;
4          function B() public payable {
5          }
6          function() public payable {
7                  test ++;
8                  A(msg.sender).withDraw();
9          }
10         function showAccount() public returns(uint) {
11                 amount = this.balance;
12                 return this.balance;
13         }
14         function sendMoney(address addr) {
15                 A(addr).receiveEther.value(1 ether)();
16         }
17         function reentry(address addr) {
18                 A(addr).withDraw();
19         }
20  }
```

Fig. 7. Contract B is used in case 1, case 2, case 3 and case4

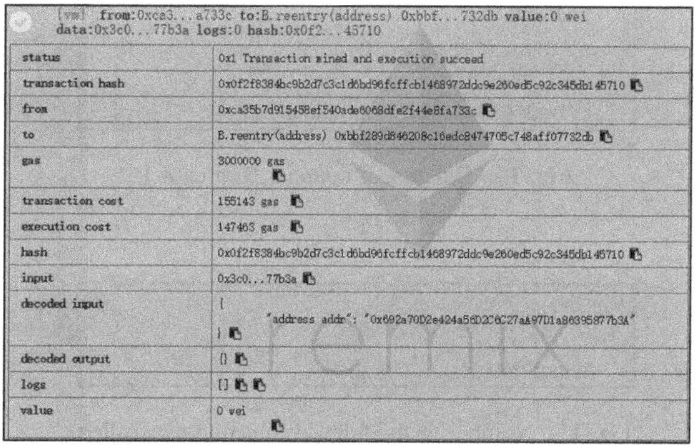

Fig. 8. Reentrant attack launched successfully

The specific experimental results of this experiment are shown in Figs. 13, 14 and 15. Figure 13 shows error after contract B launches reentrant attack, this is because the statement to be executed in the fallback function of contract B costs more than 2300 gas, and transfer() transfers have 2300 gas limit. Therefore, the statement in the contract B fallback function cannot be executed, causing the normal transfer to fail.

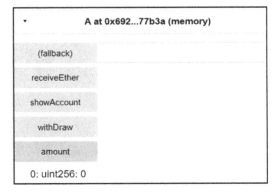

Fig. 9. Balance of contract A in case 1

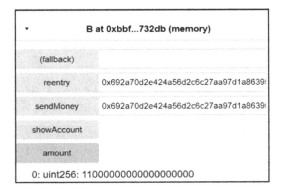

Fig. 10. Balance of contract B in case 1

Fig. 11. Number of the fallback function was called

Figure 14 shows that after contract B launches reentrant attack, the balance of contract A is 11 Ether; Fig. 15 shows that after contract B launches reentrant attack, the balance of contract B is 0 Ether.

```
1    contract A {
2         mapping(address => uint) public userBalance;
3         uint public amount = 0;
4         function A() public payable {
5         }
6         function withDraw() {
7              uint amount = userBalance[msg.sender];
8              if(amount > 0) {
9                   msg.sender.transfer(amount);          Change call.value() to
10                  userBalance[msg.sender] = 0;                  transfer()
11             }
12        }
13        function receiveEther() public payable {
14             if(msg.value > 0) {
15                  userBalance[msg.sender] += msg.value;
16             }
17        }
18        function showAccount() public returns(uint) {
19             amount = this.balance;
20             return this.balance;
21        }
22        function() public payable {
22        }
23   }
```

Fig. 12. Contract A is used in case 2

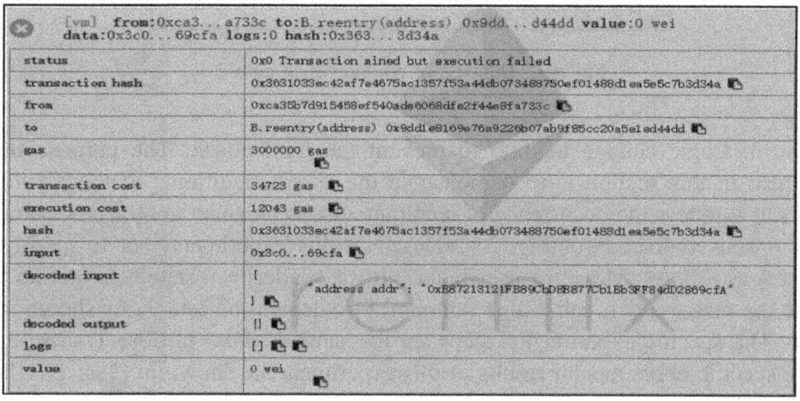

Fig. 13. Experimental results of using transfer()

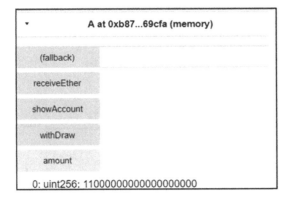

Fig. 14. Balance of contract A in case 2

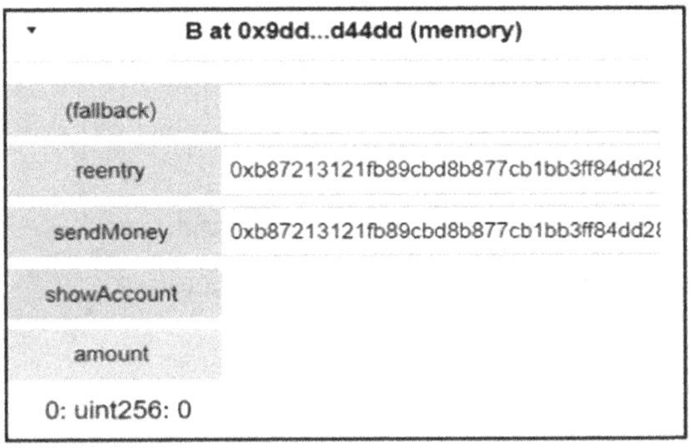

Fig. 15. Balance of contract B in case 2

Case 3: Logic change method to prevent reentrant attack. The purpose of the experiment in this section is to demonstrate the use of traditional methods—logical changes to suppress the occurrence of reentrant attacks on smart contracts. Contract A of Fig. 6 and contract B of Fig. 7 still used in this experiment, but to modify the contract A as follows: Move the userBalance [msg. sender] = 0 statement on line 10 to precede the msg. sender. call. value (amount) () statement on line 9. As shown in the Fig. 16. The specific experimental steps are the same as those in Case 1, Case 2.

The specific experimental results of this experiment are shown in Figs. 17, 18 and 19. Figure 17 shows that after contract B launches reentrant attack, the result is not wrong; Fig. 18 shows that after contract B launches reentrant attack, the balance of contract A is 10 Ether; Fig. 19 shows that after contract B launches reentrant attack, the balance of contract B is 1 Ether. The reason for the result of the experiment is: contract B only deposits 1 Ether into contract A initially, after contract B initiates a reentrant attack, determine the account balance of contract B in contract A firstly, and then update the account balance in time. Detected that contract B has 1 Ether in contract A, then contract B is retrieved. When reenter the transfer function, since contract B's balance in contract A is already 0 Ether, it is no longer executed.

```
1    contract A {
2           mapping(address => uint) public userBalance;
3           uint public amount = 0;
4           function A() public payable {
5           }
6           function withDraw() {
7                   uint amount = userBalance[msg.sender];
8                   if(amount > 0) {
9                       userBalance [msg. sender] = 0
10                      msg. sender. call. value (amount) ()
11                  }
12          }
13          function receiveEther() public payable {
14                  if(msg.value > 0) {
15                          userBalance[msg.sender] += msg.value;
16                  }
17          }
18          function showAccount() public returns(uint) {
19                  amount = this.balance;
20                  return this.balance;
21          }
22          function()  public payable {
22          }
23   }
```

Change the order of the two lines

Fig. 16. Contract A is used in case 3

Case 4: The solution proposed in this paper. The goal of this experiment is to demonstrate the effectiveness and feasibility of using this scheme to prevent reentrant attacks. This experiment uses contract A and contract B, contract A is Fig. 5 in Sect. 3.2 and contract B is Fig. 7. The specific experimental steps are the same as those in Case 1, Case 2 and Case 3. The specific experimental results of this experiment are shown in Figs. 20, 21 and 22. Figure 20 shows that after contract B launches reentrant attack, the result is not wrong; Fig. 21 shows that after contract B launches reentrant attack, the balance of contract A is 11 Ether; Fig. 22 shows that after contract B launches reentrant attack, the balance of contract B is 0 Ether. The main reason for the results of this experiment is: The require method we use in the modifier, which is one of the error handling functions in the Solidity, instead of the traditional method if…throw method. Satisfying the condition will continue to execute, if the condition is not met, the execution will be terminated and the current state will be rolled back. On the other hand, blockchain is a globally shared distributed transactional database, which indicates that all the transactions done are valid or invalid. So, through this method, it can suppress the occurrence of reentrant attacks effectively, but contract B will not be able to retrieve the 1 Ether deposited in Contract A originally.

Fig. 17. The experimental result of logical change

Fig. 18. Balance of contract A in case 3

Fig. 19. Balance of contract B in case 3

[vm] from:0xca3...a733c to:B.reentry(address) 0xd45...66bc0 value:0 wei data:0x3c0...e3967 logs:0 hash:0xfe2...a6af5	
status	0x1 Transaction mined and execution succeed
transaction hash	0xfe24821f3763f0361f4d366a2783485996eec6e431b166e8849d3b01d52a6af5
from	0xca35b7d915458ef540ade6068dfe2f44e8fa733c
to	B.reentry(address) 0xd45968f99ce42c63b2ee728bf4ccf63c19166bc0
gas	3000000 gas
transaction cost	45922 gas
execution cost	58106 gas
hash	0xfe24821f3763f0361f4d366a2783485996eec6e431b166e8849d3b01d52a6af5
input	0x3c0...e3967
decoded input	{ "address addr": "0xB05DF6af0073Fd592D8f6EE3D5C8AcOfF12e3967" }
decoded output	{}
logs	[]
value	0 wei

Fig. 20. The experimental result of this method

A at 0xb05...e3967 (memory)	
(fallback)	
callValue	uint256 _amount
receiveEther	
showAccount	
withDraw	
amount	
0: uint256: 11000000000000000000	

Fig. 21. Balance of contract A in case 4

B at 0xd45...66bc0 (memory)	
(fallback)	
reentry	0xb05df6af0073fd592d8f6ee3d5c8ac0ff12e
sendMoney	0xb05df6af0073fd592d8f6ee3d5c8ac0ff12e
showAccount	
amount	
0: uint256: 0	

Fig. 22. Balance of contract B in case 4

4.3   Experimental Analysis

In this section, we will make a comparative analysis of Transfer() and Send() methods for anti-reentrant attacks, logical change methods for anti-reentrant attacks and the scheme in this paper.

First, we compare the feasibility, effectiveness, comprehensibility, logical correctness, COP and the loss of Contract B as shown in Table 2. As can be seen from Table 2, the Transfer() and Send() method for anti-reentrant attacks are feasible and effective, the programming logic is correct, but not easy to understand, nor based on COP mode, and contract B loses 1 Ether; The logic change method for anti-reentrant attacks is also feasible and effective, but the programming logic is incorrect and not easy to understand. It is not based on COP mode, but contract B does not lose Ether; The scheme in this paper is also feasible and effective, the programming logic is correct, easy to understand and based on COP mode, but contractB loses 1 Ether. Compared with the other three methods, the scheme of this paper is better obviously.

Table 2. Anti-reentrant attack index comparison analysis table

Method	Feasibility	Effectiveness	Comprehensibility	Logical correctness	COP	Contract B loss
Transfer()	√	√	X	√	X	1eth
Send()	√	√	X	√	X	1eth
Logical change	√	√	X	X	X	0eth
Scheme of this paper	√	√	√	√	√	1eth

Then, we make a comparative analysis of Gas consumption. For the Solidity and the Ethereum environment, executing the same code and steps consumes the same Gas. We tested the transaction cost and execution cost of each solution. We executed 10 times for each solution. Since the consumption per execution is the same, we only record the results of one execution, as shown in Table 3 and Fig. 23.

Table 3. Gas consumption statistics (unit: gas)

Method	Transaction cost	Execution cost	Total cost
Transfer()	34723	12043	46766
Send()	24806	17126	41932
Logical change	44783	37103	81886
Scheme of this paper	45922	58106	104028

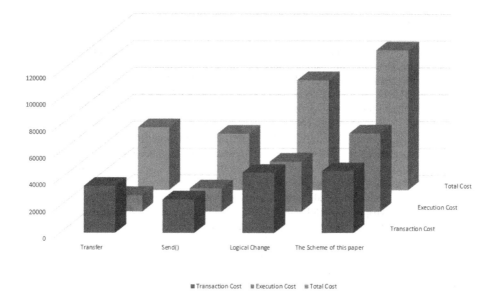

Fig. 23. Gas consumption comparison chart

As can be seen from Table 3 and Fig. 23, the total Gas consumed by "Transfer()" method is 46766 gas, the total consumption of the "Send()" method is 41932 gas, the total Gas consumption of "logical change method" is 81886 gas, the total Gas consumption of "the scheme in this paper" is 104028 gas. The Gas consumption is lower than the Gas maximum limit of 3000000 gas, which is within an acceptable range.

5   Conclusion

For the reentrant attack vulnerability of smart contracts based on Solidity, we propose a reentrant attack solution based on "state variable + modifier" using condition-oriented programming mode. Through testing, the scheme can effectively suppress reentrant attacks in smart contracts while the contract is running normally, and modify it from the Solidity, which is more convenient and mature than other schemes, and more structured. However, there is still a problem in this scheme. The ether currency originally deposited by the attacker will never be retrieved due to the problem of the Solidity mechanism. In the following work, we will continue to improve the smart contract structure against reentrant attacks, to achieve reentrant attacks that can prevent smart contracts, and to break the impediment of the Solidity mechanism.

Acknowledgements. This work is supported by National Natural Science Foundation of China under grants 61373162, Sichuan Science and Technology Support Project under grants 2019YFG0183, and Visual Computing and Virtual Reality Sichuan Provincial Key Laboratory Project under grants KJ201402.

References

1. Shuai, W., Liwei, O., Yong, Y., Xiaochun, N., Xuan, H., Feiyue, W.: Blockchain-enabled smart contracts: architecture, applications, and future trends. IEEE Trans. Syst. Man Cybern. Syst., 1–12 (2019). https://doi.org/10.1109/tsmc.2019.2895123
2. Yong, Y., Feiyue, W.: Blockchain: the state of the art and future trends. Acta Autom. Sin., 481–494 (2016). https://doi.org/10.16383/j.aas.2016.c160158
3. Haiwu, H., Zehua, C.: Survey of smart contract technology and application based on blockchain. J. Comput. Res. Dev., 112–126 (2018). CNKI:SUN:JFYZ.0.2018-11-010
4. A peer-to-peer electronic cash system. http://www.bitcoin.org/bitcoin.pdf
5. A Next-Generation Smart Contract and Decentralized Application Platform. https://github.com/ethereum/wiki/wiki/White-Paper
6. A secure decentralised generalised transaction ledger (eip-150 revision). https://github.com/ethereum/yellowpaper/raw/2c6fba1400e321734ccec19cb5d9cb32a51ffc44/paper.pdf
7. Making sense of blockchain smart contract. https://www.coindesk.com/making-sense-smart-contracts
8. Alexander, M., Markus, F.: Security vulnerabilities in ethereum smart contracts. In: Proceedings of the 20th International Conference on Information Integration and Web-based Applications & Services, pp. 375–380. ACM, New York (2018). https://doi.org/10.1145/3282373.3282419
9. Néstor, A.D., Jordi, H.J., Pino, C.G.: Smart contracts based on blockchain for logistics management. In: Proceedings of the 1st International Conference on Internet of Things and Machine Learning. ACM, New York (2017). https://doi.org/10.1145/3109761.3158384
10. Konstantinos, C., Michael, D.: Blockchains and smart contracts for the Internet of Things. IEEE Access, 2292–2303. https://doi.org/10.1109/access.2016.2566339
11. Schrans, F., Eisenbach, S., Drossopoulou, S.: Writing safe smart contracts in Flint. In: Programming 2018 Companion Conference Companion of the 2nd International Conference on Art, Science, and Engineering of Programming, pp. 218–219. ACM, New York (2018). https://doi.org/10.1145/3191697.3213790
12. Nick, S.: Smart Contracts: 12 Use Cases for Business & Beyond. Chamber of Digital Commerce (2016)
13. Liwei, O., Shuai, W., Yong, Y., Xiaochun, N., Feiyue, W.: Smart contracts: architecture and research progresses. Acta Autom. Sin., 445–457. https://doi.org/10.16383/j.aas.c180586
14. Shuang, S., Ke, W., Hyong, S.K.: Smartsupply: smart contract based validation for supply chain blockchain. In: 2018 IEEE International Conference on Internet of Things, Canada. IEEE (2018). https://doi.org/10.1109/cybermatics_2018.2018.00186
15. Bhabendu, K.M., Soumyashree, S.P., Debasish, J.: An overview of smart contract and use cases in blockchain technology. In: 2018 9th International Conference on Computing, Communication and Networking Technologies (ICCCNT), India. IEEE (2018). https://doi.org/10.1109/icccnt.2018.8494045
16. A new programming language for writing smart contracts on Ethereum. https://solidity.readthedocs.io/en/develop/
17. Santiago, B., Henrique, R., Marcus, D., Stéphane, D.: SmartInspect: solidity smart contract inspector. In: 2018 International Workshop on Blockchain Oriented Software Engineering (IWBOSE), Italy. IEEE (2018). https://doi.org/10.1109/iwbose.2018.8327566
18. Hegedűs, P.: Towards analyzing the complexity landscape of solidity based ethereum smart contracts. In: 2018 IEEE/ACM 1st International Workshop on Emerging Trends in Software Engineering for Blockchain (WETSEB), pp. 35–39. https://doi.org/10.1145/3194113.3194119

19. Hildenbrandt, E., Saxena, M., Rodrigues, N.: KEVM: a complete formal semantics of the ethereum virtual machine. In: 2018 IEEE 31st Computer Security Foundations Symposium (CSF), UK, pp. 204–217. IEEE. https://doi.org/10.1109/csf.2018.00022
20. Ence, Z., Song, H., Bingfeng, P., Jun, S., Yashihide, N., Kazuhiro, Y.: Security assurance for smart contract. In: 2018 9th IFIP International Conference on New Technologies, Mobility and Security (NTMS), France, pp. 1–5. IEEE. https://doi.org/10.1109/ntms.2018.8328743
21. Karthikeyan, B., Antoine, D.L., Cedric, F., Anitha, G., Georges, G.: Short paper: formal verification of smart contracts. In: 11th ACM Workshop on Programming Languages and Analysis for Security (PLAS), pp. 91–96
22. Condition-Orientated Programming. https://medium.com/@gavofyork/condition-orientated-programming-969f6ba0161a
23. Chao, L., Han, L., Zhao, C., Zhong, C., Bangdao, C., Bill, R.: ReGuard: finding reentrancy bugs in smart contracts. In: Proceedings of the 40th International Conference on Software Engineering: Companion Proceedings, pp. 65–68. ACM, New York (2018). https://doi.org/10.1145/3183440.3183495
24. Maximilian, W., Uwe, Z.: Smart contracts: security patterns in the ethereum ecosystem and solidity. In: 2018 International Workshop on Blockchain Oriented Software Engineering (IWBOSE), Italy, pp. 2–8. IEEE (2018). https://doi.org/10.1109/iwbose.2018.8327565
25. Ardit, D.: Ethereum Smart Contracts: Security Vulnerabilities and Security Tools. Norwegian University of Science and Technology (NTNU)
26. Delmolino, K., Arnett, M., Kosba, A., Miller, A., Shi, E.: Step by step towards creating a safe smart contract: lessons and insights from a cryptocurrency lab. In: Clark, J., Meiklejohn, S., Ryan, P.Y.A., Wallach, D., Brenner, M., Rohloff, K. (eds.) FC 2016. LNCS, vol. 9604, pp. 79–94. Springer, Heidelberg (2016). https://doi.org/10.1007/978-3-662-53357-4_6
27. Michael, C.: Obsidian: a safer blockchain programming language. In: Proceedings of the 39th International Conference on Software Engineering Companion, USA, pp. 97–99. IEEE Press (2017). https://doi.org/10.1109/icse-c.2017.150
28. Loi, L., Duc-Hiep, C., Hrishi, O., Prateek, S., Aquinas, H.: Making smart contracts smarter. In: Proceedings of the 2016 ACM SIGSAC Conference on Computer and Communications Security, pp. 254–269. ACM, New York. https://doi.org/10.1145/2976749.2978309
29. A comprehensive list of known attack methods and common defense patterns. https://ethfans.org/posts/comprehensive-list-of-common-attacks-and-defense-part-1
30. Ethereum Reentrant Attack Paradigm. https://blog.csdn.net/Programmer_CJC/article/details/85987234

CoT: A Secure Consensus of Trust with Delegation Mechanism in Blockchains

Sai Lv[1], Hui Li[1,2(✉)], Han Wang[1,2], and Xiangui Wang[1]

[1] Shenzhen Graduate School, Peking University,
Beijing, People's Republic of China
1701213616@sz.pku.edu.cn, lih64@pkusz.edu.cn,
wanghan2017@pku.edu.cn
[2] Peng Cheng Laboratory, Shenzhen, People's Republic of China

Abstract. The consensus algorithm is a key part of blockchains, which significantly influences the performance of security and efficiency. The PoW consensus guarantees the security of decentralized systems by competing to solve a puzzle, while with serious energy waste and low throughout. Follow-up consensus algorithms adopt delegation mechanisms to improve throughput and scalability. However, these delegation mechanisms, which are essentially partly decentralized, have security risks. This paper presents a consensus algorithm based on trust relationship between nodes, called Consensus of Trust (CoT), and introduces real-time credit of nodes into the delegation mechanism of the blockchain system. Firstly, CoT quantifies the trust relationship between nodes based on interactive transactions and generates the corresponding credit graph and matrix. It then uses the iterative algorithm, a variant of PageRank, to calculate the credit value of each node from the trust matrix. The nodes with high credit value are selected as the delegated nodes to participate in the block generation. We finally analyze the security performance that CoT can tolerant more than 33% of nodes to be malicious. We also prove the effectiveness and consistency in CoT.

Keywords: Blockchain · Delegation mechanism · Consensus algorithm · Security

1 Introduction

With the scientific and technological revolution and industrial transformation, the Internet has gradually developed. The information on the network is open and transparent, with the possibility of tampering and becoming untrustworthy. The trust guarantee provided by the third party is required. However, the third-party platform still has the possibility of becoming untrustworthy. In order to solve the trust problems, the blockchain technology [1] comes into being. It is an integrated application mode of distributed data storage system, peer-to-peer transmission (P2P), consensus mechanism, encryption algorithm and other technologies. It can realize trust and value transfer on the Internet, which cannot be realized in the traditional Internet. Based on cryptography principle, the blockchain enables any parties in the network to deal

© Springer Nature Singapore Pte Ltd. 2020
X. Si et al. (Eds.): CBCC 2019, CCIS 1176, pp. 104–120, 2020.
https://doi.org/10.1007/978-981-15-3278-8_7

directly without the participation of third-party intermediaries. On the other hand, there is almost no single point of failure in blockchains. The data on the chain is stored on countless machine nodes around the world, making the data stable, credible and tamper-proof. The data on the blockchains worth trusting.

The blockchain is decentralized. Nodes in the blockchain network may be malicious and can interfere with the normal operation of the blockchain. Therefore, each node in the network needs to follow a protocol to ensure the consistency of node data. That protocol is called consensus algorithm. It is often described as the classic Byzantine general problem [2]. In the Byzantine Roman empire, Byzantine generals are distributed in different places. Due to the existence of traitor generals and unreliable communication conditions during the war, how to ensure the consistency of decisions of Byzantine generals to achieve common attack or retreat is a very complicated problem.

The most typical consensus algorithms PoW [3] used in the Bitcoins [4] achieves complete decentralization of the system by proving computation power. It has the advantages of simplicity of implementation, but suffering from resource waste and poor performance. It requires malicious nodes to account for less than 50% of the total network capacity. In the application of small scale blockchain network, a few nodes are easy to grasp the computation power greater than 50%, which will degrade the decentralized PoW to centralization and even affect the security of the consensus, according to the analysis of Namecoin [5] project in paper [6].

PoS [7] has been put forward to optimize the problem of resource waste in PoW through the mechanism of equity certification. However, similar to the concentration of PoW in a few nodes, PoS will degenerate into centralized consensus due to the concentration of interests, which leads to low security. In addition, another typical algorithm BFT can also be used to optimize the problem of resource waste in PoW. BFT has the characteristics of high throughput and low latency. But using BFT alone is a way of poor scalability, with the communication cost of $O(n^2)$.

Of all optimization methods, the delegation mechanism is the most widely used. It is an effective way to optimize performance. Selecting part of the nodes to participate in the consensus can reduce the cost of network. There are some exiting typical consensuses based on it, including DPoS [8], dBFT [9]. DPoS adopts an authorized stock certification mechanism on the basis of PoS. Nodes authorize their own rights to other nodes, and the first 101 nodes with the highest interests become delegated nodes. Each delegated node has same right and takes turns to obtain accounting rights. DPoS can reduce the operation cost of the network and improve the rate of block generation by using the delegation mechanism to select some nodes to participate in the consensus. However, using rights and interests as the voting method to select delegated nodes is easy to concentrate accounting rights in a few "rich people", which still destroys the decentralized feature of the blockchain. dBFT selects the delegated nodes according to rights, and then reaches consensus through Byzantine fault-tolerant algorithms (BFT). Adopting delegation mechanism based on BFT [2], like dBFT, is good way to get better scalability while having high efficiency. However, dBFT still having the same security problem like DPoS.

Since the consensus algorithm directly affects the security and efficiency of the upper blockchain products, a consensus algorithm with security and efficiency is worth studying. Referring to the idea of trust relationship transmission in human society, this paper innovatively introduces trust mechanism in the blockchain, to propose a consensus algorithm Consensus of Trust (CoT) based on trust relationship between nodes. CoT quantifies the trust as credit value between nodes through the transactions between nodes and block data, and then selects nodes with high credit value as the delegated nodes to participate in the final consensus process. The consensus phase of CoT is based on the PBFT [10]. PBFT is an optimization of BFT, and it can achieve millisecond delay. In general, CoT has good efficiency and security.

2   Network Model of CoT

The blockchain is a distributed ledger that combines technologies such as P2P, cryptography, and databases. Multiple computers connected to each other constitute a P2P, which operates in coordination according to the consensus protocol and together processes the requests submitted by users. In P2P, each node is in a peer position, with same functional features. It changes the server-centric C/S architecture in the Internet (see Fig. 1).

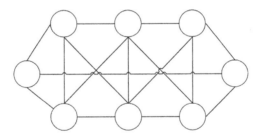

Fig. 1. Structure of P2P network.

The decentralized architecture of P2P networks fits well with blockchains. Information interaction between nodes does not require the access of intermediate servers. Therefore, it has good scalability and autonomy. For a peer network, the number of nodes is usually not fixed, and the nodes may join or leave the network at any time. In addition, it has the advantage of high network fault tolerance, because services can be performed on different nodes independently. It makes attacks on some nodes have limited impact on the whole network.

CoT is designed based on the P2P network architecture described in Fig. 1, adding some assumptions in it. Figure 2 describes the network model of CoT. Nodes are connected to each other through unreliable networks. The data that nodes interacted with can be lost, duplicated, delayed, and out of order. Moreover, there may be some untrusted malicious nodes in the network. Malicious nodes can refuse to respond to the interaction information of other nodes, and even falsely respond to the request of other nodes. However, the behaviors of malicious nodes are independent of each other and cannot cooperate. In the network model of CoT, the number of malicious nodes is f, and the total number of nodes is n. The hypothesis is that $n > 3 * f + 1$. Malicious nodes have limited computing power, cannot break the encryption information by force to forge signatures.

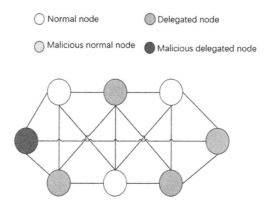

Fig. 2. The network model of CoT.

In order to reduce the cost of consensus and improve the efficiency, CoT selects some nodes with high credit value to participate in the consensus through the trust relationship between nodes. These nodes become delegated nodes. Therefore, the network model of CoT includes four kinds of nodes, namely normal node, malicious normal node, delegated node and malicious delegated node. Encryption technology is used to secure communication between nodes. Each message contains key signature, summary, and verification information. Malicious nodes cannot break encrypted messages by force, forge signatures, or find messages with the same abstract.

In CoT, all the nodes quantify the trust relationship with other nodes by monitoring transactions and block data that interact with them. CoT calculates the credit value of each node according to the trust relationship of all the members. The nodes with high credit value are selected as the delegated nodes. Generally speaking, the credit value of delegated nodes is very high, but in order to further ensure the security of the algorithm, CoT runs PBFT in the final phase of the consensus process to further ensure the reliability of the algorithm. The complete consensus process of CoT is presented in the following section in detail.

3   The Process of CoT

The basic process of CoT is shown in Fig. 3. It consists of four steps, including quantifying the trust relationship between nodes, generating the credit graph and credit matrix, computing the credit value of nodes for selecting the delegated nodes, and generating a new block after the delegated nodes obtaining accounting right. In CoT, the node quantifies the trust relationship as a real number between 0 and 1 by monitoring the transactions and block data of neighboring nodes. The higher the value, the higher the trust value. Once a node has sent valid transactions and block information to others, the trust value between them increases, and vice versa. Then, CoT constructs a credit graph and a credit matrix based on the trust relationship of nodes in the whole network. Referring to the idea of ranking web pages of search engines, nodes are similar to web pages, and the trust relationship of nodes is similar to the hyperlink relationship of web pages. PageRank is used to compute the credit value for each node iteratively. The nodes with high credit value are selected as delegated nodes, which have the opportunity to obtain accounting right to generate a new block. CoT runs PBFT among delegated nodes to further ensure the security and efficiency. Each phase of process is described in detail in the following sections.

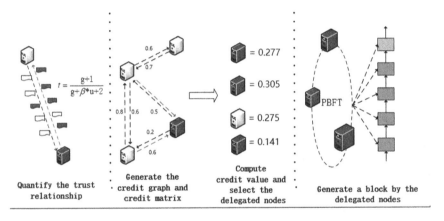

Fig. 3. The basic process of CoT.

3.1 Quantify the Trust Relationship

CoT introduces credit mechanism into the blockchain. So the key step is to quantify the trust relationship.

In human society, trust is a complex and abstract relationship that is usually an expression of experience and difficult to define and quantify. In the field of computer research, trust usually means that a node can independently, safely and reliably perform a specified function in a specific environment. Credit evaluation is complex, but not impossible, according to specific business scenarios. At present, some credit models have been proposed, mainly studying the description of trust relationship, quantification and computation by credit value. Paper [11] proposes a credit model based on authentication technology, which mainly uses the principle of digital signature. Paper [12] proposes a trust model based on local trust and external recommendation, and gives a equation for computing local credit value and external recommendation. In Paper [13], a credit model based on global and semi-global is proposed, achieved by dividing resource boundaries based on groups. Paper [14] presents a multi-granularity trust model based on grouping, which divides nodes into different groups for more accurate credit value computation. Paper [15] considers the relationship between trust and time, and the concepts of short-term trust and long-term trust, and finally obtains the credit evaluation results.

In P2P network, there is no central node, and the number of nodes in the network is not fixed. Also, Nodes have no fixed online time and can join or exit the network at any time. As a result, the link relationship between nodes in P2P network is unstable and the network topology changes dynamically. It is very difficult to evaluate the trust relationship between nodes in P2P network. This paper assumes that the trust relationship always exists between two nodes, and the credit value is of different degrees. Each node independently evaluates the credit values of other nodes, which means different nodes may have different credit values for the same node. The credit value will change dynamically under the influence of node behavior and time. However, the nodes in the network are usually in the state of mutual interaction, so the credit evaluation can be carried out by collecting the interaction performance of the nodes. In the network model assumed in this paper, the credit value of any node is essentially a probability, and it is the basis on which other nodes quantify trust.

In the blockchain network, nodes are constantly interacting with transactions and the blockchain data, continuously processing the transaction requests submitted by the user, verifying the validity of the transaction, and broadcasting valid transactions to other nodes. Most of the attacks on blockchains are related to transactions and blocks, mainly including malicious behaviors such as rejecting user requests, creating false transactions, broadcasting invalid transactions, creating false blocks and broadcasting invalid blocks. Since transactions and blocks that interact between nodes are the most important data, CoT can quantify the trust relationship of nodes based on them.

Figure 4 describes how to quantify trust relationship between nodes according to the transaction and block data. The node will check the data information of its neighbors' interaction during the running process. It is supposed that a node receives g valid transactions and blocks from a node and u invalid transactions and blocks in a certain period of time. The credit value of this node can be quantified by the Eq. (1). Due to the large size of the blockchain network, there are many nodes that do not have interactive behaviors. In this case, the degree of trust relationship between these nodes is quantified as 0.5.

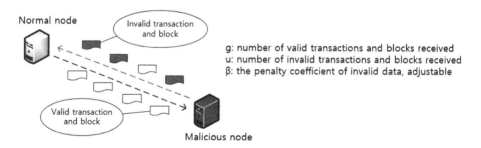

g: number of valid transactions and blocks received
u: number of invalid transactions and blocks received
β: the penalty coefficient of invalid data, adjustable

Fig. 4. Quantify trust relationship of nodes.

$$t_{ij} = \frac{g_{ij} + 1}{g_{ij} + \beta * u_{ij} + 2} \tag{1}$$

Once node i receives the invalid transaction and invalid blocks sent by node j, the credit value of node i to node j will decrease, and vice versa. g_{ij} is the number of times that node i receives valid transactions and valid blocks from node j, and u_{ij} is the number of times that node i receives invalid transactions and blocks from node j. β is an adjustment parameter, also called penalty factor, representing the penalty coefficient of invalid data. It is usually greater than 1, indicating that the receipt of invalid data has a greater impact on the degree of trust relationship than the receipt of valid data. The larger β, the heavier penalty.

3.2   Generate Credit Graph and Credit Matrix

The second step of CoT is to generate credit graph and credit matrix. In the world wide web, web pages are linked to each other through hyperlinks. Valuable web pages are usually linked by many web pages, and vice versa. Search engines sort relevant web pages according to the link relationship between web pages and present them to users in an appropriate order. In CoT, a node is analogous to a web page, and the trust relationship is analogous to the hyperlink relationship. It generates a credit graph of nodes based on their mutual trust relationship. Figure 5 depicts a very simple credit graph containing four nodes A, B, C, and D. It quantifies the degree of trust relationship between nodes according to the method described in Sect. 3.1. In Fig. 5, credit values of nodes are assumed at random. The red node indicates the malicious node, so other nodes have a low credit evaluation of this node.

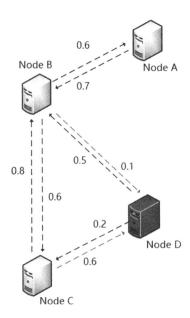

Fig. 5. Credit graph of nodes.

The credit matrix D of nodes is generated from the credit graph in Fig. 5. D_{ij} represents the degree of trust relationship between node i and node j. The credit degree of the node itself is 0, for example, $D_{ij} = 0$. The credit degree of nodes without transaction and block interaction is 0.5, for example, D_{20} and D_{30} is 0.5.

$$D = \begin{bmatrix} 0 & 0.7 & 0.5 & 0.5 \\ 0.6 & 0 & 0.6 & 0.1 \\ 0.5 & 0.8 & 0 & 0.2 \\ 0.5 & 0.5 & 0.6 & 0 \end{bmatrix} \tag{2}$$

In order to prevent malicious nodes from influencing the selection of the final delegated nodes by giving higher credit degree D_{ij} to other malicious nodes and lower trust degree to normal nodes, Eq. (3) uses regularization to process the credit degree between nodes. Finally, credit matrix C is obtained.

$$C_{ij} = \frac{D_{ij}}{\sum_j D_{ij}} \tag{3}$$

$$C = \begin{bmatrix} 0 & 0.7/1.7 & 0.5/1.7 & 0.5/1.7 \\ 0.6/1.3 & 0 & 0.6/1.3 & 0.1/1.3 \\ 0.5/1.5 & 0.8/1.5 & 0 & 0.2/1.5 \\ 0.5/1.6 & 0.5/1.6 & 0.6/1.6 & 0 \end{bmatrix} \tag{4}$$

3.3   Compute the Credit Value

Section 3.1 describes the quantification of trust relationship between nodes by recording transaction and block interaction records between nodes. Section 3.2 generates the credit graph and the credit matrix by regularization. In this section, the credit value of nodes is computed by referring to the idea of page sorting of PageRank algorithm. Nodes are similar to web pages, and the trust relationship between nodes is similar to the hyperlink relationship between pages.

In addition to directly obtaining the trust relationship of other nodes by monitoring their behavior, nodes can also use the credit information provided from other nodes to further evaluate the credit value of a specific node. Equation (5) describes that a node uses its neighbors as indirect nodes to conduct credit evaluation on other nodes. d_{ij} represents the credit degree of node i to node j. Node k is connected to node i. Accordingly, d_{ik} represents the credit degree of node i to node k, and d_{kj} represents the credit degree of node k to node j. The numerical relation of d_{ij}, d_{ik}, d_{kj} is shown as

Eq. (5). Therefore, the credit degree of nodes can be computed by according to the trust relationship of all network nodes.

$$d_{ij} = \sum_k d_{ik} d_{kj} \tag{5}$$

The final credit value of one node is computed using the iterative relationship described in Eq. (6). C represents the credit matrix. T is a column vector, and T_i represents the credit value of the node. The number of elements is n, the same as the number of nodes.

$$T_t = C^T T_{t-1} \tag{6}$$

Each element in the trust matrix C represents a direct trust relationship between nodes. The credit value of the relationship with high degree is close to 1, the credit value of the relationship with low degree is close to 0, and the credit value of the relationship with few interactions between nodes is close to 0.5.

Algorithm 1 describes the process of computing node credit value. It initializes the credit value of the node as $1/n$ and the convergence of error as ε. According to the Eq. (6), it keeps iterating until convergence. Paper [16] proved the convergence of PageRank. Section 4.1 will further prove that the credit matrix C has good randomness, irreducibility, and the entire iteration process can finally converge to compute the credit value for each node.

Algorithm 1 Compute credit value of each node with PageRank algorithm

Input:
   1: C: credit matrix;
   2: T_0: initial credit value of each node;
   3: ε: absolute convergence error;
Output: optimal T^*
   4: initial $T_0 = \vec{e}/n$ and k = 1;
   5: **repeat**
   6: compute the result of k iteration $T_k = C^T T_{k-1}$;
   7: compute the error from the previous result $\sigma = \|T_k - T_{k-1}\|$

The process of PageRank calculating the credit value of nodes is shown below based on the trust relationship of nodes described in Fig. 5. It is supposed that the system is initialized with n nodes, and the credit value of each node is the same, so the initial value of T is a column vector with all $1/n$. The credit matrix is C. Transposing C and multiplying it by the initial credit value of the node can get the computation result of PageRank iteration in the first round, as Eq. (7).

$$T_1 = C^T T_0 = \begin{bmatrix} 0 & 0.6/1.3 & 0.5/1.5 & 0.5/1.6 \\ 0.7/1.7 & 0 & 0.8/1.5 & 0.5/1.6 \\ 0.5/1.7 & 0.6/1.3 & 0 & 0.6/1.6 \\ 0.5/1.7 & 0.1/1.3 & 0.2/1.5 & 0 \end{bmatrix} \times \begin{bmatrix} 1/4 \\ 1/4 \\ 1/4 \\ 1/4 \end{bmatrix}$$

$$= \begin{bmatrix} 491/2496 \\ 5131/16320 \\ 3998/14144 \\ 1672/13260 \end{bmatrix} \approx \begin{bmatrix} 0.2768 \\ 0.3144 \\ 0.2826 \\ 0.1261 \end{bmatrix} \tag{7}$$

After a round of iterative calculation, it can be seen that the credit value of the node has changed, no longer as the initial 0.25. The credit value of node B has increased to 0.3144, while the credit value of node D has decreased to 0.1261. After that, continue to use Formula 6 to obtain T_2, T_3, T_4, and so on. It will finally converge. If the results of the two iterations are very similar, the iteration will be stopped. Table 1 lists the iterative process of calculating the credit value of nodes, and the iteration error is set to 0.000001. Each iteration will calculate the new credit value. After 12 iterations, the credit value of each node converges obviously, and finally the credit value of each node is obtained.

Table 1. The iterative process of node credit value calculation.

Iteration times	T(A)	T(B)	T(C)	T(D)
1	0.25	0.25	0.25	0.25
2	0.276843	0.3144	0.282664	0.126094
3	0.278733	0.304153	0.273817	0.143298
4	0.276431	0.305589	0.276095	0.141886
5	0.277412	0.305414	0.275551	0.141623
6	0.277068	0.305446	0.275661	0.141825
7	0.277182	0.305426	0.27565	0.141741
8	0.277143	0.305441	0.275643	0.141772
9	0.277158	0.305431	0.27565	0.141761
10	0.277152	0.305437	0.275646	0.141765
11	0.277155	0.305434	0.275648	0.141763
12	0.277153	0.305436	0.275647	0.141764

CoT refers to the idea of PageRank, but there are many differences. The hyperlink relation of web page ordering is only linked and unlinked, respectively represented by 0 and 1, while the credit between nodes in CoT is the real number between 0 and 1. In the ranking of PageRank pages, when the network link graph is not a strongly connected graph or some web pages do not have hyperlinks to other pages while having hyperlinks to themselves, the iterative relationship will not converge. However, there is a credit value between 0 and 1 among the nodes in CoT, so there will be no non-convergence.

Therefore, credit graph can be constructed by quantifying the trust relationship between nodes, and finally credit value of each node can be computed. The node with high credit value is selected as the delegated node and has the opportunity to obtain the accounting right. The delegated nodes usually have high credit values, which can reduce the probability of errors.

3.4   Block Generation Protocol

Consensus algorithm of blockchains should have security and availability. CoT defines a Byzantine fault-tolerant network model. It is supposed that the number of participating consensus protocol nodes is n, and f is the number of malicious nodes that can be tolerated. When $f < n/3$, the security of the consensus protocol can be guaranteed. The communication cost of the PBFT is $O(n^2)$, which limits the number of participating consensus nodes. CoT evaluates trust relationship between nodes, and selects the first k nodes with high credit value as delegated nodes based on mutual trust relationship to participate in PBFT on behalf of nodes, which can improve the scalability of the system. In CoT, only the delegated nodes participate in the consensus process. Normal nodes cannot generate blocks, but they can watch the full consensus process. The delegated node receives and forwards the transaction data of the whole network independently.

In each round of consensus, CoT randomly selects a node from the delegated node as the primary node. The primary node is responsible for packaging effective transaction data to generate a block, and then achieving consensus with other delegated nodes, and finally writing the block into the blockchain. The main process of selecting a primary node is show in Algorithm 2. The primary node may be a malicious node or may break down during the consensus process. In this case, the primary node needs to be replaced. Fault tolerance in primary node selection can be achieved by introducing the concept of view. View is a collection of all the data used in a round of consensus.

Algorithm 2 The main process of selecting the primary node

Input:
    1: n: the number of consensus delegated nodes;
    2: h: the current height of the blockchain;
    3: v: the current view;
Output: the primary node number p;
    4: initial $v = 0$;
    5: numbers of the delegated nodes according to the credit values, from 0 to $n - 1$;
    6: the number of current primary node is $p = (h + v)\%n$;
    7: if the primary node is malicious or down, let $v = v + 1$, and send change view message to other consensus nodes;
    8: when receive more than $2n/3$ change view message, compute the current message with primary node number $p = (h + v)\%n$;

When a node starts working, it first synchronizes the block data through other nodes in the network. It monitors incoming transactions, independently verifies the validity of transactions, stores valid transactions in the transaction pool, broadcasts them to other nodes, and discards invalid transactions. After the node obtains the accounting right, it selects several transactions from the transaction pool to generate a block, and records the hash value of the parent block is in the block header to ensure the orderliness of the block. In CoT, the period of selecting the delegated nodes is T, and the period of generating a block is t. When the transaction pool is empty and there is no valid transaction, empty blocks will be generated according to the normal process. After being verified by other delegated nodes, the block finally is added to the blockchain. Considering the latency of network transmission, the interval from the generating block to the finishing adding to the blockchain is ∇t. $t > \nabla t$, which means that when a new round of consensus begin, the other nodes have already received data from the previous block.

The final phase of CoT runs PBFT among delegated nodes, including three phases.

(1) Pre-Prepare. The primary node with the accounting right sends a Pre-Prepare request to all consensus nodes, containing the height of the current block (h), view (v), the number of the primary node (i), block content, and the signature of the block ($block_p$). The node verifies the accuracy of the message after it receives a Pre-Prepare request from the primary node. If the Pre-Prepare request is not valid, the view is proposed to be changed to reselect the primary node. When a node receives a legitimate Pre-Prepare request, it will send a Prepare request to other nodes and enter the Prepare state itself. The Prepare request contains h, v, i, and the signature of the block ($block_i$).

(2) Prepare. When a node receives a Prepare message, it enters a Commit state and sends a Commit message to other nodes. The Commit request contains $block_i$.

(3) Commit. When the node receives 2f Commit messages, the consensus is considered to be complete and the block is written into the blockchain.

The Pre-Prepare message contains the complete block. After receiving the Pre-Prepare of the primary node, the nodes will locally store the block contents of this consensus, and then replace the block with hash value in the Prepare and Commit phases to reduce the communication cost.

4 Proof and Analysis

This paper proposes a trust-based consensus algorithm CoT, which introduces credit mechanism in the blockchain and quantifies the trust relationship of nodes according to the transactions and block data in the blockchain. This section mainly analyzes its effectiveness, consistency, security, and performance. The proof and analysis are based on the following hypotheses.

Hypothesis 1. Transactions and blocks are the most important data in the blockchain. CoT currently quantifies the trust relationship between nodes based on the transactions and block data of nodes. It can monitor malicious behaviors related to false transactions and invalid blocks. In the practical application of blockchains, parameters that affect credit can be appropriately added to improve the accuracy of credit quantification. Therefore, the quantification of trust relationship between nodes is effective.

Hypothesis 2. Each node independently quantifies the trust relationship of other nodes. The more data the node interact with, the more effective it is, the higher the credit value of the node is. On the contrary, the trust relationship between two nodes is reduced.

Hypothesis 3. Hypothesis 1 and Hypothesis 2 are the judgment of trust relationship between two nodes. However, for the whole the blockchain network, if a node is recognized by more nodes with high credit value, then the credit of this node will be higher.

4.1   Effectiveness of Credit Mechanism

CoT generates credit graph and credit matrix according to trust relationship between nodes, as shown in Fig. 5. And then it refers to iterative algorithm PageRank to compute the credit value for each node. The node with high credit value is elected as a delegated node. Paper [13] has proved that when the credit matrix C satisfies the properties of random matrix, irreducible matrix and aperiodic matrix, Eq. (6) can be guaranteed to converge.

(1)   Random matrix. The random matrix requires that all elements of the credit matrix C should be greater than or equal to 0, and that the sum of elements in each row should be 1. Obviously, the degree of trust relationship between two nodes quantified according to Eq. (1) is always greater than or equal to 0. Also, normalization ensures that the sum of elements in each row is 1.

(2)   Irreducible matrix. The irreducible matrix requires that the credit graph corresponding to the credit matrix C is a strongly connected graph. Strongly connected graph requires that for every pair of nodes i, j, there is always a path from i to j. Since CoT assumes that there is always a trust relationship between any two nodes, the trust matrix C satisfies the property of irreducible matrix.

(3)   Aperiodic matrix. The aperiodic matrix requires that in the credit graph there is no situation where a node only has its own trust relationship, but no trust relationship with other nodes. Clearly, the credit matrix C is aperiodic.

In general, the algorithm always converges. The credit mechanism of CoT can always find delegated nodes with high credit value, that is, the credit mechanism is effective. In addition, in order to ensure the normal operation of CoT, PBFT is used to manage accounting rights of the nodes in the final block generation phase, further guaranteeing the effectiveness of the algorithm.

4.2   Consistency of Data

The blockchain is a decentralized distributed ledger, similar to a distributed database in a narrow sense of storage. In the distributed field, the classic CAP theory and BASE model are often used to guide the design of distributed systems. The CAP theory proves that the three basic requirements, consistency, availability and partition tolerance cannot be met simultaneously in distributed systems, meaning that trade-offs in business characteristics is needed. The BASE model is the result of trade-offs between consistency and availability in CAP theory in engineering practice. Its core idea is to emphasize basic availability of the system, while supporting partition failure, soft state and eventually consistency. The BASE model allows the system to be out of sync in a short time, but satisfies the consistency of the final data. In contrast, the ACID model of traditional relational databases requires high consistency and availability. Blockchains achieve data consistency of nodes in untrusted decentralized network. It is also impossible to meet the CAP characteristics at the same time.

CoT professionalizes accounting nodes through credit mechanism, which reduces the cost of consensus and improves the efficiency. The data of all network nodes in the consensus process of CoT is not consistent at all times, but meet the final consistency. The consensus network of CoT allows nodes to join and exit, and the nodes always process user requests and generate blocks according to established rules. After the network fails and recovers, the whole network node recognizes the longest chain as the main chain, which suffers temporary blockchain forks. However, after a period of synchronization, the final consistency of data can be guaranteed. It can handle network partition failures. In a word, from the perspective of CAP theory, at the little expense of the consistency of PBFT, CoT improves the extensibility and efficiency of consensus and achieves the final consistency at the same time.

4.3 Security and Fault Tolerance

Block chain technology has the characteristics of decentralization and high security. In the unreliable network with asymmetric information, it does not need any third party intermediary to participate. It realizes distributed ledger with decentralized and high security through encryption algorithm and consensus algorithm. Consensus algorithm is a key technology of block chain to ensure data security and unmodifiability. As described in the previous section, CoT effectively guarantees the consistency of data in the blockchain. Malicious nodes in the network may try to affect the security of the blockchain by interfering with the consensus process, making the security of the blockchain consensus algorithm is not absolute. Consensus algorithms need not only to be secure, but also to be fault-tolerant.

CoT sets that the total number of nodes in the network is n, the number of malicious nodes is f, the number of delegated nodes is k, and the number of malicious delegated nodes is m. In CoT, only the security of PBFT between delegated nodes needs to be guaranteed. CoT sets $k \geq 3m + 1$, by which the security can be well guaranteed, and the fault tolerance capacity is greater than $1/3n$. In addition, The delegated nodes in CoT are not randomly selected, but strictly selected based on the trust relationship between nodes that have high credit value. Therefore, CoT is with high security.

4.4 Performance Analysis

Due to server failure, network unreliability and malicious attack behavior, achieving a consensus protocol with security, decentralization and high performance is crucial to blockchains. This section will analyze the performance of CoT from the following perspectives.

(1) Decentralization. CoT does not rely on any third-party institutions. It is similar to DPoS in that it selects some delegated nodes as professional accounting nodes, which can be called as a delegation mechanism. However, the CoT consensus selects delegated nodes according to the trust relationship of nodes. The selection period of delegated nodes is T. It means that any node that works strictly and honestly will have the opportunity to be a delegated node, obtaining the accounting rights to generate blocks. Although CoT is a consensus protocol based on the delegation mechanism, it has a better decentralized feature than the equity-based delegation mechanism similar to DPoS.

(2) High performance. PBFT itself has good performance, but its communication cost $O(n^2)$, which limits the number of nodes in the network. It lacks scalability. CoT improves the scalability of the algorithm through the delegation mechanism and professionalizing accounting node. In the delegation mechanism of CoT, only delegated nodes participate in the PBFT consensus process, while other nodes do not. CoT refers to the concept of keeping the longest chain as final chain to ensure the consistency of node data, which reduces the strong consistency of PBFT itself to the final consistency. Therefore, compared with PBFT, the trust-based delegation mechanism of CoT greatly improves the scalability of the consensus, but also increase the delay of transaction confirmation.

(3) Not relying on tokens. CoT and DPoS both reduce the cost of consensus and provide efficiency of node consensus through delegation mechanism, but they have different ways of selecting delegated nodes. The delegation mechanism of DPoS is voting by equity. CoT selects the node with high credit value as the delegated node based on the trust relationship. DPoS relies on the token system of the blockchain and tends to concentrate accounting power among a few "rich people". By monitoring the transaction between nodes and the validity of data on the blockchain, CoT selects nodes with high credit value as the delegated node, and does not rely on the token system. Therefore, it has a broader application prospect.

(4) Consensus price. PoW is a consensus mechanism based on computing power. It punishes malicious nodes in an economic way, increasing the cost of attacks. It is secure, but consumes a huge amount of electricity. At present, the mainstream blockchain consensuses all intend to reduce resource consumption. CoT introduces trust evaluation by monitoring the effectiveness of transaction and block data. Its consensus cost is relatively small.

5 Conclusion

Consensus algorithm is a key part of blockchains, which is directly related to the performance of its upper application. Secure and efficient consensus algorithm is an important research content in the blockchain field. This paper compares the characteristics of different consensus. PBFT has a fault-tolerant capacity of 33%. Using the delegation mechanism that select some nodes as delegated nodes to participate in the consensus process can reduce the communication traffic in the network and effectively improve the efficiency and expansibility of the consensus. However, existing consensus algorithms, such as DPoS and dBFT, use the method of selecting delegated nodes based on equity, which tends to concentrate the accounting rights on a few "rich people". To solve the security problem, this paper refers to the idea of trust relationship transmission in human society, and then innovatively introduces credit mechanism in the blockchain to propose the consensus algorithm CoT. Its delegation mechanism is different from other mainstream consensus. CoT quantifies the trust relationship of nodes according to the transactions and block data of all nodes to compute the credit value of each node, and selects delegated nodes with high credit value. In the final part, this paper analyzes CoT from the aspects of effectiveness, consistency, security, and performance. It sacrifices little throughput and latency advantage of PBFT to improve the extensibility of the consensus. The number of nodes in the network does not affect the efficiency of the PBFT running by delegated nodes. Considering the relative stability of trust relationship between nodes, the selection period of delegated nodes is usually larger than the generation period of a block, which can further improve the efficiency of consensus. Furthermore, CoT always choose the nodes with high credit value as the delegated nodes, which makes the consensus securer. In general, CoT combines the advantages of the delegation mechanism and PBFT, having good consensus efficiency and expansibility while having security that can tolerant more than 33% of nodes to be malicious.

Acknowledgement. This work is supported by the Natural Science Foundation of China (NSFC) (No. 61671001), GuangDong Prov., Key Program (No. 2019B010137001), PCL Future Regional Network Facilities for Large-scale Experiments and Applications (PCL2018KP001), National Keystone Program of China (No. 2017YFB0803204), Shenzhen Research Programs (JCYJ20170306092030521), and the Shenzhen Municipal Development and Reform Commission (Disciplinary Development Program for Data Science and Intelligent Computing).

References

1. Marc, P.: Blockchain Technology: Principles and Applications. Social Science Electronic Publishing, Rochester (2015)
2. Lamport, L., Shostak, R., Pease, M.: The Byzantine generals problem. ACM Trans. Program. Lang. Syst. **4**(3), 382–401 (1982)
3. Gervais, A., Karame, G.O., Wüst, K.: On the security and performance of proof of work blockchains. In: The 2016 ACM SIGSAC Conference (2016)
4. Nakamoto, S.: Bitcoin: a peer-to-peer electronic cash system (2008)
5. Kalodner, H.A., Carlsten, M., Ellenbogen, P.: An empirical study of Namecoin and lessons for decentralized namespace design. In: WEIS (2015)
6. Ali, M., Nelson, J.C., Shea, R.: Blockstack: a global naming and storage system secured by blockchains. In: USENIX Annual Technical Conference, pp. 181–194 (2016)
7. King, S., Nadal, S.: Peer-to-peer crypto-currency with proof-of-stake. Self-published paper (2012)

8. Luo, Y., Chen, Y., Chen, Q.: A new election algorithm for DPos consensus mechanism in blockchain. In: 2018 7th International Conference on Digital Home (ICDH). IEEE (2019)
9. NEO. https://neo.org/. Accessed 19 Mar 2019
10. Sukhwani, H., Martinez, J.M., Chang, X.: Performance modeling of PBFT consensus process for permissioned blockchain network (hyperledger fabric). In: 2017 IEEE 36th Symposium on Reliable Distributed Systems (SRDS). IEEE (2017)
11. Liang, Z., Li, T.: Computation model for global trust values in P2P networks. J. Bengbu Univ. **3**, 001 (2016)
12. Zhang, X., Meng, K., Xiao, C.X.: A reputation n-based system model in peer-to-peer networks. Comput. Sci. **33**(9), 55–65 (2006)
13. Zhong, Y., Bhargava, B., Lu, Y.: A computational dynamic trust model for user authorization. IEEE Trans. Dependable Secur. Comput. **12**(1), 1–15 (2015)
14. Mujtaba, K., Partha, D., Kyung, D.: A role-based trust model for peer-to-pee r communities and dynamic coalitions. Comput. Sci. **7**(4), 141–454 (2004)
15. Dubey, J., Tokekar, V.: Bayesian network based trust model with time window for pure P2P computing systems. In: 2014 IEEE Global Conference on Wireless Computing and Networking (GCWCN), pp. 219–223. IEEE (2014)
16. Page L.: The PageRank citation ranking: bringing order to the web. Stanford Digital Libraries Working Paper, vol. 9, no. 1, pp. 1–14 (1998)

A Uniform Payment System for Hyperledger Fabric Blockchain

Qingshu Meng[1], Shubing Hou[2], Zhenxiong Li[2], and Songfeng Lu[2,3(✉)]

[1] Tianyu Research Institute, Wuhan Tianyu Information Industry Co., Ltd.,
Wuhan 430074, China
[2] School of Cyber Science and Engineering,
Huazhong University of Science and Technology, Wuhan 430074, China
lusongfeng@hust.edu.cn
[3] Shenzhen Huazhong University of Science and Technology Research Institute,
Shenzhen 518063, China

Abstract. The payment scheme of Fabric 2.0 alpha is threatened by counterfeit tokens and its users are client apps, not the end consumers. In this paper, a uniform payment system is designed with the following advantages. (1). By limiting the token-minting right to a designated token-minting bank and the design of label, our system prevents the counterfeit token problem. (2). A complete transaction is divided into Bitcoin-level part and Fabric-level part. The Bitcoin-level part constructs inputs and outputs and signs these inputs, outputs and a nonce with a private key. This makes a micro enterprises or an end consumer can enjoy the payment service as the Bitcoin-level operation can be implemented on a mobile phone. The double-spending problem is prevented by the Fabric-level mechanism. (3). The system is easy to expand. When there is a new payment application, only one sub-function is added to the payment contract to implement the payment application, and a call to the sub-function is added. (4). Compared with Bitcoin, the unlockcode of UTXO only needs to be stored once, instead of being stored with each UTXO, thus reducing the sizes of transactions.

As an application, based on the uniform payment system, we design an application of cash-on-delivery without any trusted third party. It provides technology support for any two persons to trade without any trusted third party. Similar to the payment system, a system for asset confirmation, asset transfer and redemption is designed.

Keywords: Bitcoin · Fabric · Token payment · Asset confirmation · Smart contract

1 Introduction

With the rising price of Bitcoin [1], the blockchain technology behind it has been gradually recognized. Its payment function can be used for low-cost international

Supported by the Science and Technology Program of Shenzhen of China under Grant No. JCYJ20180306124612893, JCYJ20170818160208570 and JCYJ2017030 7160458368.

exchange. Its non-tampering characteristics can be used for proof of existence, anti-counterfeiting, notarization and something like. Smart contracts can coordinate between parties credibly and collectively. Decentralized autonomous organization (DAO) [2] can be formed at the coordination of smart contracts between parties. By replacing people with machines and algorithms, the operation cost of DAO can be reduced.

According to the access control type, blockchains can be divided into public blockchains with Bitcoin and Etherem [3] as its representatives, consortium blockchains with Hyperledger Fabric [4] (Fabric for short) as its representative, and private blockchains. A public blockchain has no access control and anyone can access it. Only the registered user can access a consortium blockchain while a private blockchain is open only within an organization.

There are four types of payments [5] in Bitcoin: P2PK, P2PKH, P2SH and P2WSH (pay to witness script hash) that supports segregated witness. Among them, the most flexible type is P2SH, which uses the hash of the lock script as the UTXO address. When you spend UTXO, put the signature script and lock script together to be interpreted and executed by a virtual machine. If the running result is true, the transaction is valid, otherwise the transaction is invalid. By designing different signature scripts to define different payment applications. The signature script needs to be stored in the transaction as the input of the transaction. When the size of signature script is large, it will burden both storage and communication.

As the representative of consortium blockchains, Fabric is an IBM-led open-sourced blockchain project. Its ledger consists of two parts, a non-tampering file storing transaction logs and a world state database storing transaction results. Fabric with version 1.x does not provide the payment function directly, but the key-value pairs in its world state database can be used to implement payment function. The key is used as an account, and the amount of funds is the value. However, the payment function based on the account model has one problem. Under Fabric's transaction process, in one block an account cannot be paid two times. It is unacceptable for retailers who would do transactions with a high frequency. The UTXO model can solve the problem. A basic payment function based on the UTXO model is introduced in [4]. An UTXO can be implemented as (key, value) = (txid$_j$, (amount, owner, label), which represent that the UTXO with 'amount' tokens is from the jth output of the transaction with txid as its transaction ID, belongs to a person with address 'owner', is labeled with 'label', like Dollar or CNY. The latest version of Fabric 2.0 Alpha [6] provides the functions of asset-issuing, asset-transferring and asset-redemption. It uses the UTXO model and uses MSP (membership service provider)x to authenticate the identities of asset holders. The issuance policy can be defined and the current policy is that anyone with the write access right to the channel can issue any asset. An asset holder transfers an asset to another person by signing a statement that the asset I have now is bound to the person with this specific address. Redemption is the transfer of tokens from the holder to an address that cannot be spent for ever. There are two problems. The first, there is no confliction check on names of issued assets, no binding between the assets and their issuers. This will lead to the counterfeit tokens. The second, the users of the payment function now are client apps, not the ordinary consumers. That is to say, a user needs to run a client app to pay tokens. This limits the wide application of the payment function.

Based on the world state database and the smart contract function provided by Fabric, we design a payment system for Fabric. A complete transaction is divided into Bitcoin-level part and Fabric-level part. Bitcoin-level part can run on a mobile phone. Unlike Bitcoin, tokens do not come from mining, but is minted by a publicly recognized bank organization. It supports three payment types of P2PK, P2PKH and P2SH. With the help of P2SH, a new payment application can be added by adding a sub-function implementing the new payment application and adding a call to it into the payment contract. For asset confirmation, the assets and its issuer is bound through the design of the label. Even if the design of asset label cannot eliminate the asset name confliction, its impact is limited within the organization itself.

2   The Uniform Payment System

2.1   The Secure Token-Minting Function

Fabric 2.0 alpha treats assets and tokens equally. Our design differentiates assets from tokens. The token-minting right of an application system is crucial and should be controlled. Generally, it is only the management institution with a specific identity recognized by the public that has the token-minting right. For example, for Facebook's Libra [7] system and Wal-Mart's stable token system, their token-minting rights should belong to institutions designated by Facebook and Wal-Mart respectively.

Based on the analysis above, the main process of token-minting is shown in Fig. 1. Its explanation is as follows.

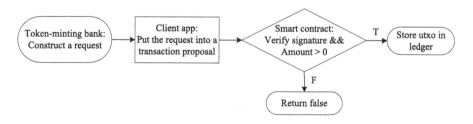

Fig. 1. Main process of token-minting.

(1). A bank with token-minting right constructs and sends a request = (output$_1$, ..., output$_m$, sig) to a client app, where each output$_i$ is defined as (amount, owner, label), which means a person with address 'ower' will be issued 'amount' of token with name 'lable'. The 'Owner' can be a public key, the hash value of a public key, or the hash of a lockparameters. The 'sig' is the signature of (output$_1$ $\|\dots\|$output$_m\|$ nonce) by the minting bank with its private key.

(2). The client app packages the request into a transaction proposal and sends it to some designated Fabric peers.

(3). These peers run a specific smart contract to verify the signature with the public key of the token-minting user that is hard-coded into the smart contract. If the verification is successful, check the amount of tokens in each output$_i$ is greater than zero. If all checks are valid, goto step (4);

(4). The smart contract generates the UTXOs as (txid$_i$, output$_i$), i = $1, 2, \dots, m$, and stores them into the world state database.

Security analysis: The minting right belongs to an institution which has the private key. As long as its signature verification is valid, the institution can issue tokens at its will, whether only one kind of tokens or many kinds of tokens, without to worry about token name confliction. The security can be reduced to the security of private key. This is a traditional problem and can be solved in traditional ways.

2.2   The Token Transferring Function

In the designed payment system, three payment types of P2PK, P2PKH and P2SH are supported. For the first two types, the receiver public key and the hash of the receiver's public key are used as the owner address respectively. The script address of a P2SH transaction is defined as hash (lockparameters) $\|$ unlockcodename.

The main process is shown in Fig. 2. The explanation is as follows.

Construct Request. The transaction initiator constructs a request $=$ (inputs; outputs; unlockparas), where inputs $= [\text{in}_1; \text{in}_2; \dots; \text{in}_m]$ is the transaction input and in$_i$ is in the form of txid$_j$, indicating that the UTXO comes from the jth output of the transaction txid, i = $1, 2, \dots, m$; outputs $=$ [(amount$_1$, owner$_1$, label$_1$); (amount$_2$, owner$_2$, label$_2$); $\dots$; (amount$_m$, owner$_m$, label$_m$)] is the outputs of the transaction and (amount$_i$, owner$_i$, label$_i$) is the value part of each output, i = $1, 2, \dots, m$; unlockparas $=$[unlockpara$_1$; unlockpara$_2$; $\dots$; unlockpara$_m$] denotes the unlock parameters that is constructed according to the type of addresses given in the inputs.

When the address type in the inputs is P2PK, unlockpara only contains the signature of (inputs$\|$outputs$\|$nonce) signed with the corresponding private key, where the nonce is a random number; When the address type in the inputs is P2PKH, unlockpara only contains the corresponding public key and the signature of (inputs$\|$outputs$\|$nonce) signed with the private key; When the address type in the inputs is P2SH, unlockpara contains the unlock parameters corresponding to the input address and is the parameters to the unlockcode. The unlockcode is programmed according to its functionality.

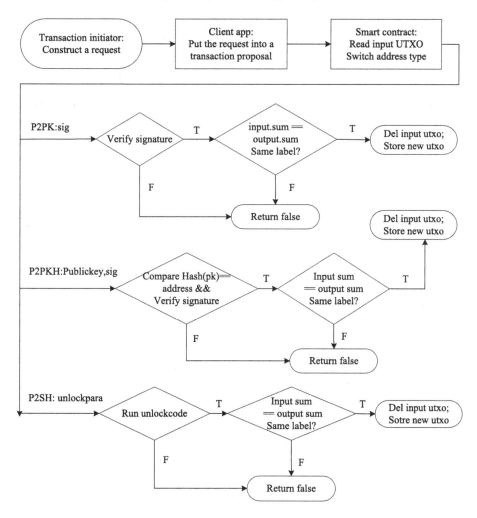

Fig. 2. Main process of token-transferring.

The transaction initiator then sends the request to a client app, which constructs a transaction proposal of fabric type and submits it to the fabric network.

One specific smart contract (in Fabric it is named chaincode) processes the request as follows.

(1). The smart contract parses the request and executes the function GetState(in$_i$) to obtain UTXO corresponding to each input in$_i$ in the request. If the input UTXO cannot be read, it indicates that the input UTXO has been spent, then the transaction is invalid; if it is read, the UTXO is valid.

(2). Determine the type of address included in UTXO. If the type is P2PK, use the public key to verify the sig. If the type is P2PKH, calculate the hash of the public key and compare it with the address. If they are equal, use the public key to verify the sig. If the type is P2SH, run the unlockcode specified in the address with input parameter unlockpara$_i$ for some i. If the result is true, the UTXO can be used, otherwise the UTXO cannot be used. If any UTXO cannot be used the transaction is invalid.

(3). Check that the sum of the input amount equals the sum of the output amount; check that the labels of the input and output are consistent; If any of the checks is invalid, the transaction ends.

(4). Run the function DelState (in$_i$) to delete the input UTXO from the state database; run the function PutState() to store output UTXO into the world state database.

Users can define various payment applications according to their business needs, and implement them by writing sub-functions. That is, a uniform payment system is designed.

Compared with Bitcoin's transactions, the unlockcode does not need to be stored directly in UTXO. It only needs to be installed once in the channel. This saves the storage.

Fabric 2.0 alpha designed an asset redemption function, by letting the owner of the asset sign a statement that the asset belongs to an address without unlock parameters. In our design, if you want to redeem tokens, you can transfer them directly to a user, such as the token-minting bank, who can return you fiat tokens.

A complete transaction in our payment system now is divided into Bitcoin-level part and Fabric-level part. For the Bitcoin-level part, a mobile phone can construct inputs and outputs and sign them. This design makes it possible for mobile phone users to enjoy the blockchain services provided by Fabric. In Fabric 2.0 alpha, client apps are the users of the Fabtoken functionality. It is not convenient for micro enterprises because they have to run a client app.

2.3   Conditional Payment and Its Application

In order to increase the transaction speed, the lightning network for off-chain payment is built. One important tool is HTLC (hash time lock contract) [8]. There are two basic elements. One is to generate a random number R, and let H' = Hash (R) be in the lockscript. The other is to set a time T in the lockscript. The unlockscript can be defined as follows. If someone can provide R before the agreed time T such that Hash (R) == H', the person can spend the money. After the agreed time T, the money is returned to the payer by binding it to the payer's public key. This is a conditional payment contract. Based on this basic contract, other functionalities can be added depending on the needs of applications.

Based on the uniform payment system, we design a conditional payment contract with the application cash-on-delivery as an example. The application needs to satisfy the following requirements: the buyer pay UTXOs to a designated address. If the seller delivers the goods before the agreed time, the UTXO bound to the designated address belongs to the seller, otherwise the UTXO still be owned by the buyer.

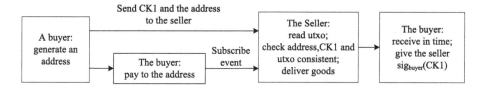

Fig. 3. Main process of cash-on-delivery.

The main process is shown in Fig. 3. Its explanation is as follows.

(1). The buyer generates an address = hash (seller's public key‖buyer's public key‖goods information hash‖time)‖unlockcodename, and sends CK1 = (seller's public key‖ buyer's public key‖goods information hash‖time) and the address to the seller, where the 'time' represents the time before which the good should be delivered, unlockcodename represents the name of the unlockcode that define under what condition the UTXO can be spent and how to spend, and goods information hash can uniquely identify the goods and goods information can be defined as any information related to the goods. The buyer pays the UTXO to the address by using the uniform payment system.

(2). Delivery process: Seller's application subscribes to the transaction event above, read UTXO and check CK1, the address and the UTXO are consistent. Store the UTXO in form $txid_j$ locally, and then delivers the goods;

(3). Receiving process: After the buyer receives the goods before the agreed time, the deliverer presents CK1 in a two-dimensional code. The buyer scans the code to get CK1 and signs it. The deliverer scans the code to get (CK1: sig_{buyer} (CK1)), and gives it to the seller to complete the delivery task. The seller records the triple ($txid_j$, CK1, sig_{buyer} (CK1)) locally. If the seller fails to deliver the goods before the agreed time, the smart contract is designed to return the UTXO to the buyer.

Next, we discuss how to spend the UTXO.

The payer constructs request = (inputs,outputs,$txid_j$ ‖ CK1‖ sig(inuts‖ outputs‖ nonce)‖ sig_{buyer}(CK1)); and submits it to a client app; The client app puts the request into a transaction proposal and then submits the proposal to Fabric peers. The uniform payment system will process it as follows. According to the inputs, it queries the ledger to obtain the UTXO and gets the unlockcode. Call the unlockcode with parameter '$txid_j$‖CK1‖sig(inuts‖outputs‖nonce)‖sig_{buyer}(CK1)' and see if the result is true. If true, construct an UTXO and store it into the ledger, else the transaction fails.

The main steps of the unlockcode is depicted in Fig. 4.

The cash-on-delivery application has wide applications. It provides the technology support for any two persons to trade without any trusted third party.

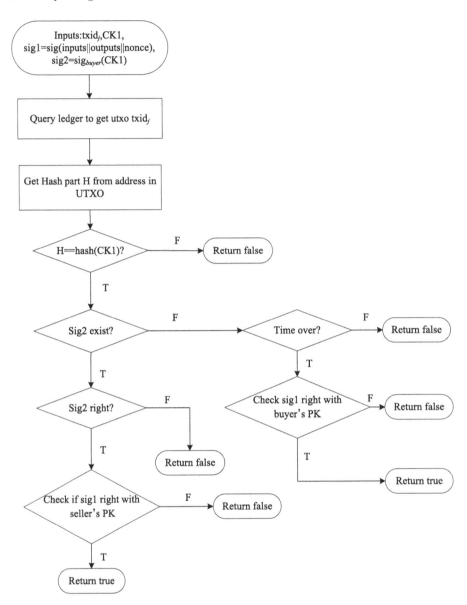

Fig. 4. The main steps of unlockcode.

Because of the flexibility of Fabric smart contract, it is easy to design other conditional payment applications with more branches depending on the uniform payment system.

2.4 Security Analysis

The security of the uniform payment system can be analyzed in two level. The Bitcoin-level includes token-minting security, token-transferring security and token-redemption security. The token-minting security aims to eliminate the possibility of forging. Our design gives the token-minting right to the only institution. If the private key is secure, nobody can impersonate the institution. Further, in our design the structure of asset label is different from the structure of token label. This eliminates the possibility to use assets as tokens. So our design prevents the counterfeit token problem. The security of each UTXO depends on the security of its private key, which is protected by each owner. In short, token-transferring and token-redemption are similar to the bitcoin-transferring, whose security is already proved by time and practice.

The transaction security of Fabric-level is ensured by the design of Fabric. For example, the double-spending problem can be prevented by the transaction mechanism provided by Fabric. In short the uniform payment system can prevent the counterfeit token and double-spending problems and is secure.

3 The Design of Digital Assets

Similar to the uniform payment system, we can design the issuance, transfer and redemption functions for digital assets. In the architecture design, the UTXO model is still used, and the initiator of asset transaction constructs a request, and client app encapsulates the request into Fabric transaction proposal, which will be submitted to the blockchain network and the smart contract will process the transaction proposal.

But there are difference in some steps between the design of digital assets and the design of tokens.

As for the issuance of digital assets, it is designed to allow anyone with write access right to the channel to issue digital assets because every enterprise or even an individual has the need to issue digital assets. Since asset-issuing is the source of trust, the identity of an asset issuer must be verifiable. The identity of an asset issuer can be generated with the MSP and placed in the inputs in the request. The asset label is defined as (producer identification‖asset type‖ asset identification), where the producer identification is abstracted from the producer's public key certificate. The asset identification can be the hash of the video, image and/or text information of the asset while the information itself can be stored in local storage. The structure of label avoids the confliction between digital asset names and token names. Before the smart contract verifies the signature in the request, the producer identity should be verified first. However, since the identity of the initiator is encapsulated in the request, the existing Fabric transaction process cannot be directly used to do the authentication. It is necessary to redesign the authentication mechanism. Based on the analysis of Fabric code, we propose the following functions are added: an API IsIDValidate with input parameter userID is added to core/chaincode/shim/handler. Add a function HandlerValidateId to core/chaincode/handler to verify that the input userID is valid for the corresponding CA.

For asset-transferring, this process is consistent with the transfer of tokens. For asset-redemption, the owner of the asset signs a statement that the asset belongs to an address which has no unlock parameters.

4 Conclusion

Depending on the state database and the smart contract functionality, we design a uniform payment system based on UTXO model for Fabric. It has three kinds of addresses: P2PK, P2PKH and P2SH. P2SH is a general payment type. When there is a new payment application, only one sub-function is added to the payment contract to implement it, and a call to the sub-function is added too.

Compared with Bitcoin, tokens are minted by a designated token-minting bank, rather than mined by POW. The unlockcode of tokens only needs to be stored once, instead of being stored with each UTXO all times.

A complete transaction is divided into Bitcoin-level part and Fabric-level part. Even a mobile phone users can easily implement Bitcoin-level transaction that constructs the inputs and outputs and then sign them. In this way, even micro enterprises can enjoy the blockchain payment services. As an example, based on the uniform payment system, we design an application of cash-on-delivery, which provides the technology support for any two persons to trade without any trusted third party. Based on the payment function, the functions of asset confirmation, asset transfer and redemption can be similarly designed.

The uniform payment system and the cash-on-delivery application are implemented and will be deployed in one company in Shanghai.

Fabric is widely recognized as the representative of consortium blockchains. It is necessary and useful to design a convenient, secure and efficient payment system for it.

References

1. Nakamoto, S.: Bitcoin: A peer-to-peer electronic cash system (2008). https://bitcoin.org/bitcoin.pdf
2. Chohan, U.W.: The decentralized autonomous organization and governance issues. SSRN Electron. J. (2017)
3. Vitalik, B.: Ethereum: a next generation smart contract and decentralized application platform (2013). https://github.com/ethereum/wiki/wiki/White-Paper
4. Androulaki, E., Barger, A., Bortnikov, V., et al.: Hyperledger fabric: a distributed operating system for permissioned blockchains (2018)
5. https://bitcoin.org/en/developer-glossary (2019)
6. https://github.com/hyperledger/fabric/releases/tag/v2.0.0-alpha (2019)
7. Zachary, A., Ramnik, A., Shehar, B., et al.: The Libra blockchain white paper (2019). https://www.cnblogs.com/books2read/articles/11065500.html
8. Poon, J., Dryja, T.: The bitcoin lightning network (DRAFT Version 0.5) (2015). http://lightning.network/lightning-network-paper-DRAFT-0.5.pdf

Identity-Based Cross-Domain Authentication by Blockchain via PKI Environment

Jiahe Wang[(✉)], Shasha Li, and Songjie Wei

School of Computer Science and Engineering,
Nanjing University of Science and Technology, Nanjing 210094, China
{jhwang,lishasha,swei}@njust.edu.cn

Abstract. To tackle the difficulty of immediate identity revocation in the identity-based cryptography (IBC) authentication system, this paper proposes an identity signature scheme by security mediator (MED), which can revoke entity. Besides, aiming at cross IBC domains authentication under large-scale network architecture, an efficient identity-based cross-domain authentication protocol via public key infrastructure (PKI) environment is presented, combining blockchain. It reduces effectively complexity by consortium blockchain, thus more available for authentication in large-scale network. Through security and performance analysis, the evaluation results show the proposed scheme introduces lower overhead in computation and communication by blockchain, with resisting various attacks and excellent security in the process of authentication, compared with other authentication protocols.

Keywords: Identity-based signature · Blockchain · Security mediator · Cross-domain · Identity authentication

1 Introduction

With user behaviors expending from the offline social interactions to the online social network, which brings security problems of potential threats such as identification or authentication for information services entity (ISE). Hopefully, identity authentication technology is an important mechanism to guarantee cyber space security [1]. Moreover, identity authentication based on public key infrastructure (PKI), is the most commonly used. Concretely, certification authority (CA), can establish a secure network environment by PKI to manage keys and certificates, but only satisfying authentication in a certain trust domain. In decentralized network, different trust domains will form relatively independent CAs, causing users not access to each other's resources. Presently, identity-based cryptography (IBC) architecture develops rapidly as well [2], which possesses more advantages than PKI framework in communication, but exiting immediate revocation difficulty of identity in IBC system, which usually stops key generation center (KGC) from updating private key for entities to key revocation, without promptness. In order to ensure the legitimacy of users' access to resources, it's necessary to design revocable signature scheme in IBC system, and to achieve cross domains authentication in multi-trust domains.

© Springer Nature Singapore Pte Ltd. 2020
X. Si et al. (Eds.): CBCC 2019, CCIS 1176, pp. 131–144, 2020.
https://doi.org/10.1007/978-981-15-3278-8_9

Blockchain technology implements decentralized peer-to-peer transactions in distributed systems where nodes do not need to trust each other by means of time stamping and distributed consensus. Also, cryptographic principle is used to ensure all data cannot be falsified and unforgeable, ultimately forming a decentralized shared ledger [3]. Hence, blockchain technology is expected to subvert the traditional authentication approach to achieve across trust domains via PKI environment. Specifically, on the basis of hierarchical PKI, we construct the root CA (RCA) by consortium blockchains, so RCAs of PKI domains can issue transactions as initiators and receivers, respectively to realize authorized trust. Moreover, in every IBC authentication system, identity signature based on security mediator (MED) can effectively achieve immediate identity revocation. In the process of key management, KGC divides private key into two parts, kept by MED and entity itself. By ordering MED to stop generating signature signals, identity revocation and key renewal can be realized.

According to above analysis, this paper summarizes the advantages of identity authentication based on PKI and IBC, designs an identity-based cross-domain authentication scheme by MED and blockchain. It aims at frequent interaction between different ISEs and users in large-scale heterogeneous network. Within a trust domain, we use IBC to achieve efficient authentication. In addition, we improve the SM9 digital signature algorithm for a revocable identity signature. Among different trust domains, to overcome IBC's unsuitable for large-scale architectures, the decentralized authentication combined with PKI and blockchain is achieved. Through security analysis and experiments, the protocol in this paper can realize secure communication. What's more, compared with other authentication protocols, it reduces communication load and storage burden of users and ISEs on the promise of cross-domains authentication process, which performs good practicability in identity authentication.

2 Related Work

In terms of the distributed network environment, currently, cross-domains authentication mainly includes three types of architectures, that is based on symmetric cryptography, PKI and IBC. PKI is mature and widely used, suitable for large-scale networks, but mutual communication between entities cause problems such as high computation or communication. IBC can solve above problem, but hard to achieve cross-domain authentication. Hence, how to achieve cross-domain authentication of IBC or PKI, and improve the efficiency of authentication have attracted wide attention of scholars. Arfaoui et al. proposed an adaptive anonymous authentication and key agreement scheme, realizing anonymous authentication and session key establishment [4]. Ghoreishi et al. proposed several secure and efficient identity-based and pairing-free without certificate two party key agreement protocols [5]. Yao et al. proposed cross heterogeneous domain authentication model based on PKI, and achieved cross domain authentication, supporting mutual authentications [6]. Hua-Xi proposed an identity-based signcryption scheme, and an authentication model for multi-domain and mutual entity authentication protocol based on IBC [7]. Wang et al. presented a new efficient authenticated key agreement protocol which can be shift between PKI and IBC, it can efficiently resist kinds of active attacks [8]. Wang et al. proposed a blockchain-based cross-domain authentication model to ensure safety and efficiency to access resources belonging to different domain, which performs more efficient than the existing PKI cross-domain authentication schemes [9].

However, all above schemes had no consideration on immediate identity revocation in IBC authentication system. Moreover, above cross-domain authentication schemes based on PKI or IBC require much computational overhead and complex communication to ensure security. Although the research of blockchain technology in the field of identity authentication has been paid attention to, the problem of cross-domain authentication has not yet been solved. As a result, there are still many problems of cross-domain authentication in complex network to be solved.

3   Technical Background

3.1   Identity-Based Cryptography

Identity-based cryptography is public key cryptosystem, whose goal is to achieve the binding of the public keys and identities without another certification services. In the IBC cryptosystem, there is a trusted party called KGC, responsible for generating private key corresponding to identity information for the users. When a user joins the system for the first time, KGC verifies the identity information. After confirming, the private is generated for the user, and the private key is secretly transmitted to the user. When a user needs to use the public key of a user in the system, he or she only need to know the identity information of the user, without having to obtain and verify the public key certificate of the user.

SM9 algorithm is an identity-based cryptography designed by bilinear pairing, which constitutes an important part of Chinese commercial cryptography system [10]. In such a system, the user's private key and public key may be extracted from user's identity and KGC's parameters. The main contents of SM9 includes digital signature algorithm, key exchange protocol, key encapsulation mechanism and public key encryption algorithm, specifically as subsequent chapters. It is mainly used for digital signature, key exchange, identity authentication, etc. SM9 algorithm is resistant to various existing attacks and has sufficient security and was released as China's national cryptographic industry standard in 2015.

3.2   Hierarchical PKI Authentication System

Hierarchical PKI authentication system means a PKI based on the subordinate relationship of CAs, as shown in Fig. 1. Under this system, all users trust the RCA that is the center of trust. When the user is authenticated, both users provide digital certificates and signatures, and the CA verifies the validity and authenticity of certificate. When both users who have issued certificates by different CAs communicate, cross-domain authentication should be performed under the hierarchical authentication system. Note that Hierarchical PKI authentication system exits some advantages due to its simple structure and one-way trustworthy relationship. Specifically, it is easier to upgrade and increase new authentication users in a domain, because we only need to establish a trust relationship between RCA in current and target domain. However, there exists a very big drawback, that is, difficult to build a trusted root CA.

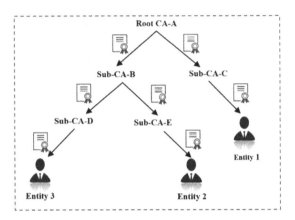

Fig. 1. Hierarchical PKI authentication architecture

3.3   Blockchain Technology

3.3.1   Blockchain Structure

Blockchain is a specific data structure that combines data blocks in a chain by chronological order. It integrates key technologies of distributed storage, modern cryptography, peer-to-peer network, consensus mechanism and smart contract to ensure decentralized and unforgeable decentralized public ledgers. In blockchain technology, data is permanently stored in blocks, and the block consists of the block header and the block body, as shown in Fig. 2. Specifically, the block header includes version number, timestamp, a hash value of last block, and a total hash value of transaction data, etc. The hash value of last block is to hash the data of each module in the head of it, and blocks are connected by such hash values in a loop. The block body records all transaction data from the time when the blockchain was created to the time when current block was generated [11].

3.3.2   Blockchain Characteristics

The scheme proposed in this paper mainly utilizes the decentralization, collective maintenance and tamper-proof characteristics of blockchain, introduced below.

Decentralization Characteristics. The blockchain system node is based on a distributed point-to-point structure. Each node stores all transaction data in the system, the damage of any node does not affect the operation of the whole system, thus the blockchain system possesses high redundancy and excellent robustness.

Collective Maintenance Characteristics. The blockchain constructs a complete set of protocol mechanisms. Nodes not only participate in recording data, but also participate in verifying the correctness of data recorded by other nodes. Data can only be credited to the block if multiple key nodes recognize correctness of data.

Tamper-Proof Characteristics. The blockchain uses a hash algorithm to perform integrity protection on the data of the recorded blocks, and connects the data blocks in a chain structure and stores them in all nodes in the system. If a block is changed, then each subsequent block will be changed. The more data blocks on the blockchain, it is almost impossible to change the data in a certain block and block.

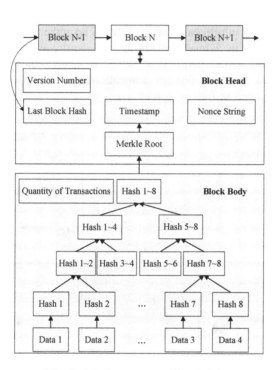

Fig. 2. Block structure of blockchain

4 Cross-Domains Authentication Scheme

4.1 Authentication Overall Architecture

In order to realize the frequent interaction between different ISEs and users in large-scale heterogeneous network environment, this paper designs a new cross-domain authentication model, the overall architecture is shown in Fig. 3.

In each of trust domains, IBC is used to achieve efficient identity authentication due to the large number of users and ISEs. In addition, in order to solve the problem that the entity cannot be revoked immediately, this paper adopts identity revocation mechanism based on MED, and improves SM9 algorithm and design an identity revocable signature scheme. Because of IBC unsuitable for large-scale network environment, we use PKI to achieve mutual authentication between domains, and utilizes blockchain technology to solve efficiency problem of cross-domain authentication. Combining the advantages of IBC and blockchain, this paper proposes a cross-domain authentication model for ISEs to realize the interaction between ISEs and users in large-scale heterogeneous network environments.

In this model, the users and ISEs are distributed across multiple IBC trust domains. The intra-domain entities adopt identity-based authentication manner, as shown as Fig. 3 (marked with black, and route mark with red meaning the whole procedure of cross-domains). The information service entity itself is its public key. KGC splits its private key pri_{id} into two parts, pri_{id}^{Med} and pri_{id}^{ISE}, and sends the pri_{id}^{Med} to the mediator agency, the pri_{id}^{ISE} to the information service entity. The authentication server manages the entity information in the domain and verifies the identity of the visitor. At the same time, it exchanges blockchain certificates for inter-domain authentication and assists intra-domain entities for cross-domain authentication. The specific authentication process will be described in following sections.

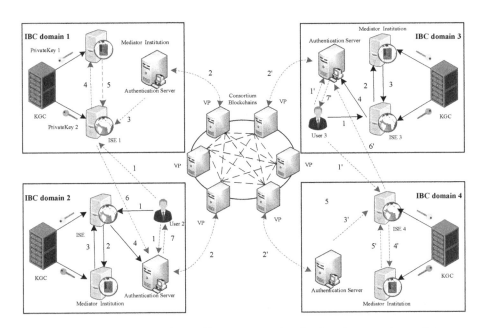

Fig. 3. Identity authentication architecture cross-domains based on security mediator

4.2   Cross-Domains PKI Authentication Model

Based on the above cross-domain analysis, this section proposes a cross-domain authentication model established by the RCA based on blockchain technology on the basis of PKI, as shown in Fig. 4. This model draws on distribution of consortium blockchain, and builds the authentication model of multiple PKI trust domains to join consortium blockchain platform. Also, this model ensures that internal architecture and hierarchy authentication logic of the original PKI trust domain remain unchanged. To implement cross-domain authentication, the trust anchor RCAs join the consortium blockchain. The RCA that joins the consortium blockchain is trusted, and self-generating RCA blockchain certificate, and the hash value of the certificate is recorded in the blockchain, as the trust certificate of each domain. If a domain no longer seeks cross-domain needs, or the domain is no longer trusted, the license to join the consortium blockchain is revoked to achieve the exit.

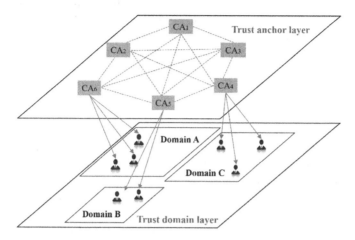

Fig. 4. Cross-domains PKI authentication model

4.3 Blockchain Certification

On the basis of X.509 digital certificate 3.0, this paper designs a blockchain certificate, as shown in Fig. 5. According to reference [12], interface that the certificate is written into the blockchain is defined as $put(action, hash(Cert))$, the query interface is defined as $get(hash(Cert))$. The query returns *action* indicating the current state of certificate, respectively *issue* and *revoke*. The scheme proposed in this paper can use the certificate to generate a hash value to quickly and efficiently query *action* on the blockchain. The blockchain certificate does not set the CRL, but the certificate validity period limits the certificate lifetime.

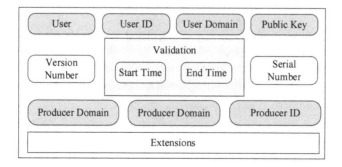

Fig. 5. Blockchain certification

5 Cross-Domains Authentication Protocol

5.1 Identity-Based Signature Scheme

In order to implement cross-domain authentication in IBC system, this paper proposes a revocable identity-based signature scheme based on the SM9 algorithm, namely mIBS. KGC divides the private key of entity into two parts, which are respectively stored by MED and the entity, by stopping the signature for the entity by commanding MED, revoking identity quickly. mIBS includes parameter generation (*Setup*), key generation (*KeyGen*), signature (*Sign*) and verification algorithm (*Verify*).

(1) *Setup*

Let $(G_1, +), (G_2, +), (G_T, \times)$ be a cyclic group with three orders of prime numbers p, P_1 is the generator of G_1, P_2 is the generator of G_2. There exists a homomorphic mapping $\varphi : G_2 \to G_1$ so that $\varphi(P_2) = P_1$. Bilinear pairing e is mapping of $G_1 \times G_2 \to G_T$, which satisfies non-degenerate and computability.

Select hash function $H_1 : \{0,1\}^* \to Z_p$ and $H_2 : \{0,1\}^* \to Z_p$.

KGC generates a random number $K \in [1, p-1]$ as master key, and calculates $P_{pub} = K \cdot P_2$ as public key, so the master key pairing is (K, P_{pub}). KGC saves K secretly, publishing $(p, P_1, P_2, G_1, G_2, e, P_{pub}, H_1, H_2)$.

(2) *KeyGen*

KGC uses a string *Str* as a unique identifier for private key generation function and publishes it. Let ISE be identified as *id*, KGC calculates $t_1 = H_1(id \parallel Str, p) + K$ and $t_2 = K \cdot t_1^{-1}$, then we get its private key and public key as follows.

$$pri_{id} = [t_2]P_1 = [K/H_1(id \parallel Str, p) + K]P_1 \tag{1}$$

$$pub_{id} = [H_1(idStr \parallel, p)]P_2 + P_{pub} \tag{2}$$

KGC then randomly selects $K_1 \in [1, p-1]$ to get part private key of ISE, calculated as formula (3).

$$pri_{id}^{ISE} = [K_1/H_1(id \parallel Str, p) + K]P_1 = [K_1/t_1]P_1 \tag{3}$$

Therefore, another part private key is calculated as formula (4), sending pri_{id}^{ISE} to ISE, and pri_{id}^{MED} to MED secretly.

$$pri_{id}^{MED} = pri_{id} - pri_{id}^{ISE} = [(K - K_1) \bmod p/t_1]P_1 \tag{4}$$

(3) *Sign*

Suppose the message to be signed is bit string A, in order to obtain the digital signature (m, S) of A, signature process is as shown in Algorithm 1. Note that before ISE signs A, we need to randomly select integer $I\epsilon[1, p-1]$. Then, calculating $B = e(P_1, P_{pub})^I$ in G_T, and converting data type of B to bit string. After that, calculating $m = H_2(A \parallel B, p)$ and $Q = (I - m) \bmod p$, if $Q = 0$, we reselect P_1 and I.

Algorithm 1	Digital signature process
Input	Sign request $R = (id, Q)$
Output	Digital signature (m, S)
1	while $id =$ 'valid' do
2	Mediator signature $S_{MED} = [Q] \cdot pri_{id}^{MED}$;
3	Send S_{MED} to ISE;
4	ISE signature $S_{ISE} = [Q] \cdot pri_{id}^{ISE}$;
5	Calculate $S = S_{MED} + S_{ISE}$;
6	Calculate $pub_{id} = [H_1(id\|Str, p)]P_2 + P_{pub}$;
7	$B' = e(S, pub_{id}) \cdot e(P_1, P_{pub})^m$;
8	if $B' = B$ then
9	Output digital signature(m, S) of A;
10	end if

(4) *Verify*

Verification process is shown in Algorithm 2, in which $f, u \epsilon G_T$.

Algorithm 2	Signature verifying process
Input	$P_{pub}, id, A', (m', S')$, public parameters
Output	Verifying result 'true' or 'false'
1	while m' $\in [1, p-1]$ do
2	while $S' \in G_1$ do
3	$pub_{id} = [H_1(id\|Str, p)]P_2 + P_{pub}$;
4	$f = e(P_1, P_{pub})^{m'}$;
5	$u = e(S, pub_{id})$;
6	$B' = f \cdot u$;
7	$m'' = H_2(A'\|B', p)$;
8	if $m'' = m'$ then
9	Output result = 'true';
10	end if

5.2   Cross-Domains Authentication Protocol

According to above authentication architecture, blockchain certificate and revocable identity signature scheme, an authentication protocol cross-domains based on security mediator and blockchain is present. It can support two-way authentication and session key agreement between different IBC trust domains, which realizes immediate revocation of identity and improves the efficiency of cross-domains authentication. Cross-domain authentication is achieved by blockchain certificate via PKI environment in each IBC domain, while intra-domain authentication is based on IBC authentication. Taking one-way authentication as an example, Table 1 is the symbolic description of authentication protocol for this model.

Table 1. Symbolic description for authentication protocol

Symbol	Implication
U_x	User in IBC_x domain
ISE_x	Information service entity in IBC_x
AS_x	Authentication server in IBC_x
$Cert_x$	Certificate of U_x
$BCert_x$	Blockchain certification of U_x
$A \rightarrow B : C$	A sends message C to B
$IBE : \{\}pub_U$	Identity-based encryption with pub_U

Note that KGCs use the same public parameters $(N, P_1, P_2, G_1, G_2, H_1, H_2)$, only differs in the master key pairing (K, P_{pub}). Assume KGC, MED, and authentication server are honest in each IBC trust domain. When U_2 in IBC_2 applies for access to ISE_1 in IBC_1, the specific protocol is as follows.

Step1. $U_2 \rightarrow ISE_1 : \{id_{U2}, requset\}$

$$U_2 \rightarrow AS_2 : \{id_{ISE1}, id_{U2}, T_1, IBS\{id_{ISE1} \parallel id_{u2}\}pri_{U2}\}$$

Step2. AS_2 verifies the signature of U_2, and $AS_2 \rightarrow AS_1$

Step3. $AS_1 \rightarrow AS_2 : R_1(random\ number)$

Step4. $AS_2 \rightarrow AS_1 : \{Cert_{PAS_2}, Sign_R, R_1\}$

Step5. AS_1 verifies R_1 and $Sign_R$ through $Cert_{PAS_2}$ and R_1, then defines trust anchor RCA_2 of PAS_2 in IBC_2.

Step6. $AS_1 \rightarrow RCA_2$

Step7. $RCA_2 \rightarrow AS_1 : \{BCert_{RCA_2}, R_2\}$

Step8. AS_1 verifies R_2, and analyzes $BCert_{RCA_2}$ for checking validation, then hash $BCert_{RCA_2}$.

Step9. AS_1 queries transactions about hash result through local authentication server on the blockchain.

The above steps are to implement the inter-domain authentication, the following is authentication process in IBC domain.

Step10. AS_2 calculates session key $W = H_1(id_{U2} \parallel id_{ISE1}) \cdot [K_2] \cdot P_{pub1}$, AS_1 calculates $W' = H_1(id_{U2} \parallel id_{ISE1}) \cdot [K_1] \cdot P_{pub2}$, evidently $W = W'$.

Step11. As above mIBS,

$$ISE_1 \rightarrow MED_1 : R = (id_{ISE1}, Q) \text{for message } M$$

Step12. $MED_1 \rightarrow ISE_1 : S_{MED1} = [Q] \cdot pri_{ISE1}^{MED}$
Step13. ISE_1 gains (m, S), and calculates $V = M \oplus W'$,

$$ISE_1 \rightarrow AS_2 : \{V., (m, S)\}$$

Step14. AS_2 use W to decrypt V sent by ISE_1, and verifies (m, S) by mIBS. After verification, AS_2 believes that $W = W'$ is shared between AS_2 and ISE_1.

6   Security Analysis

This part mainly analysis security of scheme present from the following aspects.

Resistance to Internal Attacks. The consortium blockchain model can guarantee the trustworthiness of node servers due to non-tampering, traceability and other characteristics, and the security of inter-domain authentication process. Moreover, through improved mIBS key generation algorithm based on security mediator, we can also achieve immediate identity revocation and private key escrow. The authentication scheme proposed in this paper judges the validity of identity by querying blockchain certificates, so resisting internal attacks effectively.

Resistance to Counterfeiting Attacks. During procedure of identity authentication between ISEs and users through blockchain certificate, the attacker cannot imitate users to obtain information service entities. In addition, the authenticated parties can authenticate the identity of the other party only after the signature verification has passed. Therefore, the attacker cannot forge valid signature messages, so also not to carry out counterfeit attacks.

Resistance to Replay Attacks. In the process of cross-domain authentication, because of timestamp characteristics of blockchain, interactive information between information service entities and users is guaranteed by timestamp to ensure the freshness of messages. The reason why replay attacks can be effectively prevented is that the timestamp cannot be tampered with. If an attacker reuses the intercepted message, the validation will fail because the timestamp is invalid.

Resistance to Man-in-the-Middle Attacks. In the process of authentication, interactive messages between entities are signed by own private keys. If an attacker tampers with the message, the signature message cannot be verified by the receiver and effectively resist the man-in-the-middle attack.

Resistance to DDoS Attacks. The distributed architecture of blockchain naturally has the characteristics of point-to-point and redundancy. Even if one node fails, the other nodes will not be affected, so there is no single point failure problem. It is more flexible than centralized system in the way of denial of service attack [13]. Once the node fails, users connected with the failed node will not be able to access the system.

7 Performance Analysis

In order to verify the efficiency of scheme, experiments were carried out on the computer configured with 64-bit OS, CPU I5-4590 with 4 cores, 3.3 GHz. Table 2 shows time consumption of various operations, which means the average of the experimental results after 50 experiments. Assuming that the message length is 80bits, identity size is 80bits, the timestamp length is 16bits, group size for identity-based encryption scheme is 160bits, certificate ciphertext is 160bits and hash summary information size is 160bits.

Table 2. Calculating time consumption

Operation	Time/ms	Operation	Time/ms
T_{PM}	0.0018	T_{IBS}	1.0664
T_H	0.0015	T_{IBV}	1.2468
T_e	0.0889	T_{AE}	0.3375
T_{SE}	0.0042	T_{AS}	0.4291
T_{IBE}	1.4526	T_E	0.0026

Specifically, $T_{PM}, T_H, T_e, T_E, T_{SE}, T_{IBE}, T_{IBS}, T_{IBV}, T_{AE}, T_{AS}$ means time consumption of dot product, hash, bilinear pairing, exponential operation, symmetric encryption and decryption, identity-based signature and verifying, asymmetric encryption and decryption, and signature respectively. Among them, $T_{IBE}, T_{IBS}, T_{IBV}$ are constructed with bilinear logarithmic groups, and T_{AE}, T_{AS} uses dot product and hash function based on elliptic curve, so costing longer time.

In addition, we compared this scheme with others in cross-domain authentication protocols [14], but the premise of this work is assuming that they adopt the same cryptographic algorithm, that is, all IBC domains adopt the same identity-based encryption/signature algorithm, the consortium blockchain adopts the same asymmetric encryption/signature algorithm as well as all PKI domains. Table 3 shows specific performance comparison in authentication protocols.

From Table 3, we can know that time consumption spent by our scheme is between EIMAKP-II and 3PAKE. Obviously, EIMAKP-II need the lowest communication traffic, but with the highest computational complexity, the reason is that it requires strong computing and communication capabilities of user, so more suitable for mainstream users in the trust domain, such as resource-constrained portable mobile terminals. In addition, the computational complexity of 3PAKE performs the lowest, however, all messages are sent in plaintext, which is vulnerable to counterfeit and secret key leakage attacks. Therefore, this scheme trades security for communication complexity. However, the scheme proposed in this paper uses the untamperable property of blockchain to complete the whole cross-domain authentication, with security mediator to assist identity revoking in the IBC domain. All the process integrates the advantages of IBC and PKI to build a cross-domain model of complex networks, with lower computational burden than EIMAKP-II. In terms of computation, the scheme is designed based on the consortium blockchain architecture. At present, it is known that the consortium blockchain can settle down thousands to tens of thousands of transactions in parallel every second, so is easier to meet functional requirements of cross-domain authentication in communication burden.

Table 3. Calculation of time consumption

		Computation/ms	Communication/bit
EIMAK P-II	User	$2T_H + 2T_{AS} + 2T_{AE} + T_{SE} + T_{IBE}$	1056
	ISE	$2T_{SE} + T_{IBE} + T_E$	
	Others	$4T_{AE} + 3T_{AS} + T_{IBE} + T_{IBV}$	
3PAKE	User	$3T_{PM} + 2T_H$	1664
	ISE	$3T_{PM} + 2T_H$	
	Others	$2T_{PM} + 8T_H$	
Ours	User	T_{IBS}	1496
	ISE	$T_{PM} + 2T_H + 2T_E + 2T_e$	
	Others	$T_{AE} + T_{IBV} + 2T_H + 2T_{PM} + T_e + T_{IBE}$	

In addition, when the number of cross-domain authentication requests increases, since the proposed scheme is based on a distributed consortium blockchains, the it will not cause the number of public key algorithms increasing, but objectively there will be an increase in the number of hash operations due to the collective maintenance of the ledger by blockchain. However, when tested on a machine with the same configuration, ECDSA-192 takes about twice as long as RSA-1024, and RSA-1024 takes about 10 times as much as SHA-256, so the calculation speed of the hash algorithm is much higher. Therefore, even in a multi-domain environment, this model has the potential to achieve the efficiency and carrying capacity of cross-domain authentication. Therefore, this protocol has obvious performance advantages in cross-domains.

8 Conclusion

Aiming at frequent cross-authentication between different kinds of ISEs and users in large-scale heterogeneous network, this paper summarizes the advantages of identity authentication based on PKI and IBC, designs an efficient authentication scheme cross-domains based on security mediator. To overcome IBC's unsuitable for large-scale architectures in cross-domains, an authentication protocol combined with PKI environment and blockchain is present. It can communicate securely cross different IBC domains with immediate identity revocation, both with lower computation and communication load. Further, we will continue to simplify the authentication process, for more efficient cross-domain authentication, and applying the proposed scheme in practices.

Acknowledgments. This material is based upon work supported by the NSFC fund No. 61472189 and CERNET Innovation Project No. NGII20180103. Opinions expressed are those of the authors and do not necessarily reflect the views of the sponsors.

References

1. Guanqun, B.A.O., Libonate, B., Counterman, R.C.: Network-based authentication and security services. U.S. Patent Application 10/084,780, 25 September 2018
2. Lozupone, V.: Analyze encryption and public key infrastructure (PKI). Int. J. Inf. Manage. **38**(1), 42–44 (2018)
3. Templin, F.L., Viswanathan, K.: Secured data transmission using identity-based cryptography. U.S. Patent Application 10/326,743, 18 June 2019
4. Arfaoui, A., ben Letaifa, A., Kribeche, A., et al.: Adaptive anonymous authentication for wearable sensors in wireless body area networks. In: 2018 14th International Wireless Communications & Mobile Computing Conference (IWCMC), pp. 606–611. IEEE (2018)
5. Ghoreishi, S.M., Razak, S.A., Isnin, I.F., et al.: New secure identity-based and certificateless authenticated key agreement protocols without pairings. In: 2014 International Symposium on Biometrics and Security Technologies (ISBAST), pp. 188–192. IEEE (2014)
6. Yao, Y., Xingwei, W., Xiaoguang, S.: A cross heterogeneous domain authentication model based on PKI. In: 2011 Fourth International Symposium on Parallel Architectures, Algorithms and Programming, pp. 325–329. IEEE (2011)
7. Hua-Xi, P.: An identity-based authentication model for multi-domain. Chin. J. Comput. **8** (29), 8 (2006)
8. Wang, C., Liu, C., Niu, S., et al.: An authenticated key agreement protocol for cross-domain based on heterogeneous signcryption scheme. In: 2017 13th International Wireless Communications and Mobile Computing Conference (IWCMC), pp. 723–728. IEEE (2017)
9. Wang, W., Hu, N., Liu, X.: BlockCAM: a blockchain-based cross-domain authentication model. In: 2018 IEEE Third International Conference on Data Science in Cyberspace (DSC), pp. 896–901. IEEE (2018)
10. Cheng, Z.: Security analysis of SM9 key agreement and encryption. In: Guo, F., Huang, X., Yung, M. (eds.) Inscrypt 2018. LNCS, vol. 11449, pp. 3–25. Springer, Cham (2019). https://doi.org/10.1007/978-3-030-14234-6_1
11. Banga, V., Kshirsagar, A.C.: Ephemeral blockchain data structure. U.S. Patent Application 15/419,765, 2 August 2018
12. Tsai, W.T., Yu, L., et al.: Blockchain application development techniques. J. Softw. **28**(6), 1474–1487 (2017)
13. Tian, Y.L., Peng, C.G., Ma, J.F., et al.: Game-theoretic mechanism for cryptographic protocol. J. Comput. Res. Dev. **51**(2), 344–352 (2014)
14. Xie, Y.R., Ma, W.P., Luo, W.: A new cross-domain authentication model for information service entities. Comput. Sci. **45**(09), 177–182 (2018)

Blockchain-Based Content Name Search Mechanism in NDN

Jinshan Shi, Ru Li$^{(\boxtimes)}$, Jianghui Zhang, and Bo Cui

College of Computer Science, Inner Mongolia University,
Hohhot 010021, China
`csliru@imu.edu.cn`

Abstract. Named Data Networking (NDN) is one of the strong competitors of the next generation network architecture, meeting the needs of today's users for the network. One problem with NDN is that the content requester does not know if there is any content in the network when it sends out the interest package, and it does not know where the target is. This problem is currently solved by the domain name resolution service, but the existing solution does not apply to the NDN architecture. Because the content in the NDN is identified by a human-readable name, the NDN architecture does not require an additional name resolution system. In this paper, we propose a blockchain-based Content Name Search Mechanism (BCNSM) by binding the content producer and the human-readable content name as the unique identifier of the content, and then using the blockchain as a trusted organization to store content information, and dynamically stores the information through the smart contract, thereby mapping the content name and the storage location to each other. BCNSM provides users with content name search services and name to the content provider resolution services. Then the model was built for the BCNSM using the colored petri net, and the model process is verified by the model simulation to meet the expectations, and the state space analysis proves that the BCNSM has no deadlock. Finally, a prototype of the smart contract was implemented in Ethereum's testnet, and the storage and Gas overhead of content name registration and content cache address update were tested.

Keywords: Named Data Networking · Blockchain · Content name search · Smart contract · Colored Petri Net

1 Introduction

Nowadays, users' demand for the network has been changed from computing resource sharing to content acquisition and distribution. Therefore, Named Data Networking (NDN) has been proposed as an implementation of Information Centric Networking (ICN) thinking [1, 2]. However, there is a problem in the NDN: the content consumer does not know whether there is any content in the network when sending the interest packet, and does not know where the target is, but passively searches through the routing process of the NDN architecture, that is, through name-based longest prefix match lookup in each NDN routers [3–5].

X. Si et al. (Eds.): CBCC 2019, CCIS 1176, pp. 145–155, 2020.
https://doi.org/10.1007/978-981-15-3278-8_10

This problem has been solved by the Domain Name System (DNS) under the TCP/IP network architecture. The DNS provides a domain name directory for the user, and maps the IP address to the domain name so that the user can find the corresponding host according to the directory [6]. However, the lack of DNS is also obvious. DNS is a distributed database with a central tree structure, so it is vulnerable to DDoS attacks, and the closer the attack target is to the center, the greater the impact. At the same time, DNS has the disadvantage that information is easily falsified and registration fees are high.

In view of the problems in the design of DNS centralization, two decentralized schemes proposed by researchers at the blockchain are proposed. Ethereum Name Service (ENS) [7] and Open Data Index Name (ODIN) [8]. The decentralized architecture of the blockchain greatly increases the difficulty of DDoS attacks. ENS is a distributed domain name system built on the Ethereum. It maps the addresses and domain names on Ethereum to each other. ENS is a decentralized application built on the ethereum blockchain. The purpose of the ODIN project is to create a decentralized DNS. ODIN is an open system for identifying and exchanging data content indexes on a Bitcoin blockchain architecture. Currently ODIN is used in ICN as a directory for data content. The core of ICN is information, or called content or data, that identifies each unit of information by its name. ODIN gives the content a unique name and is not readable, for example: ppk:305678.568/ISBN2890321345#1.0.

However, the content in the NDN is identified by a human-readable name, and the content is named using a hierarchical structured naming method, so that the current NDN architecture does not need to rename the content. Therefore, we propose a blockchain-based Content Name Search Mechanism (BCNSM) to solve the above problem. BCNSM creates a content name directory and maps the content name to its storage address. In BCNSM, the content name is not resolved to other types of permanent identifiers, but is directly identified with the content name and content producer as the unique identity of the content.

The main contribution of this paper is to design a content name search mechanism that is tightly coupled with the NDN without adding an additional identifier to the content. The content name is mapped to the content provider that stores the content, providing the user with the location of the target content. The irrelevance of the network address that NDN has is oriented to the application layer. For the bottom layer, the content still has a storage location.

2 Background

Currently, the content search in the NDN relies on passive search with the router and its forwarding rules, so the user cannot know whether there is a corresponding data packet in the network before sending the interest packet. The same problem exists under TCP/IP. The thin waist of the TCP/IP structure is IP, and the user needs to find the target host conveniently. Therefore, the researchers designed the DNS to provide users with a domain name directory, mapping the IP address and the domain name so that the user can find the corresponding host according to the directory [6].

However, due to the serious security problems caused by its centralized design, some researchers have proposed to use a decentralized blockchain instead of DNS. As a distributed decentralized computing and storage architecture, blockchain can solve the trust problem between multiple agencies [9, 10]. The open source project ODIN released by the PPkPub development team, the purpose of ODIN is to create a decentralized DNS. ODIN is a completely open and decentralized naming identification system based on the blockchain. It is an open system for autonomously naming and exchanging data content indexes in the network environment [8]. At present, ODIN is used in the ICN network environment as a directory of data content in the ICN network, and a blockchain location in which the content name is registered is used as a unique identifier.

Another solution in the blockchain environment is the ENS, a distributed, open naming system based on the Ethereum. ENS maps the user address and account address in Ethereum to a domain name that is simple and easy to remember. ENS is a decentralized application provided by the Ethereum Foundation. Its purpose is to convert a series of complicated and difficult hash addresses in Ethereum into human-readable domain names, which facilitates the use of Ethereum. The ENS consists of three main modules, the registry, the resolver, and the registrar. The registry is the immutable part of the system core, and the resolver is finally implemented by the user. The registrar is a smart contract that assigns a subdomain according to the rules [7]. Hirai conducted formal verification for the contracts in ENS [11].

3   Blockchain-Based Content Name Search Mechanism

3.1   Application Scenario

The application scenario is an NDN environment, which provides a content name search service for the user, so that the user can know whether there is content that the user wants in the network and the location of the node that can provide the content before sending the interest packet. Did not consider converting the content name to a domain name, because the naming of the content in the NDN itself is readable, not a bunch of meaningless hash characters. nor does it consider creating a unique identifier for the content, because we believe that a content can be uniquely identified through the content producer and content name. Although NDN is content-centric and does not require end-to-end connectivity, we believe that transparently providing users with the location of content caching nodes can make content routing more efficient than blind passive routing.

There are five types of roles in the network. Among them, the blockchain node consists of three main functional modules: blockchain database, Ethereum Virtual Machine (EVM), and content name search module. The blockchain database is used to store the complete blockchain, the EVM is used to execute the smart contract, and the content name search module is used to query whether there is content named by the name in the network. The content name search module is not a smart contract running on the blockchain, so the search rate is not affected by the blockchain consensus speed. The description of other roles is shown in Table 1.

Table 1. Functional description of the main role

Name	Functional description
Blockchain node	Provide search services to users, store and execute smart contracts
Content producer	The node that generates the content, generates the smart contract corresponding to the content, and publishes the smart contract to blockchain
Content consumer	The node requesting the content, searching for the node of the content name to the blockchain
Content cacher	The node that stores the content in the cache and also initiates a transaction to update the information of the smart contract. Generally assumed by the NDN router
Content provider	Consisting of content producers and content cachers, can provide content for consumers

3.2   Architectural Design

The network architecture of the BCNSM is shown in Fig. 1. The content producer publishes the content name in the form of a smart contract to the blockchain before publishing the content to the NDN. Smart contracts automatically maintain a list of content cacher addresses.

Then, the content name search algorithm running on the blockchain node collects all the content names stored in the blockchain to construct a mapping of content names to smart contract addresses. When the content consumer wants to search for the content of the name in the network, the content name search module can be used to quickly find out whether the content of the name exists. If the content exists, the content name search module will give the address of the corresponding smart contract. And then get a list of content provider addresses through the smart contract.

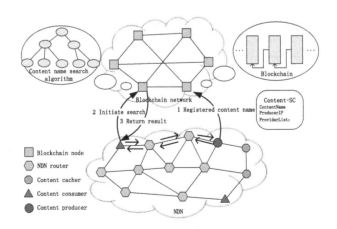

Fig. 1. Schematic diagram

In this way, the content consumer can know whether there is a named content in the network and the location of the data source of the content.

The BCNSM is divided into three parts: the publish-subscribe mechanism, the content cache address update mechanism and the content name search algorithm. These three parts are combined by the blockchain.

3.3 Publish-Subscribe Mechanism

The publish-subscribe mechanism provides a registration service for content names and a content name search service. The blockchain acts as a message manager in the publish-subscribe mechanism. It mainly consists of two key parts: the design of the smart contract for registered content name, and the publish and subscription process.

Smart Contract Design. When the content producer generates the content, it also generates a smart contract for the content. The content producer publishes the content name and related information by deploying the smart contract on the blockchain. Choosing each content to generate a smart contract instead of processing all content through a smart contract is mainly due to the following factors: First, the network will generate and disappear a large amount of content at the same time, so the update and maintenance of database is a great burden for single smart contract. Second, it is more secure, content producer can be signed in smart contracts, while preventing malicious users from forging information.

A smart contract can be a collection of code and data. The information and functions stored in the smart contract are as follows:

1. The name of the content, because the content is determined by name in the NDN.
2. Content producer address, because the name is not mandatory globally unique in the NDN, so the producer's address needs to be recorded while the name is recorded to make a distinction.
3. Producer signature, for security reasons, producers will sign smart contracts to ensure that smart contracts are not forged by malicious users.
4. The address list of the content cachers. Associate the content name with all content providers for that content. Automatically update the list by initiates transactions through the content cacher.

Publish Subscription Process. The process of publishing in the publish-subscribe mechanism is to register the content name with the blockchain. The content producer publishes the content name and other related information through the smart contract, and the content cacher publishes the location where the content copy is stored by the cache address update mechanism. The process of subscribing is the content consumer requesting content information from BCNSM. The specific process is as follows:

The First Step: Publish Smart Contract. As shown in Fig. 1. The content producer does not directly publish the content, but generates the corresponding smart contract at the same time. Then publish the smart contract in the blockchain. After the smart contract is deployed successfully, the address of the smart contract and the contract interface are added to the content data package, so that the NDN router can send the transaction synchronization information to the smart contract after receiving the content data package.

The Second Step: Subscription Content. The content consumer sends a subscription request message to the blockchain node to request a content provider address of a content, and the subscription request message is represented as a dual group (content name, source address), wherein the content name is used to identify the subscribed content, and the source address is passed to the smart contract lets it return a message to the content consumer.

The Third Step: Search Content Name. After receiving the subscription request message, the blockchain node reads the content name in the message, and then uses the content name search algorithm to search for the smart contract of the content in the blockchain, and if so, reads the address of the content provider stored in the smart contract, generate a subscription reply message and return it to the content consumer.

The Fourth Step: Return Messages. The subscription reply message is represented as a quad (content name, content producer, requester address, target node address list). The content name and content producer are combined to be used as the unique identifier of the content, because the name in the NDN is not mandatory to be globally unique, so there may be cases where the content names are the same. The requester address is used to locate the target node of this message. The target node address list provides possible destination node addresses for user.

3.4   Content Cache Address Update Mechanism

After the NDN route node caches a certain content, the smart contract address and the contract interface in the content data package are read, and then the transaction that updates the "content cacher address list" in the content smart contract is sent to the blockchain. Add the address of the content cacher. When the node that caches the content deletes the content, a transaction is sent to the blockchain to delete the address of the node in the "content cacher address list" in the smart contract.

3.5   Content Name Search Algorithm

The content name search algorithm uses the blockchain as the data source of the content name, reads the smart contract stored in the blockchain, and collects all the content names to construct a mapping of the content name to the smart contract address. The data structure of the index database is selected using the prefix tree, because the purpose of the search is to find the address of the smart contract based on the content name, so the keyword is the content name, and the hierarchical naming method is used in the NDN, so the search only needs to match the longest common prefix. Provided that an exact match is found, the content exists in the network and then directly returns the corresponding smart contract address to publish-subscribe mechanism.

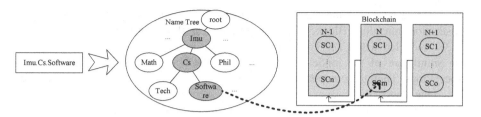

Fig. 2. Schematic diagram of content name search algorithm

Figure 2 shows a search schematic of an application using a hierarchical naming method. The content name is the path of the content of the Imu/Cs/Software search in the name tree. Each node represents a mapping of a smart contract, and finally the target contract is found based on the smart contract address mapped by the Imu/Cs/Software node. The specific algorithm is as follows: (Algorithm 1):

Algorithm 1. Content name search algorithm

Input:	BlockChain(t) ,cn$_i$ // Blockchain at t time, content name
Output:	ContractAddress$_{sc}$ // Smart contract address
1	(1) Initialize the name tree:
2	NameTree(t)=TreeInitialise(BlockChain(t))// Construct a name tree based on the blockchain at time t
3	(2)Periodically update the name tree
4	While *Blockchain consensus* do
5	Scan new blocks and update the name tree
6	End while
7	(3) Content name search:
8	Longest prefix match on the name tree
9	If (*the node exactly matches the content name cn$_i$*) then
10	Return ContractAddress$_{sc}$
11	Else
12	The content name is not in the blockchain
13	End if

4   Modeling and Analysis

We use formal verification of BCNSM through Colored Petri Net (CPN), which is modeled using hierarchical CPN due to the complexity of the mechanism. The top-level model is shown in Fig. 3. It consists of four substitution transitions, nine places, and 16 arcs. The subpage model of the substitution transitions Consumer is shown in Fig. 4. The substitution transitions Producer subpage model is shown in Fig. 5.

The subpage model of the substitution transitions provider is shown in Fig. 6. The substitution transitions Blockchain subpage model is shown in Fig. 7.

We modeled with CPN Tools and performed simulation and state space analysis. The simulation of the model verified that the BCNSM process was in line with expectations. Then the complete state space of the model is calculated by CPN Tools. Due to the length of the paper we do not display a complete state space analysis report. The state space analysis report proves that our model has no deadlock.

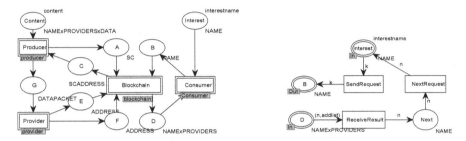

Fig. 3. Top-level module   **Fig. 4.** Content consumer module

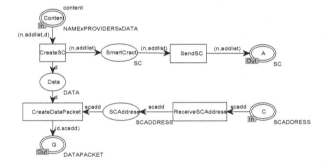

Fig. 5. Content producer module

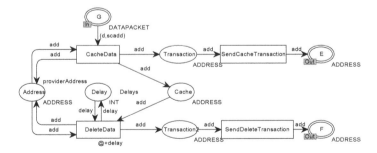

Fig. 6. Content cacher module

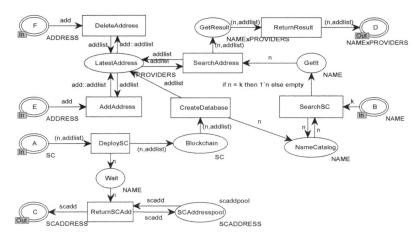

Fig. 7. Blockchain module

5 Cost Assessment and Experiment

In Ethereum, the cost of calculation and storage is relatively large. Therefore, the average cost of publishing smart contracts and storing data through experimental testing is required. We use the Solidity language to write a smart contract issued by the content producer to register the content name.

Smart contracts are compiled in bytecode and deployed in Ethereum. Ethereum uses Merkle Patricia Trie as a data organization to store the status and data of smart contracts, so we can not directly test the storage overhead of smart contracts, but through the smart contract bytecode is used to represent it. Table 2 shows the storage overhead of the registered content name smart contract. A typical registered smart contract size is 13,033 bytes; the add content cacher transaction (ACCT) and the delete content cacher transaction (DCCT) are both 200 bytes.

Table 2. Storage overhead

Name	Storage overhead (bytes)
Smart contract	13033
ACCT	200
DCCT	200

Next, the gas overhead of the smart contract is tested experimentally. As shown in Fig. 8, the gas overhead is divided into transaction overhead and execution cost. The transaction overhead is the Gas required to initiate the transaction, and the execution cost is the gas required to execute the transaction. The execution cost of deleting a content provider transaction is only 382Gas because the transaction does not need to write additional data to the account store, only changes the state of the stored data in the smart contract, while the other two need to write data to the account store.

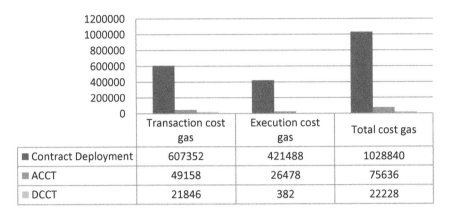

	Transaction cost gas	Execution cost gas	Total cost gas
■ Contract Deployment	607352	421488	1028840
▨ ACCT	49158	26478	75636
▨ DCCT	21846	382	22228

Fig. 8. The gas cost of contract deployment and transaction

6 Future Work and Summary

The current work provides a content name search service for the user, and the user can know whether there is any content in the network before sending the interest package, and can also know the location of the content provider of the content. The next work plan will be to design a routing algorithm based on the content name search. The BCNSM can obtain the storage location of the required content, so the routing algorithm combined with the BCNSM does not need to search for the content data packet through the routing process.

This paper proposes a blockchain-based BCNSM, which provides users with content name search services in the NDN environment, so that users can know whether there is content in the network and the storage location of the content. Then, the BCNSM was modeled by colored Petri nets, and the correctness of the mechanism was proved by formal methods. Finally, the storage and Gas overhead of the smart contract in the mechanism were evaluated through experiments.

Acknowledgments. This work has received funding from the Inner Mongolia Autonomous Region science and technology planning project (No. 201702019).

References

1. Zhang, L., Afanasyev, A., Burke, J., et al.: Named data networking. ACM SIGCOMM Comput. Commun. Rev. **44**(3), 66–73 (2014)
2. Jacobson, V., Smetters, D.K., Thornton, J.D., et al.: Networking named content. In: Proceedings of the 5th International Conference on Emerging Networking Experiments and Technologies, CoNEXT, Italy, pp. 1–12. ACM (2009)
3. Wang, Y., He, K., Dai, H., et al.: Scalable name lookup in NDN using effective name component encoding. In: 2012 IEEE 32nd International Conference on Distributed Computing Systems, ICDCS, Macau, China, pp. 688–697. IEEE (2012)

4. Wang, Y., Zu, Y., Zhang, T., et al.: Wire speed name lookup: a GPU-based approach. In: USENIX Symposium on Networked Systems Design & Implementation, NSDI, Lombard, pp. 199–212. ACM (2013)
5. Huang, K., Wang, Z., Xie, G.: Scalable high-speed NDN name lookup. In: Proceedings of the 2018 Symposium on Architectures for Networking and Communications Systems, ANCS, Ithaca, pp. 55–65. ACM (2018)
6. Mockapetris, P., Dunlap, K.J.: Development of the domain name system. In: SIGCOMM 1988 Symposium Proceedings on Communications Architectures and Protocols, vol. 18, pp. 123–133. ACM, New York (1988)
7. ENS. https://docs.ens.domains/en/latest/. Accessed 05 Oct 2018
8. ODIN. https://github.com/ppkpub/docs/blob/master/PPT_PPk_ODIN_Introduce_20180322. pdf. Accessed 05 Oct 2018
9. Alansari, S., Paci, F., Sassone, V.: A distributed access control system for cloud federations. In: 2017 IEEE 37th International Conference on Distributed Computing Systems (ICDCS), pp. 2131–2136. IEEE (2017)
10. Di Francesco Maesa, D., Mori, P., Ricci, L.: Blockchain based access control. In: Chen, L.Y., Reiser, H.P. (eds.) DAIS 2017. LNCS, vol. 10320, pp. 206–220. Springer, Cham (2017). https://doi.org/10.1007/978-3-319-59665-5_15
11. Hirai, Y.: Formal Verification of Deed Contract in Ethereum Name Service (2016)

Dizar: An Architecture of Distributed Public Key Infrastructure Based on Permissoned Blockchain

Qianyi Dai[✉], Kaiyong Xu, Leyu Dai, and Song Guo

Zhengzhou Information Science and Technology Institute, 450001 Zhengzhou, China
`qianyi_dai@outlook.com`

Abstract. With the current blockchain-based Public Key Infrastructure (PKI) being in its early stage of R&D, it is suffering from many shortcomings, such as its reliance on the centralized Certificate Authority (CA), the faulty identity registration and verification mechanism, and the difficulty in certificate management. As a result, the existing blockchain based PKI has trouble in adapting to a distributed network. Therefore, we have proposed Dizar: A distributed PKI architecture based on permissoned blockchain. Dizar architecture is designed with a distributed ledger operation system that can verify security. Based on no certificate authentication, electronic certificates with legal identities in the network are registered in a secure and verifiable permissioned blockchain, thus realizing the full-cycle management of the issued electronic certificates. The performance of Dizar is analyzed and compared with previous protocols. The results show that the Dizar architecture has better adaptability to a distributed network.

Keywords: Distributed PKI · Permissioned blockchain · Distributed ledger · No-certificate authentication

1 Introduction

PKI refers to an infrastructure system based on public key theory. It manages terminals or applying corresponding public and private key pairs, and is used to verify the legal relationship between the subject and the corresponding key pairs. The PKI model widely used now issues legal electronic certificates to public key subjects through a Certificate Authority (CA) based on a Certificate Policy (CP) and a Certificate Practice Statement (CPS), providing authentic, integral and confidential cryptographic services to the public key subjects. However, given the frequent incidents in recent years (e.g., Stuxnet [9], Comodo [19], DigiNotar [6] and Trustwave [7]), the fragility of the traditional CA-based centralized PKI is fully demonstrated. Besides, the applications of PGP-based certificate information model in the distributed network still needs to be improved due to its short trust chain and coarse granularity in measuring trust levels. Therefore,

© Springer Nature Singapore Pte Ltd. 2020
X. Si et al. (Eds.): CBCC 2019, CCIS 1176, pp. 156–186, 2020.
https://doi.org/10.1007/978-981-15-3278-8_11

a new distributed PKI architecture is needed to solve the flaws of existing PKI and PGP, so as to adapt it to the dynamically changing distributed networks.

Originally proposed by Nakamoto [17], a blockchain aims at building a tamper-proofing and traceable block data structure in an open Peer to Peer (P2P) network through transparent and credible rules, to realize data sharing, auditing and management in a network composed of multiple sites or institutions. Any node can query the transaction history through blockchain transactions. Since a P2P network is a distributed system among peers, each peer node has the same access on its network, and has both client and server identities. A permissioned blockchain is an upgrade of the blockchain represented by Bitcoin, which only allows nodes with high credibility to verify transactions [2]. A permissioned blockchain is only open to specific groups. Each group is composed of a plurality of highly credible nodes and independently maintains block data within its own group domain, avoiding the risk of data disclosure caused by transparency across the network and offering high transaction throughputs and identity authentication efficiency.

A blockchain offers a credible distributed data storage platform based on multiple nodes in a distributed environment. And, it has no center. To address the over-reliance of PKI on a centralized CA, the blockchain and the PKI system are combined to realize a PKI based on blockchain, which has become a new research direction. At present, the main research protocols mainly include the following.

NameCoin [16] is an encrypted currency derived from Bitcoin. It is designed as a decentralized DNS and named after the ".bit" address. The self-signed certificate of Transport Layer Security (TLS) protocol of the node domain in Name-Coin is written into the DNS address as auxiliary information, and is recorded into the blockchain after being verified by all nodes in their mining process. During a TLS handshake, a TLS client can publicly query the TLS self-signed certificate to verify the identity of the node domain. [10] proposed a CA-free distributed PKI based on NameCoin: Certcoin. Certcoin retains the identities of the nodes, which register both online and offline key pairs for their identities. A node uses the public key to register its identity, searches, verifies and revoks the public key of the given identity, thus realizing the basic operation of a traditional PKI. [4] proposed a privacy-aware PKI model: PB-PKI. This model does not directly link a user's real identity through the public key, but protects the online key through the offline one, thus securing the user's real identity, conducting multi-party authentication the registered nodes by all nodes. Meanwhile, PB-PKI divides the user's privacy level into global privacy and proximal privacy, and discloses different degrees of privacy for different application scenarios, thus reducing the risk of disclosure. However, Namecoin, Certcoin and PB-PKI suffer the same issues: none has an authentication mechanism. Any node that first applies for an identity will own it. A malicious node, being aware of the identity registration policy of a legitimate node, can impersonate a legitimate node to cheat other users by registering the identity, and the legitimate one will not be allowed to revoke it.

The IKP protocol (a platform for automated response of unauthorized certificates), proposed by Matsumoto et al. [15], addresses the improper behaviors of a centralized CA to issue unauthorized certificates. It designs an intelligent contract based on multi-point responses to stimulate CA to issue certificates correctly, with multiple nodes jointly supervising the legitimacy of CA's behabiors of issuing certificates and actively rejecting unauthorized issuance. The IKP protocol legally issues certificates through providing economic incentives to the CA, imposes penalties on unauthorized CA issuance, and rewards whistle-blowers who report unauthorized issuance. However, this protocol still uses a small number of CA to issue certificates, and still has inherent defects of a traditional PKI based on centralized CA, e.g., high centralization, single failure point, performance bottleneck and high cost.

[14] proposes a certificate-based PKI authentication system based on Ethernet. By defining multi-point authentication contracts, it addresses the excessive communication loads in traditional PKI certificate management, Certificate Revocation List (CRL) and Online Certificate Status Protocol (OCSP). The current X.509 Certificate Standard only issues certificates for user identities, yet unable to sign certificates for fined-grained identity attributes. To Address this issue, Al-Bassam [1] improved it based on intelligent contracts, and improved its authentication of attribute information. The attributes corresponding to the user's identity are trustworthy should the identity be authenticated, and the transfer of trust between the user's identity and attributes is realized. However, the certificate management protocols proposed by [1,14] are complicated, and the whole cycle management process is not perfect: the process of certificate revocation and recovery is not defined.

By constructing a certificate management platform based on blockchain in cloud, [8] ensured the security and reliability of certificate authentication with the security and reliability consistency of blockchain technology. By doing this, it solved the issues of identity and certificate management in personal cloud, and improved the efficiency and security of authentication before interoperability among different clouds. [25] proposed an efficient cross-domain authentication protocol based on blockchain technology, increasing the efficiency of the existing protocols. This protocol is designed with a trust model based on blockchain CA to improve the efficiency of certificate authentication. However, [8] and [25] are also based on B/S authentication mechanism. Such reliance will cause performance bottlenecks and distributed denial of service (DDoS).

In view of the above-mentioned defects in a PKI based on blockchain, a distributed PKI architecture based on permissioned blockchain is designed: Dizar. The Dizar architecture is designed with a non-certificate authentication process, and runs the permissioned blockchain in the consensus mode of the ledger designed in this article. By combining the blockchain with collective mining of block data, it offers a complete PKI platform in a distributed network. The main contributions of this article are as follows:

The design is based on non-certificate authentication, which enables the registration node to authorize the release of part of the registration information without revealing the identity. In this way, the multi-party credibility authentication of the certificate is achieved and securely registered in the permissioned blockchain.

- With the high transaction throughputs and high identity authentication efficiency of permissioned blockchain in a distributed network, the PKI function based on permissioned blockchain is realized.
- Facilitate the multi-party credibility and multi-party maintenance of PKI service contents; traceable, revocable and recoverable node identities, keys and certificates; realizing dynamic security protection of node identities.
- This article designs a permissioned blockchain operation model of verifiable security based on the ledger model. This model treats nodes with different processing efficiency indiscriminately, making them participate collectively in the multi-point authentication process of the blocks and maintaining the reliability of transaction data. However, for different services of PKI, all nodes are classified and applied to comprehensively improve the application efficiency of Dizar architecture.
- The theoretical analysis and practical tests of Dizar architecture in this article show that the platform has good operation efficiency and scalability.

2 Relevant Researches on Blockchain

A blockchain is composed of a series of data blocks generated by cryptology associations. A data block comprises of a Block Header and a Block Body. The block header contains block height, current version code (version), Previous Block's Address (Prev-block), Target Hash Value (Bits) of the current block, random number (nonce), Hash Target, Merkle Root, Timestamp, etc. The block body records all previous transaction records and economic reward value (Gas), and all previous transaction information values are recorded in the Merkle Tree in the form of root nodes. The change of any root node recorded will affect the value of the whole Merkle Tree. The legal existence of transaction information can be verified as per the binary tree. A typical blockchain network is composed of nodes based on P2P networks. Each node maintains the consistency of the ledger data by executing a consensus algorithm.

The blockchain is operated as follows: when user A is making a transaction with user B, user B will generate his private key and address (that is, the result of the public key encoded by Base58) through the address generation algorithm. By digital signature, user B sends the wallet address to user A. User A initiates a transaction to user B's address. Meanwhile, user A will generate a corresponding block, and send the transaction with his own digital signature authorization to user B. Then, user A broadcasts the transaction to all nodes in the whole network. Miner nodes in the network begin to compete for bookkeeping rights until the confirmation authorization time of the block expires. The process of competing for bookkeeping rights is as follows: first, the hash value of Merkle root node is calculated; second, the nonce in the block header is continuously adjusted so that the SHA-256^2 value is smaller than the target difficulty value.

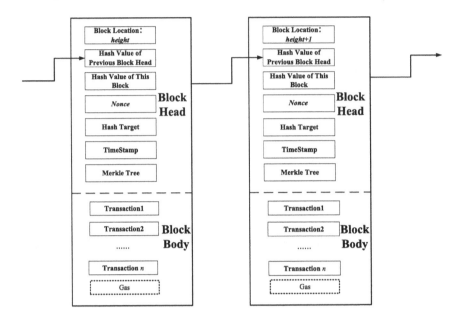

Fig. 1. Structure of a blockchain

The process of competing for bookkeeping rights is also called "mining". The calculation process requires corresponding calculation powers. Therefore, this working mechanism is called the Proof of Work (POW). The node that first calculated and released the correct nonce will be rewarded with Gas (Fig. 1).

Based on the hashing principle of the blockchain structure, the credibility of the blockchain will increase with the increasing of the blocks so long as most nodes in the blockchain are credible. If an adversary tries to tamper with the blockchain that has been saved by the nodes, he must construct a chain longer than the recognized main chain. The adversary needs to recalculate all blocks after the very block with more calculation powers than all nodes combined in the blockchain network. For a increasing blockchain, it is almost impossible for the adversary to complete the modification of the corresponding block information [5,11].

3   Blockchain Node Ledger Operation System Based on Verifiable Security

This article uses a hybrid model based on proxy and pure peer-to-peer architecture between nodes to provide routing, security and topology information. It should be noted that the status of proxy nodes in this article are equal to other terminal nodes. That is, they have the same access as others, and only play servicing and auxiliary functions in the network, instead of acting as traditional centralized management nodes. In order to achieve global credibility of block data, we designed a corresponding distributed node architecture and a blockchain operation system based on the ledger system.

3.1 Network Node Architecture

In this article, a permissioned blockchain architecture is adopted, and the bitcoin system [13,21] designed by Nakamoto is utilized. By default, the following basic facts exist in the network system:

- The nodes are linked through insecure channels;
- Any node in the network has access to the complete ledger records in the blockchain;
- There may be delays in publishing results on the blockchain between participating nodes of the protocol;
- The as-confirmed ledger records on the blockchain cannot be tampered with. The nodes are classified and their functions and characteristics are defined, as shown in Fig. 2.

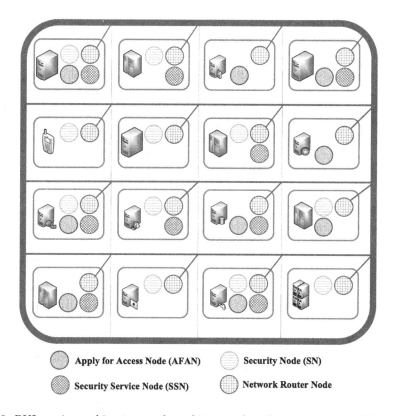

Fig. 2. PKI service architecture node architecture based on permissioned blockchain

Security Node (SN): A node whose network has been verified secure, usually refers to a mobile terminal node. If the security nodes want to authenticate each other's identities, they can issue certificate authentication requests to a security service node. An SN dynamically chooses whether to participate in the bookkeeping right competition process or whether to adopt the light node strategy according to its own resource processing capacity.

Apply for Access Node (AFAN): A node that applies for access in the network system. It may be a good node or a malicious node. Therefore, the node applying for access needs to send relevant authentication information to the Registration Nodes. It can only be recorded into the blockchain and obtain its identify access permission after its identity legitimacy are verified by all nodes.

Registration Node (RN): Responsible for user proxy node registration in the network, verifying the legitimacy of AFAN, and providing partial registration private key information for legitimate AFAN. A RN has strong data processing capability, especially in terms of bilinear pairings. It should be noted that the RN blockchain's physical infrastructure, which acts as proxy service nodes, does not have an authorization function and is not a centralized management node.

Security Service Node (SSN): Records all the published blockchain records in the network, and forms a blockchain physical infrastructure group with RN. It has strong data backup, disaster tolerance and fast blockchain retrieval capabilities. The network is composed jointly by RN and SSN, which are equal to each other. They jointly participate in the identity authentication of AFAN and in the competition of bookkeeping rights of all blocks. The legal basis of SSN data is determined by the PoW mechanism in the blockchain.

Miner Nodes (MN): The blockchain includes RN and SSN, as well as some security nodes actively join in. All the nodes in the miners' nodes adopt the same consensus mechanism and authentication protocol to jointly participate in the identity authentication of the AFAN. The generated blockchains are identical and jointly responsible for the legality and security of the data.

According to the functional features of nodes in the network, AFAN and SSN are credible nodes serving as permissioned blockchains responsible for authentication and proxy of the corresponding network access information. Based on the nature of P2P networks, miners or SSN are routing nodes, who will use Gnutella protocol to jointly participate in message broadcasting. RN can be functionally implemented as a distributed credible CA; SSN, as a credible data backup library, also participates in mutual identity authentication among SSN and keeps the same backup records as all nodes do. Besides, SSN is responsible for mutual authentication among common SSN to reduce the loads of secondary authentication on RN.

3.2   The Operating Mode of a Ledger-Based Permissioned Blockchain

The ledger-based licensing system designed in this article regards the blockchain as a credible public ledger maintained by all nodes. Each block is a set of transaction record ledgers. The Input Collection and Output Collection are recorded in the block body, and the PKI service information to be recorded in the blockchain is regarded as posting information requiring authentication by nodes across the network. During the operation, the legality of the information to be recorded is verified by proxy nodes, and is written into the input information of the block body and encapsulated in the block. Then, the block is sent to the miner nodes for multi-party authentication by competing for bookkeeping rights; when each node receives a new block, it verifies the legality of the block and the correctness of its contents. If the block is legal, it receives and stores the block and replies the correct receipt to the network. If the block is illegal, it discards the block and reply the error receipt to the network. When the node has received the correct receipts for more than half of the blocks, it writes the input records into the output, and link them to its own blockchain according to the time-stamp sequence, thus forming credible PKI service records (as shown in steps 1 to 6 in Fig. 3).

In order to further illustrate the process of a ledger-based blockchain system, we have defined, proved and analyzed its running mode.

Definition 1. *Similar to Bitcoin's trading process [21], the blockchain in this article is defined as follows:*

- *Input Collection: The information collection of the services initiated by proxy nodes in the network to the miner node group within a certain period of time. Iutput Collection is represented by "S". The types of input service elements defined in this article include node registration, public key update and key revocation, or S_0, S_1 and S_2, respectively. The specific input collection is as follows:*
  $S = \{Sx_y | Sx_y \in S$, *where x represents the input service element type of the node and y represents the number of the node requesting services.}*
- *Output Collection: A collection of legal information that has been verified by the miner node group in the blockchain within a certain period of time. Output Collection is represented by "R": $R = \{R_0, R_1, R_2, \ldots, R_M\}$. The status of each output information will only be "Unspend" or "Spend".*
- *Transaction: The process during which the nodes responsible for the corresponding services in the miner node group construct the transaction input information into corresponding blocks, and send the blocks to all the nodes in the group in order to collectively compete for bookkeeping rights. The essence of this process is the mapping from the elements of input collection to the corresponding ones of output collection, with Tr representing the transaction function: $R_i = Tr(S_i), S_i \in S$. With the different service contents in the transaction, Tr_1, Tr_2 and Tr_3 represent node registration, key update, and key revocation operation, respectively.*

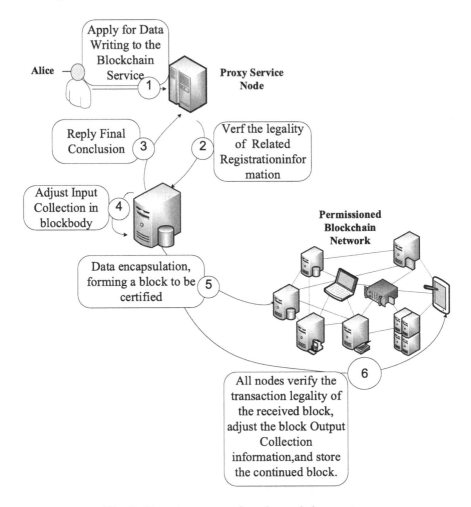

Fig. 3. Licensing process based on a ledger system

- **Round:** *The number of times a miner node, during the process of updating its own transaction book, has received a correct receipt from all miners across the network.*

Definition 2. *The legal transaction behaviors on the blockchain (commandtype) defined in this article include: commandtype → {register, update, revoke}.*

Specifically, in the multi-party verification process by a miner's node group with v nodes, the j-th node performs the PoW for the PoW initiated by the i-th miner node. The corresponding proof value given by node j is: $y_{ij} = \mathcal{F}_{HashTarget}(nounce, x_{ij}) \rightarrow \{0,1\}$, *0 and 1 represent Unspend and Spend respectively.*

Table 1. The corresponding ledge-based blocks designed in this article

Block content	Block part	Note	Strlen/bit
ID	Block head	The user ID, which is the anonymous value of the public key	8
Prev Block Hash	Block head	Hash value of the previous block head	32
TimeStamp	Block head	Timestamp, based on user system generation	4
Version	Block head	Blockchain version number, 1.0 in this paper	4
Merkle Root Hash	Block head	Merkle Root value for transaction content	32
Block Height	Block head	Block height	4
Hash Target	Block head	Hash value of the previous block head	8
Nonce	Block head	Random value to adjust the block	4
Fulfillments	Block Body	Satisfy the list of conditions, the signature value and hash value of each book	72
Operation	Block Body	Operation type register,revoke,update	2
Data	Block Body	Transaction data	–
Input Collection	Data	The data of all pending transactions	–
Output Collection	Data	Transactions that have been certified by multiple parties as legitimate	–
Data_Hash	Data	Hash value of the Data	32
Gas	Data	Competitive accounting awards	4
Payload	Input Collection	Data load, related data values	–
Declarative Signature	Output Collection	Miner node has the right to sign the accouting information after successful mining	–

y_i is defined as the overall evaluation of the PoW initiated by all nodes in the network for the i-th miner node. To make a transaction legal, the Spend status of the information is proved only when it is approved by more than 51%

of the nodes. Information whose security cannot be proved $y_i = \sum\limits_{i=0}^{N} y_{ij} \geq \nu/2$ *is regarded as Unspend.*

The miner node group operates on a consensus system based on permissioned blockchain ledgers, and the process of competing for bookkeeping rights is essentially a process of constantly adjusting their own output collections. Referring to the traditional block format [20], we designed the corresponding block based on the ledger system, as shown in Table 1. When any proxy node sets up a corresponding input collection and generates a corresponding block, the block will be sent to all the nodes in the network for authentication. During network-wide multi-node authentication, the legality of input information of each block received by the miner node will be verified. If the information is legitimate, it is written into the output collection, while the corresponding local block's storage copy is adjusted and the output information is written therein; If it is illegal, the blocks will be discarded. When the correct receipts of a node exceed half of the nodes, the block can be written into its own blockchain. The consensus algorithm based on blockchain ledgers of miner nodes can be described by Algorithm 1.

Algorithm 1 is analyzed below.

Algorithm 1. Improved POW consensus base on ledgers system

Input: *Blockchain (height-1)*, S_i, R_i, round, *nonce*, HashTarget
Output: Blockchain (height)
1: **Start:**
2: The proxy node constructs the block to be authenticated: block (blockhead, S_i, R_i, nonce), $S_i = \{Tr_1, Tr_2, \ldots, Tr_n\}$, R_i = null, nonce = null,
3: round = 1
4: decided = false
5: Broadcast myReport (block (blockhead, S_i, R_i, nonce))
6: **while** true **do**
7:     The network node verifies the legitimacy of the transaction records of S_i, Write legal transaction records to $R_i = \{Tr_1, Tr_2, \ldots, Tr_m\}, m < n$
8:     Enumerate the nonce in SHA-256^2(blockhead, nonce) < HashTarget
9:     Reconstructs the block: block (blockhead, S_i, R_i', nonce')
10:    The miners node broadcasts the block information after the restructuring
11:    Continue waiting for network replies until updates are received myReport (block (blockhead, S_i, R_i', nonce'))times nonce > v/2
12:    $Blockchain(height) = Blockchain(height-1) + block(blockhead, S_i, R_i', nonce')$
13:    **if** all the myReport hasthe same R_i', **then**
14:        Broadcast Propose (block (blockhead, S_i, R_i', nonce'), round);
15:    **else**
16:        Broadcast Propose ($\perp$, round);
17:    **end if**
18:    **if** (decided == false) **then**
19:        Report myReport (block (blockhead, S_i, R_i', nonce'), round + 1)

20:        Determine decision value $R_i, R_i' = S_i$, writes the R_i into Output, broadcasts update block

21:    **end if**

22:    Adjust the local Block copy value

23:    Continue to wait for, until half round have the same Propose information

24:    **if** if (all receive block blocks are the same) **then**

25:        $R_i' = S_i$

26:        decide $=$ true

27:    **else if** (at least one block proposal contains the same as the local copy R_i') **then**

28:        $R_i' = Si,$

29:    **else**

30:        Random choose R_i, $\Pr[S_i = 1] = p$, $\Pr[S_i = 0] = 1 - p$

31:    **end if**

32:    $round = round + 1$

33:    Broadcast myReport (block (blockhead, S_i, R_i', nonce'), round)

34: **end while**

Effectiveness Analysis: Note that the effectiveness of consensus is equivalent to: if the block inputs of all nodes are S_i, it must be the last decision value assigned to R_i; Otherwise, R_i will only approve or reject, so the effectiveness will be verified automatically.

Assume that all nodes have input ledger proposals of $R_i' = S_i$, in which case all nodes start proposing S_i as the final decision value of Ri in the first round. Since all nodes can only receive the ledger proposal of $R_i' = S_i$, they will also take S_i as R_i' decision value (Line 17) and exit the loop in the next round.

Consistency Analysis: A node only sends a reply supporting the input proposal when it receives a message that more than half of the nodes contain S_i (Line 8). Therefore, it is not possible for the proposal to be approved and rejected at the same time in the same round.

Assuming T is the node whose first decision value is $R_i' = S_i$ in the r-th round, it must have received proposals from a majority of ledgers recommending r (Line 17) in the r-th round. If a node receives more than half of the ledger proposals recommending the same value, it will accept the ledger proposal (changing the local R_i to R_i') and exit in the next round. Since there is no ledger proposal recommending other results in r-th round, it can be inferred that no node will select another different ledger proposal in the same round.

Any node with $T' \neq T$ may experience the following two situations: 1. It receives more than half of the ledger proposals recommending $R_i' = S_i$ in r-th round and decides to adopt R_i'. In this case, the requirement to reach consensus is satisfied directly, and the nodes will not get stuck; 2. This node does not receive unanimous recommendation from more than half of the proposals. Since node T receives most of the ledger proposals recommending S, each node must receive messages from more than half the nodes before ending. This means that each node receives at least one ledger proposal recommending S (Line 16).

Therefore, all the nodes set their respective R_i as $R_i' = S_i$ (Line 17, 18) in r-th round. All nodes will broadcast S at the end of r-th round, so all will propose $R_i' = S_i$ at $r+1$ round. The nodes already decide to adopt this proposal in r-th round will terminate running in round $r+1$ and send an additional myReport message (Line 13).

All other nodes will receive S recommended by more than half of the nodes in round $r+l$, and decide to adopt in this round. Meanwhile, they also send a myReport message. In this way, some nodes would have already terminated running in round $r+2$, and the remaining nodes would have received enough myReport messages (Line 6). These nodes send a Propose message and a myReport message, and decide to adopt the ledger proposal in round $r+2$ to terminate running.

Termination Analysis: We already know from the proof of consistency that, if a node receives more than half of the ledger proposals recommending r, all nodes will terminate their running with maximum two rounds.

Let's assume that none of the nodes has received more than half of the proposals recommending same value. In such a round, some nodes may update their values to R_i' based on a received proposal. Other nodes randomly select 0 or 1, with the probability of selecting the same value being at least p_n. A Boolean consensus can be reached within the expected time $O(2^n)$ if less than $v/2$ nodes collapse.

3.3   Security Proof of Permissioned Blockchain Based on Ledger System

Theorem 1. *Each output entry must correspond to the corresponding input entry, and the number of elements in the output collection is smaller than number of elements in the input collection; During transactions, there are individual inputs and Unspent Transaction Outputs (UTXO). That is, $m \leq n$.*

Proof. $\because R = Tr(S)$, R can only be 0 or 1, which is the unit price decision value (only Spend or Unspend)

$\therefore S \to R$, if the transaction mapping Tr is an injective mapping, the number of image set elements must be less than the number of source set elements.

$\therefore m \leq n$.

Proof is complete.

During blockchain transactions, a miner node concludes that the transaction information contained in the block is verified and the block can be written into the blockchain if it receives correct receipts when more than half of all nodes are submitting the transactions to the network. Proof is complete.

From a functional point of view, the process of combining UTXO transaction set with PKI will be regarded as CRL in a traditional PKI.

Theorem 2. *When the node data is large enough, the blockchain mode system error probability Fp(S) (Failure Probability) based on the ledger system is close to 0.*

Proof. The multi-node authentication process of the ledger system shows that this proof is equivalent to proving that the decision group composed of more than half of the nodes has error 0.

Assuming that each node gives a fixed probability of error reply to the j-th node's authentication request as p_j, a Chernoff bound is formed as all nodes in the network adopt identical protocol for the same information authenticated. The following conclusions are reached: $y_1\cdot, \ldots, y_n$, are all variables with independent and same distribution, and obey binomial distribution, i.e., $P_r[y_j = 1] = p_j$, $P_r[y_j = 0] = 1 - p_j$ and for $Y := n_j = 1y_j$.

And: $\mu : E[Y] \sum\limits_{j-1}^{n} p_j, \mu = np_j$. Here, Y is the number of nodes with correct receipts.

In particular, $0 < \delta < 1$: $P_r[Y \leq (1 - \delta)\mu] \leq e^{-\mu\delta^2/2}$.

In a network system, more than $\lfloor v/2 \rfloor + 1$ node decision groups verify the authentication tuples issued in the network. Each node with a cardinality of $\lfloor v/2 \rfloor + 1$ can form a decision group. If more than half of the decision groups are attacked by Eclipsed [24], only $\lfloor v/2 \rfloor$ nodes can work normally at most. Otherwise, there must be at least one decision group to complete the decision.In order to estimate the asymptotic failure probability of $\lfloor v/2 \rfloor + 1$ node, $F_p(S) = Pr[\lfloor Y \leq 2/v \rfloor] \leq Pr[Y \leq 2/v] == Pr[Y \leq (1 - \delta)\mu]$ can be obtained based on Chernoff inequality.

$\because \delta = p_j - p_j^2$, and if the node is considered to fail with a high probability, $1/2 < p_j \leq 1$ is taken.

$\therefore 0 < \delta \leq 1/4$, according to Chernoff bound, $F_p(S) \leq e^{-\mu\delta^2/2} \in e^{-\Omega(v)}$ is obtained.

$\lim\limits_{v \to \infty} e^{-\Omega(v)} = 0$ That is, when the number of nodes is large enough, the running error probability of blockchain based on ledger system tends to 0. Proof is complete.

4   Distributed PKI Services Based on Permissioned Blockchain

The above platform node system's security analysis shows that a blockchain based on the ledger consensus system is capable of achieving global consistency, validity and termination of all node's ledger results. Combined with the specific implementation process of a ledger-based permissioned blockchain mode, a node-based PKI full-cycle management strategy with identities at its core is realized by designing the corresponding block body structure in the account book, with the service information to be authenticated being issued by the proxy nodes, multi-party authentication being performed by miner nodes in the network, and the authenticated results being written into the blockchain (as shown in Fig. 4).

The following functions of a distributed PKI system are implemented: 1. The AFAN in that network can register the corresponding public-private key pairs and the certificates based on the identities; 2. Update the public and private keys and certificates corresponding to the previously registered identities; 3. Retrieve, update, and revoke public and private key pairs corresponding to a given identity.

The operations in Fig. 4 respectively describe the processes of AFAN and SN completing identity registration, certificate update, certificate revocation/key recovery, certificate search and key verification services through the proxy node groups. Among them, the first three are blockchain writing services and the last ones are data query services.

The process of blockchain writing services is as follows: AFAN and SN respectively send the information to be written into the blockchain to the proxy node group, which includes RN and SSN; the proxy node group checks the legality of the applicant data and generates transaction information Tx_n (Tx_1 and Tx_4 are registration applications of the nodes, Tx_2 and Tx_5 are key renewal applications, and Tx_3 and Tx_6 are key revocation applications); the proxy nodes construct blocks and uniformly write the transaction applications during a period of time into the input collection of the block body, and submit them to all the miners, who compete for bookkeeping rights. Miners throughout the network check the legality of the contents in the receiving blocks and the block input collection, and

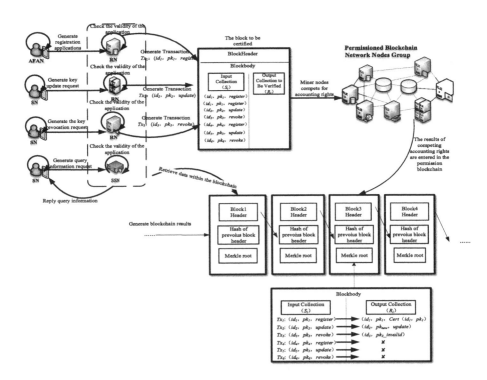

Fig. 4. PKI service system based on permissioned blockchain

exhaustively calculate nonce. Then, they write legal transaction information into the output collection and generate corresponding certificate data. Illegal information is recorded as $\times$ (Tx_1, Tx_2 and Tx_3 are written into the block output collection, and Tx_4, Tx_5 and Tx_6 are recorded as illegal information). After the calculation is completed, the blocks are connected into the local blockchain to complete the process of data writing.

The process of data search services is as follows: SN send out data query applications to the data service nodes through the security nodes; the data service nodes check the legality of the applicant information and retrieve the blockchain information if it is legal; the data service nodes query and verify the information retrieved and reply the corresponding conclusions to the SN; the service process is finished.

4.1   Description of Relevant Cryptographic Algorithms

Definition 3. *This paper adopts the relevant cryptographic algorithms in the permissioned blockchain, which are defined as follows:*

- $KFG(1^k) \rightarrow (sk, pk)$ *Key Generator Function: input security parameter k and output corresponding public key pk and private key sk.*
- $Sig(sk, \mu) \rightarrow \sigma$, *Signature Algorithm: The information μ is digitally signed with the private key sk, and the result is σ.*
- $Vrfy(pk, \sigma, \mu) \rightarrow b \in \{0, 1\}$, *Signature Verification Algorithm: Verify through the public key pk whether the digital signature σ corresponds to the signature information σ of the corresponding private key sk.*
- $Rand() \rightarrow \mathbb{R}$, *Random Number Generation Algorithm: generate random number $\mathbb{R}$. the randam numbers generated in any two times are completely random.*
- $GenCert(id, pk, T) \rightarrow Cert(id, pk)$, *Certificate Generation Algorithm: the corresponding digital certificate $Cert(id, pk)$ is generated through the corresponding id, public key pk and timestamp T.*

The certificate version refers to the X.509 version certificate [19].

$$pk_n = f_1(pk_{n-1}, sk', N) = pk_{n-1} \times sk'(mod N)$$

$$sk_n = f_2(sk_{n-1}, sk', N) = sk_{n-1}/sk'(mod N)$$

Chain Key Pair Updating Algorithm: f_1 generates new public key pkn through original public key pk_{n-1}, reserved private key sk', and random number N; f_2 generates new public key skn through original private key sk_{n-1}, reserved private key sk', and random number N. In particular, according to the construction features of a blockchain, the crypto-system is based on the secp 256 k1elliptic curve of ECDSA.

And, below facts are recognized by default:

Privacy security: In the entire permissioned blockchain network, the computing environment of each default node is secure, i.e. an adversary cannot obtain the private key information of any node.

The private key cannot be forged: the digital signatures cannot be forged. Even if the adversary possesses the public key pk, he cannot obtain the corresponding private key sk. The adversary cannot generate the signature message pair (μ, σ) in polynomial time to satisfy $Vrfy(pk, \sigma, \mu) = 1$.

Initial security: this article believes that the miner node groups are the initial security node groups, which have the initial security by default.

4.2   Identity Registration

OnlineKeyPair: $(pk_{online}, sk_{online})$ and *OfflineKeyPair:* $(pk_{offline}, sk_{offline})$ are generated by the AFAN and corresponding certificates are generated. The two sets of key pairs can be encrypted and decrypted in different application scenarios. AFAN send identity authentication information to RN, who issue partial registrated private keys to legitimate AFAN. After the AFAN generate registered private keys, the public keys, certificates and related registration information corresponding to the *OnlineKeyPair* and *OfflineKeyPair* are signed without certificate and packaged into blocks, and then released to MN node groups. After receiving the blocks, all MN verify the legality of the block contents and the non-certificate signature information and compete for bookkeeping rights. The legal blocks will be written into the main chain.

Algorithm 2. Identity Registration

1: **Start Operation**
2: **Step 0 RN Initialization Operation**
3: (1) RN Selects safety parameters k, p plane number circulation group G_1 and G_2. RN constructs bilinear mappings on elliptic curves: $ê : G_1 \times G_1 \rightarrow G_2$, P is the point on the elliptic curve, and G_1 is the Generator.
4: (2) RN random selects $\lambda \in Z_p^*$ and $g_2 \in G_1$, thereinto g_2^λ is selected as as the miner node group manager key. $Rand() \rightarrow s \in Z_p^*, sk_{RN} = s$ as a private key and stored securely, $pk_{RN} = s \cdot P \in Z_p^*$ is choosen based on multiplied point production generation public offering.
5: (3) Meanwhile, RN random selects $g \in G_1, g_1 = g^\alpha$, select four hash functions identified $H_1 \sim H_5$, $\boldsymbol{v} = (u_i)$, $\boldsymbol{\phi} = (f_i)$, $\boldsymbol{\gamma} = (g_i)$, $\boldsymbol{\omega} = (w_i)$ is a vector of character lengths as m, n, n, l. Miners node groups expose system parameters $params : = \{G_1, G_2, p, e, g, g_1, g_2, H_1 \sim H_5, \boldsymbol{v}, \boldsymbol{\sigma}, \boldsymbol{\tau}, \boldsymbol{\omega}, B_I, pk_{RN}\}$, there in B_I is the base name of group.
6: **Step 1 AFAN Executes Operation**
7: (1) AFAN generats random number: $Rand() \rightarrow \theta_1 \in Z_p^*, Rand() \rightarrow \theta_2 \in Z_p^*$, securely stores θ_1 and θ_2.
8: (2) AFAN generats the public-private key pair: $KGF(\theta_1) \rightarrow g^{\theta_1}$, $KGF(\theta_2) \rightarrow g^{\theta_2}, pk_1 = g^{\theta_1}, pk_2 = g^{\theta_2}$
9: (3) AFAN generates sequence random number and challenge random number: $Rand() \rightarrow seq_1, Rand() \rightarrow chlg$
10: (4) AFAN generates temporary anonymity: $\rho = H_1(ID_{AFAN}), PID_{AFAN} = B_I^\rho (mod p)$

11: (5) AFAN randomly accesses an RN node from the RN list, denotes as RN', AFAN sends RegistrationApplication $(PID_{AFAN}, register, T_0, seq_1, pk_1, pk_2, chlg)$ to RN'

12: **Step 2 RN' Generats Partial Private Key**

13: (1)RN' generats random number: $Rand() \to \mathcal{K} \in Z_p^*$

14: (2)RN' generats partial private key for AFAN: $\boldsymbol{v} = H_1(PID_{AFAN}, pk_1) = (v_1, v_2, v_3, \ldots, v_m), DID_{AFAN} = (D_1, D_2) = (g_2 U^k, g^k),$

15: thereinto $U = \prod\limits_{j=1}^{m} \boldsymbol{u}_j^{v_j}$

16: (3) RN' generates a verification signature for AFAN: $Sig(PID_{AFAN} ||chlg||T_0, sk_{RN}) \to \sigma_{RN'}$

17: (4) RN' sends RegistrationApplicationReply $(PID_{AFAN}, T_0, seq_1, DID_{AFAN}, \sigma_{RN'})$ to AFAN via secure channel

18: **Step 3 AFAN Generates Private Key Signature and Certificate**

19: (1) AFAN verifies the RegistrationApplicationReply legitimacy published by RN'

20: **if** $(Vrfy(pk_{RN}, \sigma_{RN'}, PID_{AFAN}||chlg||T_0, sk_{RN}) == 1)$ **then**

21: accept RegistrationApplicationReply $(PID_{AFAN}, T_0, seq_1, DID_{AFAN}, \sigma_{RN'})$ generated by RN'

22: **else**Returns to Step 2

23: **end if**

24: (2) AFAN calculates: $\boldsymbol{v} = H_1(ID_{AFAN}, pk_1) = (v_1, v_2, v_2, \ldots, v_m), \vartheta = \prod\limits_{j=1}^{m}(\phi_j)^{v_j}$

25: (3) AFAN verifies partial private key thatpublished by RN':

26: **if** $(\hat{e}(g_1, D_1) = \hat{e}(g_1, g_2)\hat{e}(D2, U))$ **then**

27: Accept partial private key generated by RN', generates AFAN's own user private $key sk = \{(\theta_1, \theta_2), (D_1, D_2)\}$

28: **else**

29: Returns to Step 2

30: **end if**

31: (4) AFAN generats random number: $Rand() \to \Psi \in Z_p^*$

32: (5) AFAN generates own certificate: $Rand() \to \mathbb{R}, Rand() \to \mathbb{Z}, KGF(1^{\mathbb{R}}) \to (sk_{online}, pk_{online}), KGF(1^{\mathbb{Z}}) \to (pk_{offline}, sk_{offline})$

33: securely stores sk_{online} and $sk_{offline}$, securely deletes $\mathbb{R}$ and $\mathbb{Z}$

34: $GenCert(ID_{AFAN}, pk_{online}, T_0) := Cert(ID_{AFAN}, pk_{online}, T_0),$

35: $GenCert(ID_{AFAN}, pk_{offline}, T_0) := Cert(ID_{AFAN}, pk_{offline}, T_0)$

36: (6) AFAN calculates: $M = Cert(ID_{AFAN}, pk_{online}, T_0)||Cert(ID_{AFAN}, pk_{offline}, T_0),$

37: $\alpha = H_4(ID_{AFAN}) = (\alpha_1, \alpha_2, \alpha_3, \ldots, \alpha_l), \Omega = \prod\limits_{k=1}^{l}(\omega_k)^{\alpha_k}, \eta = H_5(M||g^{\Psi}|| pk_1||pk_2), \beta = H_2(M||g^{\Psi}||pk_1||pk_2) = (\beta_i),$

38: $\Phi = \prod\limits_{i=1}^{n}(\phi_j)^{\beta_j}, \chi = H_5(M||g^{\Psi}||pk_1||pk_2) = (\chi_i, \Gamma = \prod\limits_{i=1}^{n}(\gamma_j)^{\chi_j}$, the signature is $\sigma_{Register}(\sigma_1, \sigma_2, \sigma_3) = (D_1^{\eta}(\Phi)^{\theta_1\eta}\Gamma^{\theta_2}\Omega^{\Psi}, D_2^{\eta}, g^{\Psi})$

39: (7) AFAN constructs Input information, issues registered blocks to the miners node group: S_i : $= \{PID_{AFAN}, Register, online\|offline, T_1, height, Cert(ID_{AFAN}, pk_{online}, T_0), Cert(ID_{AFAN}, pk_{offline}, T_0), Verification Values = (Cert(ID_{AFAN}, pk_{online}, T_0)\|Cert(ID_{AFAN}, pk_{offline}, T_0), \sigma_{Register}, ID_{AFAN})), (pk_1, pk_2), (D_1, D_2)\}$

40: **Step 4 MN Competes for Accounting Rights**

41: (1) MN verify the legitimacy of AFAN identity

42: **if** (PID_{AFAN} has been registered) **then**

43:     The transaction fails, discards the block, broadcast to the network bullitinboard report ERROR: (PID_{AFAN}, Registration), **End Operation**

44:     (2) MN extracts VerificationValues from S_i, calculates $\vartheta = \prod_{j=1}^{m}(\phi_j)^{v_j}, \Omega = \prod_{k=1}^{l}(\omega_k)^{\alpha_k}, \Phi = \prod_{j=1}^{n}(\phi_j)^{\beta_j}, \Gamma = \prod_{j=1}^{n}(\gamma_j)^{\chi_j}$

45: **end if**

46: (3) MN verifies the legality of the signature

47: **if** $(\hat{e}(g, \sigma_1) == \hat{e}(g_1, g_2)^{\eta}\hat{e}(\sigma_2, \vartheta)\hat{e}(pk_1, \Phi)^{\eta}\hat{e}(pk_2, \Gamma)\hat{e}(\sigma_3, \Omega))$ **then**

48:     Writes S_i : $= \{PID_{AFAN}, Register, T_1, height, Cert(ID_{AFAN}, pk_1, T_0), Cert(ID_{AFAN}, pk_2, T_0), Verification Values = (Cert(ID_{AFAN}, pk_{online}, T_0) \|Cert(ID_{AFAN}, pk_{offline}, T_0), \sigma_{Register}, ID_{AFAN})), (pk_1, pk_2), (D_1, D_2)\}$ into output information of R_i, rebuilds and stores the block, broadcasts $VerificationSuccess(nonce)$ and myReport($block(blockhead, S_i, R_i'$, $nonce'$), round) to the network.

49: **else**

50:     The transaction fails, discards the block, **End Operation**

51: **end if**

52: (4) MN process copy statistics

53: **if** (round $> 2/v$) **then**

54:     Continue the update block onto the blockchain

55:     **End Operation**

56: **end if**

4.3   Certificate Update

As the online public key certificate mainly used in the network, the nodes update the same type of public and private key pairs and certificates through updating operations when SN and MN in the network need to update the online key pairs and corresponding certificates to which the subject identities belong due to specific security requirements (e.g. online public and private key pair disclosure, online public key certificate's regular updates, etc.). In this case, the nodes do not need to re-register their identities, but only use the new and old public key pairs to jointly publish the updated transaction to ensure the security of the published information, thus realizing the binding of the new online keys with the old offline keys and the node identities.

Algorithm 3. Certificate Update

1: **Start Operation**
2: **Step 1 AFAN Executes Operation**
3: (1) AFAN generates sequence random number: $Rand() \rightarrow seq_2$
4: (2) AFAN randomly accesses an RN node from the RN list, denotes as RN",
   AFAN sends CertRenewalApplication $(PID_{AFAN}, certrenewal, keytype, T_1,$
   $seq_2)$ to RN"
5: **Step 2 RN" Executes Operation**
6: (1) RN" verifies CertRenewalApplication legality, return to Step 1 if is not
   valid
7: (2) RN" generates validation success signatures for illegal CertRenewalAp-
   plication: $Sig(PID_{AFAN}||CertRenewalApplicationSuccess||T_1, sk_{RN}) \rightarrow$
   $\sigma_{RN''}$
8: (3) RN" Sends CertRenewalApplicationReply$(PID_{AFAN}, T_1, seq_1, \sigma_{RN''})$ to
   AFAN via secure channel
9: **Step 3 AFAN Update the Certificate**
10: (1) AFAN Verifies an legitimacy published by RN" CertRenewalApplication-
    Reply
11: **if** $(Vrfy(pk_{RN''}, \sigma_{RN''}, PID_{AFAN}||CertRenewalApplicationSuccess||T_1)$
    $== 1)$ **then**
12:     Accept the CertRenewalApplicationReply$(PID_{AFAN}, T_1, seq_1, \sigma_{RN'})$
    generated by RN"
13: **else**
14:     Returns to Step 1
15: **end if**
16: (2) AFAN generates update key: $Rand() \rightarrow \mathbb{N}, KGF(1^{\mathbb{N}}) \rightarrow (sk_{keytype}^{new},$
    $pk_{keytype}^{new})$
17: (3) AFAN generates update certificate: GenCert$(ID_{AFAN}, pk_{keytype}^{new}, T_0)$:
    $= Cert(ID_{AFAN}, pk_{keytype}^{new}, T_0)$
18: (4) AFAN calculates $M' = Cert(ID_{AFAN}, pk_{keytype}^{new}, T_0), \eta' = H_5(M||g^{\Psi}||$
    $pk_1||pk_2)$, generates authentication value signatures
19: $\sigma_{CertRenewal} = (\sigma_1, \sigma_2, \sigma_3) = (D_1^{\eta}(\Phi)^{\theta_1\eta'}\Gamma^{\theta_2}\Omega^{\Psi}, D_2^{\eta}, g^{\Psi})$
20: (5) AFAN constructs Input information, issues the blocks to the MN
    group: $S_i : = \{PID_{AFAN}, CertRenewal, keytype, T_1, height', M' = Cert$
    $(ID_{AFAN}, pk_{keytype}^{new}, T_0), VerificationValues = (M' = Cert(ID_{AFAN},$
    $pk_{keytype}^{new}, T_0), \sigma_{CertRenewal}, ID_{AFAN})), (pk_1, pk_2), (D_1, D_2)\}$
21: **Step 4 MN Competes for Accounting Rights**
22: (1) MN extracts $VerificationValues$ from S_i, calculates $\vartheta = \prod_{j=1}^{m}(\phi_j)^{v_j}, \Omega =$
    $\prod_{k=1}^{l}(\omega_k)^{\alpha_k}, \Phi = \prod_{j=1}^{n}(\phi_j)^{\beta_j}, \Gamma = \prod_{j=1}^{n}(\gamma_j)^{\chi_j}$
23: (2) MN verifies the legality of the signature
24: **if** $(\hat{e}(g, \sigma_1) == \hat{e}(g_1, g_2)^{\eta'}\hat{e}(\sigma_2, \vartheta)\hat{e}(pk_1, \Phi)^{\eta'}\hat{e}(pk_2, \Gamma)\hat{e}(\sigma_3, \Omega))$ **then**

25:    Writes S_i : $= \{PID_{AFAN}, CertRenewal, keytype, T_1, height',$
$M' = Cert(ID_{AFAN}, pk_{keytype}^{new}, T_0), VerificationValues = (M' = Cert(ID_{AFAN},$
$pk_{keytype}^{new}, T_0), \sigma_{CertRenewal}, ID_{AFAN})), (pk_1, pk_2), (D_1, D_2)\}$ into Outout
information Ri, rebuilds and stores the block, broadcasts VerificationSuccess
(nonce) and myReport($block(blockhead, S_i, R'_i, nonce')$, round) to the network.

26: **else**

27:    The transaction fails, discards the block, **End Operation**

28: **end if**

29: (3) MN process copy statistics

30: **if** (round $> 2/v$) **then**

31:    Continue the update block onto the blockchain

32:    End Operation

33: **end if**

4.4   Certificate Revocation and Key Recovery

Certificate revocation and key recovery refer to the fact that SN or MN need to
revoke original registration information, regenerate new identities and public and
private keys and generate new certificates due to specific security requirements
(e.g. users discover that offline public and private key pairs are disclosed at the
same time). The execution process is as follows.

Algorithm 4. Certificate Invalidation and Key Recovery

1: **Start Operation**

2: **Step 1 SN**

3: (1) From RN randomly accesses an RN node from the RN list, denotes as
RN"'

4: (2) SN generats random number: $Rand() \rightarrow t \in Z_p^*$

5: (3) SN generates sequence random number and challenge random number:
$Rand() \rightarrow seq_3, Rand() \rightarrow chlg'$

6: (4) SN regenerates temporary anonymity: $\rho' = H_1(ID_{SN}||t), PID'_{SN} = B_I^{\rho'} (mod p)$

7: (5) SN regenerates the original private key signature: $Sig(PID_{SN}||PID'_{SN}),$
$sk_{online}) \rightarrow \sigma_{online}, Sig(PID_{SN}||PID'_{SN}), sk_{offline}) \rightarrow \sigma_{offline}$

8: (6) SN sends KeyRevokeApplication($PID_{SN}, PID'_{SN}, keyrevoke, T_3, seq_3,$
$pk_1, pk_2, chlg', \sigma_{online}, \sigma_{offline}$) to RN"'.

9: **Step 2 RN" Executes Operation**

10: (1) RN"' verifies the legality of KeyRevokeApplication

11: **if** $(Vrfy(pk_{online}, \sigma_{online}, PID_{SN}||PID'_{SN}) == 1 \&\&(pk_{offline}, \sigma_{offline},$
$PID_{SN}||PID'_{SN}) == 1)$ **then**

12:    Accept the KeyRevokeApplication generated by SN

13: **else**

14:    Returns to Step 1

15: **end if**

16: (2) RN"' generats the new partial private key for SN: $v = H_1(PID_{SN}, pk_1) = (v_1, v_2, v_3, \ldots, v_m), D'_{ID_{SN}} = (D'_1, D_2) = (g_2 U'^{\mathcal{K}}, g^{\mathcal{K}})$, there into $U' = \prod\limits_{j=1}^{m} u_j^{v_j}$

17: (3) RN"' generates validation signatures for SN: $Sig(PID'_{SN}||chlg||T_3, sk_{RN'''}) \rightarrow \sigma'_{RN'''}$

18: (4) RN"' sends KeyRevokeReply($PID'_{SN}, T_3, seq_3, D'_{ID_{SN}}, \sigma'_{RN'''}$) through the security channel to SN

19: **Step 3 SN Generates Private Key Signatures and Certificates**

20: (1) SN verifies the KeyRevokeReply legitimacy published by RN"'

21: **if** $(Vrfy(pk_{RN}, \sigma'_{RN'''}, PID'_{SN}||chlg||T_3, sk_{RN}) == 1)$ **then**

22:     Accepts the RegistrationApplicationReply generated by RN"'

23: **else**

24:     Returns to Step 2

25: **end if**

26: (2) SN calculates: $v = H_1(PID_{SN}, pk_1) = (v_1, v_2, v_3, \ldots, v_m), \vartheta' = \prod\limits_{j=1}^{m} (\varphi_j)^{v_j}$

27: (3) SN verifies the partial private key generated by RN"':

28: **if** $(\hat{e}(g_1, D'_1) = \hat{e}(g_1, g_2)\hat{e}(D_2, U))$ **then**

29:     Accept partial private key generated by RN"' generates SN's own user's renew private key $sk = \{(\theta_1, \theta_2), (D'_1, D_2)\}$

30: **else**

31:     Returns to Step 2

32: **end if**

33: (5) SN generates update certificate: $Rand() \rightarrow \mathbb{P}, Rand() \rightarrow \mathbb{Q}, KGF(1^{\mathbb{P}}) \rightarrow (sk_{online}^{update}, pk_{online}^{update}), KGF(1^{\mathbb{Q}}) \rightarrow sk_{online}^{update}, pk_{online}^{update})$

34: securely stores sk_{online}^{update} and sk_{online}^{update}, securely deletes $\mathbb{P}$ and $\mathbb{Q}$

35: $GenCert(ID_{SN}, pk_{online}^{update}, T_3) := Cert(ID_{SN}, pk_{online}^{update}, T_3, update)$

36: $GenCert(ID_{SN}, pk_{online}^{update}, T_3) := Cert(ID_{SN}, pk_{online}^{update}, T_3, update)$

37: (6) SN calculates: $M'' = Cert(ID_{SN}, pk_{online}^{update}, T_3, update)||Cert(ID_{SN}, pk_{online}^{update}, T_3, update)$

38: $\alpha' = H_4(ID_{SN}) = (\alpha'_1, \alpha'_2, \alpha'_3, \ldots, \alpha'_l), \Omega' = \prod\limits_{k=1}^{l} (\omega_k)^{\alpha'k}, \eta'' H_5(M''||g^{\Psi}||pk_1 ||pk_2), \beta' = H_2(M''||g^{\Psi}||pk_1||pk_2) = (\beta'_i)$,

39: $\Phi' = \prod\limits_{j=1}^{n} (\phi_j)^{\beta'_j}, \chi' = H_5(M''||g^{\Psi}||pk_1||pk_2) = (\chi'_i), \Gamma' = \prod\limits_{j=1}^{n} (\gamma_j)^{\chi'_j}$, the signature is $\sigma_{Update} = (\sigma'_1, \sigma_2, \sigma_3) = ((D'_1)^{\eta''}(\Phi)^{\theta_1 \eta''}(\Gamma')^{\theta_2}(\Omega')^{\Psi}, D_2^{\eta''}, g^{\Psi})$

40: (7) SN reconstructs the Input information, sends the Block to the MN: $S_i := \{PID_{SN}, revoke, online||offline, T_3, height, Cert(ID_{SN}, pk_{online}, T_0), Cert(ID_{SN}, pk_{offline}, T_0))\}$ and $S_i := \{PID'_{SN}, update, online||offline, T_3, height, Cert(ID_{SN}, pk_{online}^{update}, T_3, update), Cert(ID_{SN}, pk_{online}^{update}, T_3, update)$,

$$VerificationValues = (Cert(ID_{SN}, pk^{update}_{online}, T_3, update) || Cert(ID_{SN},$$
$$pk^{update}_{online}, T_3, update), \sigma_{Update}, ID_{SN})), (pk_1, pk_2), (D'_1, D2)\}$$

41: **Step 4 MN Competes for Accounting Rights**

42: (1) MN verify the legitimacy of SN identity

43: (2) MN extracts VerificationValues from S_i, calculates $\vartheta' = \prod_{j=1}^{m} (\varphi_j)^{v_j}$, $\Omega' =$

$$\prod_{k=1}^{l} (\omega_k)^{\alpha_k}, \Phi' = \prod_{j=1}^{n} (\phi_j)^{\beta_j}, \Gamma' = \prod_{j=1}^{n} (\gamma_j)^{\chi_j}$$

44: (3) MN verifies the legality of the signature

45: **if** $(\hat{e}(g, \sigma'_1) == \hat{e}(g_1, g_2)^{n''} \hat{e}(\sigma_2, \vartheta) \hat{e}(pk_1, \Phi)^{n''} \hat{e}(pk_2, \Gamma') \hat{e}(\sigma_3, \Omega))$ **then**

46:    MN publish the $S_i :$ $= \{PID_{SN}, revoke, online||offline, T_3, height,$
$Cert(ID_{SN}, pk_{online}, T_0), Cert(ID_{SN}, pk_{offline}, T_0))\}$ and $S_i := \{PID'_{SN},$
$Update, online||offline, T_3, height, Cert(ID_{SN}, pk^{update}_{online}, T_3, update), Cert$
$(ID_{SN}, pk^{update}_{online}, T_3, update)$, write $VerificationValues = (Cert(ID_{SN},$
$pk^{update}_{online}, T_3, update) || Cert(ID_{SN}, pk^{update}_{online}, T_3, update), \sigma_{Update}, ID_{SN})),$
$(pk_1, pk_2), (D'_1, D2)\}$ into Ri,reconstruct and store the block, publish
$VerificationSuccess(nonce)$ and   myReport$(block(blockhead, S_i, R'_i,$
$nonce')$, round) to the network.

47: **else**

48:    The transaction fails, discards the block, **End Operation**

49: **end if**

50: **(4) MN process copy statistics**

51: **if** (round $> 2/v$) **then** Continue the update block onto the blockchain

52:    **End Operation**

53: **end if**

4.5   Certificate Retrieval and Key Verification

Certificate retrieval and key verification are to find and verify the corresponding keys according to the nodes' identities and key types. SSN reply the latest key information currentpublickey according to the corresponding historical state of the keys. This operation is initiated by MN and SN to SSN to verify the relevant information of the nodes to be retrieved (NTBR), retrieve all transaction records in the blockchain, and output the corresponding keys. If no corresponding key type exists, the output $\perp$ process is as follows.

Algorithm 5. Certificate Retrieval and Key Verification

1: **Start Operation**

2: **Step 1 SN**

3: (1) SN randomly accesses an SSN node from the SSN list, denotes as SSN'

4: (2) SN generates sequence random number and challenge random number: $Rand() \rightarrow seq_4$

5: (3) SN generates query validation values: $Sig(PID_{SN}||PID'_{NTBR}||(Cert$
$(ID_{NTBR}, pk^{ketype}_{NTBR}, T', keytype)), sk_{online}) \rightarrow \sigma_{lookup}$

6: (4) SN sends LookupRequest $(PID_{SN}, T_4, height, seq_4, \sigma_{lookup}, PID'_{NTBR})$ to SSN'

7: **Step 2 RN" Executes Operation**

8: SSN' validates LookupRequest, extracts the Si from the Block at height, search and parse Blockbody information

9: **if** $(keytype == register \&\& Vrfy(pk_{SN}, \sigma_{lookup}, PID_{SN}||PID'_{NTBR}||(Cert$ $(ID_{NTBR}, pk^{ketype}_{NTBR}, T', keytype)) == 1)$ **then**

10:     Replies $(currentpublickey = pk^*, Cert(ID_{NTBR}, pk^*_N TBR, T', register))$, **End Operation**

11: **else if** $(commandtype == update \&\& Vrfy(pk_{SN}, \sigma_{lookup}, PID_{SN}$ $||PID'_{NTBR}||(Cert(ID_{NTBR}, pk^{ketype}_{NTBR}, T', keytype)) == 1))$ **then**

12:     Replies $(currentpublickey = pk^{new}, Cert(ID_{NTBR}, pk^{new}_{NTBR}, T',$ $updated))$, **End Operation**

13: **else if** $(renewalkeytype == revoke \&\& Vrfy(pk_{SN}, \sigma_{lookup}, PID_{SN}$ $||PID'_{NTBR}||(Cert(ID_{NTBR}, pk^{ketype}_{NTBR}, T', keytype)) == 1))$ **then**

14:     Replies $(currentpublickey = \bot, Cert(ID_{NTBR}, pk^{revoked}_{NTBR}, T', revoked))$, **End Operation**

15: **else**

16:     Replies $(currentpublickey = \bot, CertNotExisted)$, **End Operation**

17: **end if**

5 Protocol Analysis

5.1 Security Analysis

Platform Authority. Platform authority: the existence of any transaction record in the blockchain is determined by all parties in the process of consensus ledgers and cannot be denied by any node. Therefore, the blockchain results have corresponding authority. Based on the permissioned blockchain system, each node, when performing block calculations, stores the blockchain's historical transaction information like a crypto accumulator in the form of Merkle Tree, and uses SHA-256[2] to calculate. As SHA-256 algorithm has unidirectionality and collision resistance [5,12], it is capable of recording the information of all previous transactions of blockchain nodes in security. With the Merkle Tree and timestamp in the blockchain, the existence of ledger transaction records is proved based on the PoW mechanism. That is, the more trusted nodes in the network and the more nodes authenticating transaction values, the higher the results' reliability [11,24].

Unforgeability. Unforgeability means that, without obtaining the identity of a node and online and offline key pairs, an adversary cannot forge the legal identity of a node and impersonate it to access to a network based on a permissioned blockchain. In the absence of key pairs without node identities, even if the adversary uses a legitimate mobile device to send an authorization request to the RN, the identity information cannot be written into the blockchain as long as he cannot provide the corresponding two sets of public keys and the corresponding signature values. In this case, the adversary cannot access the network.

Key Security. The platform in this article verifies the identity of each node and the corresponding public key. The legal correlation between the public key and the node's identity is recorded by the ledger in the blockchain, the results of which cannot be changed. SSN are responsible for verifying the public keys, the generation of which must be subject to the process of identity verification. If the verification fails, the public keys are not verified. Moreover, even if the adversary obtains the corresponding public keys after passing platform verification, he cannot update the keys without having grasped the corresponding two sets of private keys.

Revocation Transparency. The revocation process: the emergency revocation of keys in an insecure state is supported by the platform. It can reduce the harms caused by key disclosure. Once a node discovers that the network may be attacked, or there is a vulnerability in the node's mobile application, or the node's offline private key may be compromised, a revocation operation will be triggered. The transparent revocation operation in this paper can be used either as an active defense measure or an emergency remedy measure to improve the security and controllability of the platform as a whole.

The whole revocation process in Dizar architecture is transparent and open. The revocation process in Dizar architecture is not a traditional PKI and is authorized by CA. When a valid revocation transaction is included in a new block, its validity is verified by all miner nodes. Only when all miner nodes have verified the legitimacy of the node can the status of the certificate be changed globally. Therefore, the revocation process in the Dizar architecture is ideally transparent and can be audited and verified. SN do not need CA to check the revocation status of certificates. All miners in Dizar can check and verify the final revocation status of certificates in the block at any time, thus eliminating the problems caused by relying on CA to ensure the reliability and transparency of the results.

Resistance to Aggression. The attack methods against permissioned blockchains mainly include Split-world attack, 51% attack, Eclipse attack and DDoS attack. This article copes with DDoS attacks with a permissioned blockchain implemented on a P2P network. The chain itself is a distributed architecture and is featured by decentralization and multiple redundancies. Even if some nodes in the network fail due to attaches, other nodes are not affected and there is no failure of single point. In this paper, the permissioned blockchain architecture is adopted. The node information in the network is stored in a distributed manner. The network system will not be paralyzed when several nodes in the network are attacked. Split-world attacks, 51% attacks and Eclipse attacks are applicable to the situation where the adversary is capable of providing different ledgers to the miner nodes. In a traditional PKI system, such situation only exists when there is a credible log operator and the target nodes do not exchange log views through a gossip protocol. The Dizar architecture has eliminated such attacks because it does not have an independent third-party verification authority. All miners are verification parties, all have the same and unique ledger data, and can only be updated based on the consensus of all miners.

The credibility of Dizar architecture is essentially based on its consensus mechanism. Under the assumption that the basic consensus protocol of blockchain architecture is secure, all miner nodes will have the final state of blockchain data containing certificate status. However, based on the PoW consensus mechanism, it is impossible to attack the blockchain node data. Therefore, the Dizar architecture has strong resistance to attack.

Verification of Information Rationality. In fact, we take the authentication process of the identity registration as an example to prove the mathematical rationality of the node authentication process.

Proof.

$$\hat{e}(g, \sigma_1) = \hat{e}(g, D_1^{\eta}(\Phi)^{\theta_1 \eta} \Gamma^{\theta_2} \Omega^{\Psi})$$
$$= \hat{e}(g, (g_2^{\lambda} \vartheta^{\mathcal{K}})^{\eta}) \hat{e}(g, (\Phi)^{\eta \theta_1}) \hat{e}(g, (\Gamma)^{\theta_2}) \hat{e}(g, (\Omega)^{\Psi})$$
$$= \hat{e}(g^{\lambda}, g_2) \hat{e}(g^{\eta \mathcal{K}}, \vartheta) \hat{e}(g^{\theta_1}, \Phi)^{\eta} \hat{e}(g^{\theta_2}, \Gamma) \hat{e}(g^{\Psi}, \Omega)$$
$$= \hat{e}(g_1, g_2)^{\eta} \hat{e}(\sigma_2, \vartheta) \hat{e}(pk_1, \Phi)^{\eta} \hat{e}(pk_2, \Gamma) \hat{e}(\sigma_3, \Omega)$$

Proof is complete.

Therefore, based on the rationality of the design verification algorithm and combined with the non-certificate authentication process, the global credibility authentication of the information submitted by members can be realized without the need for a third-party authentication institution and without exposing the member's relevant privacy information. The Dizar architecture has eliminated the requirement for external auditors to check their encryption consistency and behaviors, as new blocks are verified and attached to the blockchain only if all miners agree.

Decentralized Storage. The Dizar architecture has eliminated the storage problem of certificate/key centralization. We believe it is a burden for X509 V3 to manage credible CA root certificates and public keys in a centralized manner, which is also one of the main sources of security threats [18,22]: it stores CA root certificates and public keys in a centralized certificate database. However, there is no need for a separate certificate database to manage the certificates and public keys of credible CA under the Dizar architecture, which stores and maintains the certificates and public keys in distributed databases of blockchains composed of all nodes. The distributed chain storage structure of a permissioned blockchain ensures the credibility and integrity of these certificates and keys.

5.2   Platform Efficiency Test

In this section, the cost of competition for bookkeeping rights by multi-node is tested in an experiment. To not lose generality, the running of nodes is at the same level of complexity as other literature. The efficiency test is conducted on ARM FastModels(ARM,2011) in Ubuntu 10.04 environment. The hardware is Intel(R) Core(TM)i7-4510CPU2.60g Hz, 16G memory. The efficiency test uses Docker virtual technology to build permissioned blockchain nodes and uses Zeppelin to design the intelligent contract architecture of the blockchain. Each blockchain node runs in a separate Docker container with 2G memory. The contract codes to be run by each node are packaged in the Docker container, and the programs are isolated from each other with high security. The resource consumptions of the Docker containers are also independent of each other. The CPU consumption is at most about 3% and the memory consumption is not more than 100MB to test the average running efficiency of each node. The number of protocol nodes in this article is 1024, the block size is 1MB, and the ledger records are single records. Table 2 shows the efficiency comparison, in which public and private key encryption and decryption, digital signature and verification are compared, and the sum of single steps is counted.

Table 2. Comparison of efficiency of various protocols

Protocols	Average number of public and private key encryption/times	Average digital signature and verification/times	Average hash calculation times/times	Consensus mechanism	Degree of decentralization	Average registration time/s
Literature [4]	5	6	4	PoW	Distributed	65
Literature [10]	8	6	4	PoS	Decentralized	58
Literature [14]	6	4	2	PoS	Distributed	64
Literature [15]	3	5	2	Multipoint response	Decentralized	47
Dizar	4	4	3	Improved PoW	Distributed	10

Calculation Cost Analysis: Compared with [10] and [4], the public key encryption and decryption, signature verification and hash calculation of the protocol in this article have decreased, but some indexes have increased slightly compared with [14,15]. [10] and [15] are based on the multi-center certificate distribution protocol, in which the computing loads of the center nodes will increase with the increase of nodes. This article is based on the distributed private chain. The increase of proxy nodes will not lead to an increase in the average number of public key algorithms used in multi-party competition for bookkeeping rights, and there are multiple proxy nodes, which can effectively reduce the burden of a single authentication node. In addition, the protocol in this article actively screens the ledgers to be authenticated in the process of multi-node competing for bookkeeping rights, thus reducing unnecessary expenses. Tests with mining machines with equivalent computing capacity show that the average registration time is obviously shortened. Therefore, the protocol in this article is more advantageous in writing data into blockchain in a multi-node mobile environment, thus maintaining a moderate calculation overhead on the network. Compared with PoS and multi-point collaboration, this paper adopts the POW consensus approach to minimize the overall mechanism unfairness caused by the fact that a few nodes have greater decision-making powers, making the process of competing for bookkeeping rights more reliable.

Average Transaction Time: The time required to detect that a block containing an input collection passes verification and is added into the blockchain (through Algorithm 1). The running time of PKI based on blockchain and different working mechanisms is analyzed. The transaction verification time is the same order of magnitude for all transaction verification times. However, as shown in Table 2, the average transaction verification time of CertCoin protocol [10] is about 1.1 min per transaction, the one of IKP protocol [15] is 1 min, while the one of PB-PKI is 45s [4]. The verification transaction time of the blockchain will change according to the status of the network and the upgrade of the protocol version. In the running of the ledger-based permissioned blockchain in this article, the average block verification takes about 10 s. Compared with other schemes, the average running time is shortened and relatively reasonable, which helps to avoid potential false transactions from taking place in a short time and is more suitable for running in a dynamic network.

Increase in the Size of the Blockchain: The blockchain, acting as a distributed database, provides integrity and store security information to realize credibility. For the calculation, we adopt the elliptic curve encryption algorithm with smaller key size, higher performance and higher security. The block size is 256 bits. The size of Dizar's permissioned blockchain depends on the block size and the frequency of adding new blocks. The block's size increases with increase of transactions, and the block verification time depends on the consensus algorithm selected. In actual calculation, the target block time is selected to be 5 min considering the following aspects.

- The storage capacity required in a light node will increase as the block time decreases. However, most of the medium and small-sized nodes in the actual Dizar architecture have storage limitations and cannot be easily upgraded. With the increase of network mobility, we expect light nodes to become the main form of the most common Dizar architecture. Light nodes do not store blocks but only headers. The required disk space is proportional to the number of blocks. The light nodes in the Dizar architecture require only about 30 MB of disk space per year for storage.
- Full Node: The node where the whole miner nodes create new blocks. It is a part of the consensus and stores all blocks. Assume that the average certificate

life cycle is one year, all network nodes need only 150 GB of disk space to store all updated transactions (the assumption is based on the 2017 VeriSign Domain Name Industry Briefing [23], or, about 3.3 × 108 registered domain names). These calculations are based on the assumption that certificates are stored for all. Considering the fact that the price of 1 GB disk storage is about US $ 0.02 [3], the cost of storing all Dizar block data for non-mining entire nodes is about US $ 5. The extra data needed to build a blockchain will not have significant impact on the overall storage space required.

Analysis of Time Consumption Required by Blockchain Retrieval: The main challenge in PKI services in the protocol of this article is the time needed to perform the retrieval in the blockchain. The complexity of this operation is theoretically $O(v)$, v is the number of network nodes. The CertCoin [10] and the IKP [15] use a DHT and a password accumulator to reduce the retrieval complexity and time of the blockchain to $O(\log(t))$, where t represents the number of transactions in the blockchain. Therefore, proceeding from this point of view, the protocol in this article still has opportunity for improvement theoretically in terms of data retrieval. On the other hand, the actual time required to view the retrieval is as shown in Table 3.

Table 3. Average operation time of retrievals in blockchains of different sizes

	LookUp
250 MB	320 ms
500 MB	652 ms
1 G	1315 ms
2 G	2711 ms

Based on the different sizes of blockchains, we examine the time required by each transaction in all the blockchains. The worst case of the test certificate retrieval is that the transaction block is retrieved at the end of the blockchain. Our results in Table 3 show a linear increase in complexity. For the size of the representative blockchain, the certificate retrieval time is less than 3 s. However, in the actual applications, the data service nodes do not have to retrieve throughout the entire blockchain. The data service nodes usually use the latest updated information in the blockchain to improve the retrieval efficiency by adopting a fast retrieval method.

6   Conclusion

To address the existing challenges in current blockchain-based PKI, this article proposes the Dizar architecture, designs the blockchain running mode in a basic ledger system, realizes multi-party credibility of identity information based on the non-certificate authentication process, and defines the corresponding distributed PKI service process. The platform realizes distributed PKI results based on blockchain, which are featured by multi-party credibility and joint maintenance. The analysis of the simulation test results shows that its calculation cost makes it suitable for implementation in the distributed network. The platform has strong scalability and high network adaptability. Our next step is to study the fast synthesis and retrieval of block data to improve the adaptability of a distributed PKI in the network.

References

1. Al-Bassam, M.: SCPKI: a smart contract-based PKI and identity system. In: ACM Workshop on Blockchain, Cryptocurrencies and Contracts, pp. 35–40 (2017)
2. Androulaki, E., et al.: Hyperledger fabric: a distributed operating system for permissioned blockchains (2018)
3. Author: Disk storage cost. https://diskprices.com/. Accessed 28 Nov 2017
4. Axon, L.: Privacy-awareness in blockchain-based PKI (2015)
5. Camacho, P., Hevia, A., Kiwi, M., Opazo, R.: Strong accumulators from collision-resistant hashing. In: Wu, T.-C., Lei, C.-L., Rijmen, V., Lee, D.-T. (eds.) ISC 2008. LNCS, vol. 5222, pp. 471–486. Springer, Heidelberg (2008). https://doi.org/10.1007/978-3-540-85886-7_32
6. Diginotar: Diginotar. https://en.wikipedia.org/wiki/DigiNotar/. Accessed 4 Mar 2011
7. Eweek: Mozilla asked to revoke trustwave CA for allowing SSL eavesdropping. http://www.eweek.com/security/mozilla-askedto-revoke-trustwave-ca-for-allowing-ssleavesdropping/. February March 4, 2012
8. Faisca, J.G., Rogado, J.Q.: Personal cloud interoperability. In: World of Wireless, Mobile and Multimedia Networks, pp. 1–3 (2016)
9. Falliere, N., Murchu, L.O., Chien, E.: W32.stuxnet dossier. White Paper (2011)
10. Fromknecht, C., Velicanu, D.: CertCoin: a NameCoin based decentralized authentication system. Technical report, 6.857 class (2014)
11. Gervais, A., Karame, G.O., Glykantzis, V., Ritzdorf, H., Capkun, S.: On the security and performance of proof of work blockchains. In: ACM SIGSAC Conference on Computer and Communications Security, pp. 3–16 (2016)
12. Heilman, E., Kendler, A., Zohar, A., Goldberg, S.: Eclipse attacks on bitcoin's peer-to-peer network. In: Usenix Conference on Security Symposium, pp. 129–144 (2015)
13. Lesueur, F., Me, L., Tong, V.V.T.: An efficient distributed PKI for structured P2P networks. In: IEEE Ninth International Conference on Peer-to-Peer Computing, pp. 1–10 (2009)
14. Lewison, K., Corella, F.: Backing rich credentials with a blockchain PKI. Technical report, Pomian & Corella LLC (2016)
15. Matsumoto, S., Reischuk, R.M.: IKP: turning a PKI around with decentralized automated incentives. In: Security and Privacy, pp. 410–426 (2017)
16. Melin, T., Vidhall, T.: Namecoin as authentication for public-key cryptography (2014)
17. Nakamoto, S.: Bitcoin: a peer-to-peer electronic cash system. Consulted (2008)

18. Patrick Wardle, A.M.: CA threats. https://objectivesee.com/blog/blog_0x26. html/. Accessed 4 Apr 2017
19. Phillip: Comodo SSL affiliate the recent RA compromise. https://blog.comodo. com/other/therecent-ra-compromise/. Accessed 4 Mar 2011
20. Nakamoto, S.: Bitcoin blockchain size. http://blockchain.info/charts/blocks-size/. Accessed 7 Aug 2018
21. Shen, X., Pei, Q.Q., Liu, X.F.: Survey of block chain. Chin. J. Netw. Inf. Secur. **11**, 11–20 (2016)
22. Symantec Threat Intelligence: Marketscore proxyserver certificate. https:// www.symantec.com/security_response/attacksignatures/detail.jsp?asid=20804./. Accessed 4 Apr 2017
23. VerisignDECEMBER: The verisign domain name industry brief. https://www. verisign.com/en_US/domainnames/dnib/index.xhtml/. Accessed 4 Apr 2017
24. Xu, J.J.: Are blockchains immune to all malicious attacks? Financ. Innov. **2**(1), 25 (2016)
25. Zhicheng, Z., Lixin, L., Zuohui, L.: Efficient cross domain authentication scheme based on blockchain technology. J. Comput. Appl. **38**(2), 316–320 (2018)

Optimization Scheme of Consensus Mechanism Based on Practical Byzantine Fault Tolerance Algorithm

Zhipeng Gao[✉] and Lulin Yang

State Key Laboratory of Networking and Switching Technology,
Beijing University of Posts and Telecommunications, Beijing, China
gaozhipeng@bupt.edu.cn

Abstract. Blockchain was first proposed in 2009, it is a kind of distributed ledger system with peer-to-peer network, which has drawn wide spread attention because of its characteristics such as decentralization, security and credibility. The consensus algorithm of the blockchain is a mechanism for achieving agreement among the nodes in the blockchain. How to reach consensus quickly and effectively is the core issue of the blockchain. Byzantine nodes are invalid or malicious nodes in the blockchain. This paper considers the actual situation of Byzantine nodes in the blockchain. For the problem that the classical PBFT algorithm has too much communication spending and cannot dynamically follow the change of consensus nodes, an improved PBFT algorithm in this paper is proposed. In the improved Practical Byzantine consensus algorithm (IMP-PBFT), the convergence speed of the consensus process is effectively improved under the condition of the fault tolerance rate. The experiment proves the accuracy and effectiveness of the improved PBFT algorithm.

Keywords: Blockchain · Consensus · PBFT · Communication spending

1 Introduction

In 2009, Nakamoto [1] was first proposed the concept of blockchain in the paper "Bitcoin: A Peer-to-Peer E-Cash System". As the most typical application of blockchain, bitcoin uses numbers techniques such as timestamps, signatures, asymmetric cryptographic algorithms, and consensus mechanisms based on workload proofing implement a truly decentralized trustworthy trading system. Since the block chain technology cannot be tampered with, safe and reliable characteristics, it has quickly received the attention of the financial and Internet industries, and various applications based on blockchain technology have also been developed. Such as the crowd funding platform based on Ethereum [2], IBM's hyperledger fabric project [3], EOS [4] public chain and so on. With the development of blockchain technology, the blockchain has been transitioned from the 1.0 era represented by Bitcoin to the 2.0 era represented by hyperledger and Ethereum. The blockchain's application scenarios are also developed from public chains to alliance chains suitable for commercial applications.

© Springer Nature Singapore Pte Ltd. 2020
X. Si et al. (Eds.): CBCC 2019, CCIS 1176, pp. 187–195, 2020.
https://doi.org/10.1007/978-981-15-3278-8_12

The core issue of the blockchain is how to achieve an effective consensus while meeting consistency and availability. Bitcoin uses a consensus mechanism for Proof of work, in this case each node wins the billing right of the block by quizzing a random number. However, the POW [5] has obvious problems. It requires huge power costs, the consensus efficiency is very low, and the transaction delay is very high. In the case of Bitcoin, the confirmation of a transaction is about one hour after the generation of six new blocks. Therefore, it does not apply to business scenarios represented by the alliance chain. POS [6] (proof of stake) is a stake-based consensus mechanism that obtains the billing rights from the node with the highest property instead of the most powerful one, but this may cause the rights of some nodes to be too large, which also deviates from the original intention of decentralization of the blockchain. In the hyperledger project led by IBM, the PBFT [7] (practical Byzantine fault tolerance) algorithm based on Byzantine problem was used. The PBFT algorithm was first proposed by Castro and used to solve the problem of how the asynchronous distributed system agrees. The nodes reach agreement through negotiation. The algorithm can ensure that the blockchain can still operate normally when no more than one third of the nodes fail. However, in the PBFT algorithm, the client request needs to go through five stages of request, pre-preparation, preparation, confirmation, and response, which will greatly delay the consensus process, and the number of nodes must be fixed and cannot be dynamically changed. Based on the above problems, this paper proposes an improved PBFT algorithm, which can effectively shorten the consensus process and dynamically add or delete nodes while having a high fault tolerance.

2   Related Works

2.1   Practical Byzantine Fault Tolerant Algorithm

PBFT (Practical Byzantine Fault Tolerant Algorithm) [8] is a fault-tolerant algorithm based on the Byzantine general problem, which is divided into five phases to achieve consistency. PBFT solves the problem that the original Byzantine algorithm is not efficient, and makes the algorithm feasible in practical applications. In PBFT, a blockchain net of N nodes can accept byzantine nodes where $N \geq 3f + 1$. The PBFT algorithm has the following definitions:

All consensus nodes operate in a single view. Each view has a unique primary node, and the remaining nodes are called replica nodes. The corresponding number of the node is $0.1\dots n - 1$, The rule corresponding to the view of the primary node is:

$$p = v \bmod N \tag{1}$$

In this formula p is the primary node number, v is the view number, and N is the total number of nodes. PBFT's communication process [9] is as follows (see Fig. 1).

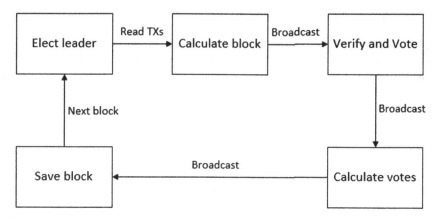

Fig. 1. The communication process of Practical Byzantine Fault Tolerant Algorithm

Request: The request is sent by the client to start the consensus process.

Pre-prepare: After receiving the request from the client, the primary forwards the prepared message to all replica nodes. The format of the message is *<pre-p, v, n, d>*, where v is the view number and n is the requested number, d is the content of the request;

Prepare: After the replica node accepts the preparation message, it enters the preparation phase. The replica node will broadcast the preparation message to all the remaining replica nodes. The message format is *<p, v, n, d, i>*, i is the replica node number. When at least $2f + 1$ preparation messages consistent with the prepared message, the node enters the confirmation phase and writes a *<d, v, n, i>* message to log.

Commit: Each node forwards an acknowledgment message to all remaining nodes. When a node receives $f + 1$ acknowledgment messages, it begins to execute the request and sends feedback to the client.

Confirm: The block will be written to the blockchain after verified. End of consensus process.

If the client does not reply within a valid time, the request will be broadcast to all replica nodes. If the request is not processed at the replica node, the replica nodes will forward the request to the primary node. If the primary node does not broadcast the request, then the primary node is considered invalid. If there are enough duplicate nodes to consider the primary node to be invalid, the view will be change.

2.2   The Overall Idea of the Algorithm

Suppose there are 3 nodes in the blockchain. N_1, N_2 are honest nodes and N_{er1} is a byzantine node. Let N_1 receive the transaction vector of N_2 as TX_{21} and receive the N_{er1} transaction vector as TX_{er1}. If the correct consistency is to be achieved, the algorithm f [10] must satisfy

$$TX_{21} = f(TX_{21}, TX_{er1})$$
$$Store(TX_{er1}) = false \tag{2}$$

The classic PBFT [11] algorithm uses a three-stage protocol to ensure consistency, but it pays a great deal of communication spending, and in PBFT the number of nodes is fixed [12]. In the scenario of the alliance chain, the consensus node has no subjective malicious motives. Only the network has a downtime, or the communication is disconnected, the Byzantine node will appear, in general, the probability of such a thing occurring is extremely low, so there is no need to conduct a three-stage broadcast every time to reach a consensus.

This paper considers the first method of using two-step broadcast [13] communication to reach a consensus, and switches to the classic PBFT algorithm if the consensus is not reached. In terms of the selection of the primary node, this paper adopts a voting mechanism to select the primary node [14]. When a node joins/exits, the voting rights are added or deleted for the node, and the current primary node remains unchanged, after the view switching protocol is triggered, all voting nodes re-select the primary node. This saves system overhead due to node changes to change views.

3   Algorithm Design

3.1   Primary Node Selection Strategy

In this paper, voting mechanism is adopted in the selection of the primary node. When the system is stable, selecting the most recognized master node of the whole network can effectively reduce the frequency of changing view; When the node changes, the system does not immediately switch the view. Instead, it waits for the primary node to make an error and then re-votes to determine the primary node. This prevents wasted time by frequently switching views. The voting strategy is as follows:

(1) Each consensus node can vote for one node, the voting is in the form of broadcast, and the node with more than half of the votes becomes the master node.

(2) If the primary node is not determined, select the three nodes with the highest number of votes and vote again, the node with the highest number of votes is elected as the primary node.

(3) The primary node determines the switching order of the views. If no nodes join/exit in the process of consensus, the views will be switched, in the determined order.

(4) If a node joins or exits, assigns a number to the new node and deletes the exit node number.

(5) When the view switching protocol is triggered, if there is a new node at this time, vote again and determine the view switching order.

3.2 Block Synchronization Strategy

When all the nodes in blockchain [15] are honest nodes, this paper uses a two-stage agreement to reach a consensus. When the Byzantine node appears, it switches to the PBFT algorithm, the IMP-PBFT algorithm uses the following strategy to reach a consensus:

(1) Select the primary node, and the primary node initiates the consistency protocol.

(2) Primary node package transaction records and send a broadcast message to the replica nodes. The message's format is $<pre, v, n, d>$, where v is the view number of the primary and n is the requested number, d is the content of the request.

(3) After receiving the primary's message, the replica nodes verify the message and send a confirmation message to the primary node. The confirmation's format is $<com, v, n, d, i>$, and i is the number of replica node.

(4) If all replica nodes are verified. the primary node packages the transaction records into block and add it to the blockchain.

(5) The replica nodes verified the block and synchronizes the block to the blockchain.

In the fourth step, when the primary node finds that there is a conflict in the response from the replica nodes or does not receive all the verified messages within one timestamp, it will consider that there is a byzantine node in the replica nodes, and triggers the PBFT algorithm. In the fifth step, if the replica node finds that the block packed by the primary node is inconsistent with the block verified by itself, the primary node will be considered to be faulty, and the view switching protocol is triggered.

3.3 Algorithm Overall Process

The overall process design of the IMP-PBFT algorithm is designed as follows (See Fig. 2).

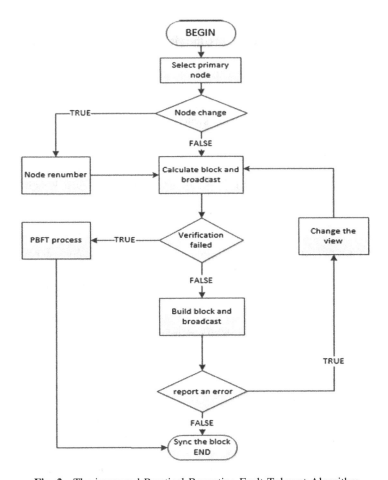

Fig. 2. The improved Practical Byzantine Fault Tolerant Algorithm

4   Experimentation and Analysis

4.1   Computing Overhead Verification

In the classic PBFT algorithm, the communication overhead in the network is

$$TS = N * N * (headsize) + N * (blocks) \tag{3}$$

TS is the total spending, N is the number of nodes, and in the IMP-PBFT, the total spending is

$$TS = N * (headsize) + N(blocks) \tag{4}$$

As can be seen from above formulas, the improved algorithm reduces the cost of a broadcast compared to PBFT. We can verify this inference from the blockchain's TPS.

In this paper we used Ethereum to build a blockchain operating environment and set the nodes to 4, 5, 6, 7, 8. Each node is configured as follows Table 1:

Table 1. The configuration of experimental environment

CPU	Intel(R) Core(TM) i5-6100 CPU @3.70 GHz
OS	Ubuntu 16.04
RAM	1 GB
ROM	20 GB

Then we observe the system throughput under different nodes, the result is shown as Fig. 3.

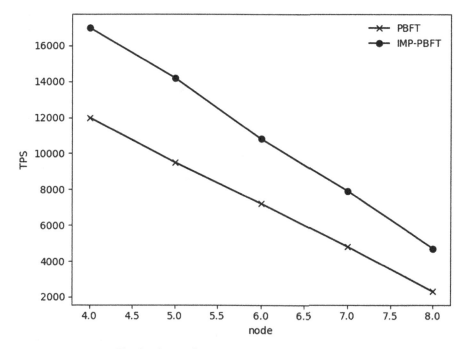

Fig. 3. Comparison of TPS under different nodes

As can be seen from the figure, due to the reduction of communication costs, the IMP-PBFT's TPS has been significantly improved compared to PBFT.

4.2   Fault Tolerance Verification

We use 8 nodes to build a blockchain and gradually increase the number of Byzantine nodes, and then observe the TPS in the blockchain. The results are shown below (Fig. 4):

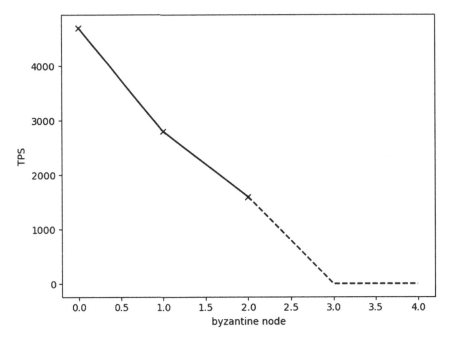

Fig. 4. Relationship between TPS and byzantine nodes

It can be seen that when there are more than 3 Byzantine nodes, the TPS is 0, which means that nodes cannot reach a consensus.

5   Conclusion

Targeted at the problems encountered by PBFT in practical application scenarios, this paper proposes an improved Byzantine (IMP-PBFT) consensus algorithm for adaptive and dynamic monitoring nodes. Compared to the classic PBFT algorithm. The improved algorithm enables faster consensus and guarantees fault tolerance. The focus of the future is to further effectively enhance the stability of the algorithm in various client environments and apply it to actual production practices.

References

1. Nakamoto, S.: Bitcoin: a peer-to-peer electronic cash system [J/OL] (2008)
2. Ethereum [EB/OL] (2017). https://www.ethereum.org/
3. Hyperledger [EB/OL] (2017). https://www.hyperledger.org/
4. EOS [EB/OL] (2018). https://eos.io/
5. Vasin, P.: Blockchain's proof-of-stake protocol v2 [J/OL] (2014)
6. Larimer, D.: Delegated proof-of-stake white paper [EB/OL]
7. Lamport, L., Shostak, R., Pease, M.: The Byzantine generals problem. ACM Trans. Program. Lang. Syst. **4**(3), 382–401 (1982)
8. Castro, M.: Practical Byzantine fault tolerance and proactive recovery. ACM Trans. Program. Lang. Syst. (TOCS) **20**(4), 398–461 (2002)
9. Sun, J., Yan, J., Zhang, K.Z.K.: Blcokchain-based sharing services: what blockchain technology can contribute to smart cities. Financ. Innov. **2**, 1–9 (2016)
10. Happe, A., Krenn, S., Lorunser, T.: PBFT and secret-shring in storage settings. In: Twenty-Fourth International Workshop on Security Protocols (2016)
11. Lamport, L.: Seminal research document related to the field of Byzantine fault tolerance (1982)
12. Lamport, L.: The part-time parliament. ACM Trans. Comput. Syst. **16**(2), 133–169 (1998)
13. Bracha, G., Toueg, S.: Asynchronous consensus and broadcast protocols. J. ACM **32**(4), 824–840 (1995)
14. Jakobsson, M., Leighton, T., Micali, S., Szydlo, M.: Fractal Merkle tree representation and traversal. In: Joye, M. (ed.) CT-RSA 2003. LNCS, vol. 2612, pp. 314–326. Springer, Heidelberg (2003). https://doi.org/10.1007/3-540-36563-X_21
15. Swan, M.: Blockchain: Blueprint for a New Economy. O'Really Media, Sebastopol (2015)

The Trojan Message Attack on the Pay-to-Public-Key-Hash Protocol of Bitcoin

Maoning Wang[1,2,3,4](✉), Meijiao Duan[1], and Jianming Zhu[1]

[1] School of Information, Central University of Finance and Economics,
Beijing 100081, China
13854139297@139.com
[2] Shanghai Key Laboratory of Integrated Administration
Technologies for Information Security, Shanghai 200240, China
[3] Key Laboratory of Computer Network and Information Integration,
Southeast University, Ministry of Education, Nanjing 211189, China
[4] Hunan Provincial Base of International Science and Technology Innovation
and Cooperation on Big Data Technology and Management,
Changsha 410205, China

Abstract. Bitcoin is the first and seemingly the most successful cryptocurrency based in a peer-to-peer network that uses blockchain technology. Given Bitcoin's growing real-life deployment and popularity, its security has aroused more and more attention in both financial and information industries. As a body containing a variety of cryptosystems, Bitcoin may also suffer from cryptanalysis attacks. This paper focuses on one of such attacks: the Trojan message attack, and presents in detail how to conduct the attack according to the structure and workflow of the Pay-to-Public-Key-Hash protocol of Bitcoin. The attack aims at forging an upcoming transaction record and results from the fact that all users' candidate input transactions are open to the attacker. The construction of the attack employs a combination of the Bitcoin transaction structure with standard Merkle–Damgard extension vulnerabilities. The conclusion of the attack shows that both the mathematical structure of the hash function itself and the public information in the blockchain are important to the security of Bitcoin. These factors should be considered in the future for the design of other cryptocurrency and blockchain systems.

Keywords: Bitcoin · Blockchain · Hash function · Trojan message attack · Pay-to-Public-Key-Hash (P2PKH) Protocol

The work is supported by the National Key R&D Program of China under Grant No. 2017YFB1400700, Beijing Natural Science Foundation under Grant No. 4194090, the National Natural Science Foundation of China under Grant No. 61702570, U1509214, the Opening Project of Shanghai Key Laboratory of Integrated Administration Technologies for Information Security under Grant No. AGK2018005, the Opening Project of Key Laboratory of Computer Network and Information Integration (Southeast University) under Grant No. K93-9-2018-05, and Open Fund of Key Laboratory of Hunan Province (2017TP1026).

X. Si et al. (Eds.): CBCC 2019, CCIS 1176, pp. 196–209, 2020.
https://doi.org/10.1007/978-981-15-3278-8_13

1 Introduction

Decentralized cryptocurrencies have generated considerable interest in recent years, as they enable users to "securely" transfer currency without the intermediation of a trusted authority. Bitcoin [1], the first distributed cryptocurrency system presented by Nakamoto in 2008, has laid the foundation for subsequent decentralized cryptocurrencies. Moreover, the technical essence of Bitcoin is a public data structure called a blockchain, which gathers transactions of currency in blocks. It is widely considered to have revolutionary application prospects, as blockchain's advantages lie in its decentralization, high efficiency, transparency, and low cost [2].

Concretely, Bitcoin is considered to be "secure", as transactions of currency are added-allowed-only to the blockchain. The consensus algorithm of Bitcoin guarantees that, for an attacker to be able to alter an existing block, the attacker must control the majority of the computational resources of the network [3]. Hence, attacks aiming at incrementing one's balance, e.g., by deleting transactions that certify payments to other users, are infeasible in practice. This security property is often rephrased by saying that the blockchain can be seen as an immutable data structure.

However, as an integration of a series of protocols, blockchain technology is confronted with challenges such as algorithmic security, protocol security, usage security, implementation security, and system security. Specially, because Bitcoin has been the most successful cryptocurrency so far, numerous research reports on threats to its security and security analysis have appeared. According to currently published research results, issues such as anonymity and privacy [4, 5], adversarial miners [6–8], double-spending attacks in special scenarios [9], network splitting [10–12], flaws in instructions of the scripting language [13], and so on [14, 15] have been discussed.

In addition to the abovementioned fields, another important aspect for researchers is based on the principle of cryptography, that is, treating the Bitcoin blockchain system as a system containing a variety of cryptoschemes and then applying cryptanalysis techniques to address and evaluate the system's security mechanism, i.e., to stand on an attacker's side for analyzing those cryptographic algorithms' structures, to find the relationships between the security strength of cryptographic schemes and the mathematical problems, to seek possible cryptosystem defects in a practical environment, to study the problems caused when cryptosystems are used overlappingly, and so on. Similar research methods have appeared in recent articles that focus on the security of many other systems containing cryptographic primitives, and even attack instances are constructed, such as a rogue CA certificate, colliding X.509 certificates for different identities, and forged PDF files, as given by Stevens et al. [16–18], and transcript collision attacks that break authentication in TLS, IKE, and SSH, as given by Bhargavan et al. [19], which extend the results given by Mavrogiannopoulos et al. [20] and Vaudenay [21]. Moreover, from the point of view of cryptanalysis, compared with the other systems mentioned above, the blockchain system in Bitcoin tends to be more vulnerable owing to the extensive application of various cryptographic techniques because any highly algorithm-intensive engineering system often brings more problems. Hence, it is necessary to apply such techniques of cryptanalysis once the security of Bitcoin is considered.

There have been numerous papers on cryptanalysis of Bitcoin and its successors. For example, Zheng et al. [22] discussed the elliptic curve digital signature algorithm (ECDSA) signature vulnerability of the current Bitcoin scheme when introducing a new backup scheme that can provide protection when an attacker manages to obtain the backup; Abusalah et al. [23] gave better time–memory tradeoffs based on Hellman's algorithm with applications to proofs of space (PoS), where PoS were suggested as a more ecological and economical alternative to proofs of work and are currently used in blockchain designs other than Bitcoin; Dinur et al. [24] constructed time–memory tradeoff attacks on the Merkle tree proof proof-of-work (PoW) scheme proposed by Biryukov et al. in 2016 [25]. Focusing on Bitcoin, for which hash functions are one of the most important foundations in ensuring its functionality and security, Giechaskiel et al. [26] specifically discussed the impact on the security of the entire Bitcoin blockchain system when the most classical hash function security criteria—preimage resistance, second preimage resistance, and collision resistance—were broken. Their conclusion is theoretically meaningful; however, it is not comprehensive enough: The three security criteria describe only the security strength of the hash functions themselves. For a hash function applied in an actual scene, in addition to its own mathematical structure, its security also depends on the particular aspects of the environment in which it works, because, in general, the application scenarios tend to bring some restrictions, making it difficult for the hash functions to establish the necessary conditions of the security criteria.

In Bitcoin, constraints such as the specified data structure of the messages, working together with the ECDSA signature, the tree-like structure of the Merkle tree hash function, and other cryptographic components, make the hash functions' security no longer an intuitively true argument but an inconclusive problem that requires more rigorous and innovative theoretical analysis.

Hence, in this paper, we focus on such security problems faced by the hash functions in Bitcoin. Concretely, the Trojan message attack on the Pay-to-Public-Key-Hash (P2PKH) protocol of Bitcoin is constructed, relying on the interaction of the Bitcoin transaction structure with standard Merkle–Damgard extension vulnerabilities. Intuitively, the Trojan message attack reduces the complexity of stealing bitcoins from a generic second-preimage attack to a collision attack. To our knowledge, this is also the first concrete cryptanalysis attack construction in the circumstance of Bitcoin.

The structure of this paper is as follows: In Sect. 2, we introduce basic knowledge about Bitcoin's blockchain system, especially the data structure and the formation principle of the P2PKH transaction records involved in the attack proposed in this paper. In Sect. 3, we introduce the model of a Trojan message attack and detail how to construct such an attack based on Bitcoin's property that all the users' available input transactions are public. In Sect. 4, we give some conclusions about the above attack.

2 Background

2.1 Basic Blockchain Principle

First, we introduce the basic workflow of the blockchain system in Bitcoin. The blockchain can be seen as a public log in which all transactions that have occurred are recorded in the form of blocks of these transactions. Specifically, each transaction uses scripting language to describe the owner of the Bitcoin involved in this transaction and is guaranteed by miners that only valid transactions can be included in the blockchain. To ensure that transactions that have occurred cannot be changed or removed, the miners will solve difficult problems to prove their workload.

Therefore, from the perspective of the transaction participants, the blockchain's workflow can be summarized as follows: The initiator of a transaction will write the transaction information in accordance with the specified data structure into a transaction record and then send the transaction record to the miner nodes; one of the miner nodes validates the transaction record by solving the difficult problem to complete the PoW to include the transaction record in the blockchain, forms a new block, and broadcasts the block to the entire network; the recipient of the transaction sees the blocks in the network and verifies the information in the block.

Simply and intuitively put, in Bitcoin the "mining" mechanism is employed to ensure that the concept of decentralization and the double-spend problem is addresses through a distributed network and hash chain mechanism. In fact, instead of electronic coins, only the transaction records exist in the Bitcoin system. That is, the monetary value is dependent on the existence of the transaction records, and the change in the user amount of coins is substantially the change in the transaction records. At the same time, this also means that, in a digital currency system such as Bitcoin, a transaction record that contains money-transferring information between different users is an important part of the whole system's security.

2.2 Data Structure of P2PKH Transaction Records

Therefore, to analyze the security of the cryptographic components involved and to identify potential security problems, we focus on the data structure of the transaction records, particularly the parts relevant to the cryptographic components. In the following, we will introduce the structure of the transaction record of the P2PKH protocol, which is the most commonly used protocol in Bitcoin. Such a transaction record can be seen as a series of inputs and outputs. Inputs are some transactions that can be used by a user, that is, transactions indicating there are Bitcoins transferred into a user's account that have not been spent by the user. An output is the address to which the currency will be transferred. The following is the process of constructing a new transaction record using the P2PKH protocol, described in the Bitcoin source code [26, 27].

Input: source transaction record outputs o_n, destination addresses *addr*, and currency
     amount *value* for each address to transfer into
Output: a transaction record

  // indicate where the currency used in this transaction is from
  For each source transaction record output o_n:
    $pub, priv \leftarrow$ the public and private key pairs obtained according to information
in o_n;
      $sig \leftarrow Sign_{priv}$(selected parts) ;
      $ScriptSig \leftarrow sig, pub$;
    Add $(o_n, ScriptSig)$ to the input list of this transaction record;
  End the loop
  // indicate one or more addresses to receive the Bitcoins in this transaction
  For each destination address *addr* :
    $ScriptPubKey \leftarrow DUP\ HASH160\ addr\ EQV\ CHKSIG$;
    Add $(value, ScriptPubKey)$ to the output list of this transaction record;
  End the loop
  Transaction record $T \leftarrow$ (version number, input list, output list, lock time)

By observing the definition of the class CTransaction in the Bitcoin source code
[27], we can see that a transaction record should contain the following components:

Integer variable nVersion has 32 bits and stores the version number of the current
system.

Array vin contains the source of the currency used in this transaction. The number
of elements in the array is that of the previous transactions that the initiator selected as
inputs in this transaction. Each element in the array is a CtxIn class object, occupying a
1344-bit space, in particular, that contains (1) a CoutPoint class object prevout, (2) a
Cscript class object scriptSig, and (3) a 32-bit integer nSequence, the latter of which is
used as a fixed identifier to show whether to enable the lock time.

The CoutPoint class object prevout occupies a 288-bit space and identifies the
source transactions and outputs; it contains a 256-bit hash value used to identify the
source transaction and a 32-bit integer used to indicate which output in that transaction,
corresponding to the symbol o_n in the pseudo-code above. The Cscript class object
scriptSig occupies 1024 bits of space and contains the signature and public key of the
initiator. Because the digital signature algorithm used in the Bitcoin system is ECDSA
(secp256k1 curve) and the public key adopts the uncompressed version, the signature
and public key pubkey in scriptSig takes 512 bits of space each, respectively.

Array vout specifies the account address and the amount of Bitcoins to be transferred in this transaction. The number of the array's elements is that of the destination
addresses. Each element in the array is a CtxOut class object that occupies 224 bits of
space; specifically, it contains a 32-bit integer nValue and a script scriptPubKey. The
form of the script scriptPubKey is as shown in the above pseudo-code: *DUP*,
*HASH*160, *addr*, *EQV*, *CHKSIG*, which is used to parse the subsequent operation.

Here, *DUP*, *HASH*160, *EQV*, and *CHKSIG* are OP opcodes, where each opcode is a 8-bit char-type constant, and *addr* is a public key address' 160-bit hash value; that is, the script scriptPubKey accounts for 192 bits of space totally.

Integer variable nLockTime occupies 32 bits of space and is usually set to 0. Only when the number representing the time that the transaction is broadcast to the network is greater than this value is the transaction record considered to be valid.

Figure 1 shows an example of the data format of the P2PKH protocol transaction record described above, where there is only one CtxIn class object in the array vin, which is quite a typical case in practice.

The process of generating a transaction record is the process in which an initiator completes going through the above pseudo-code as needed. It is worth noting that scriptSig in the source input array vin is not filled in at first. In fact, finally scriptSig should be the signature of a transaction initiator, and the signed message contains both the inputs and the outputs of the current transaction. Specifically, scriptSig is generated by the following process: First, the transaction information, i.e., the above nVersion, vin, vout, and nLockTime parts, will be filled out in the required data structure to

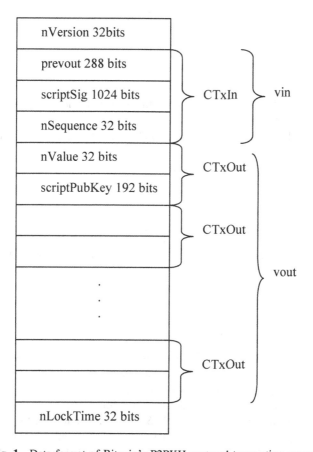

Fig. 1. Data format of Bitcoin's P2PKH protocol transaction record.

generate a temporary transaction record, in which scriptSig in vin will be filled as a temporary value—scriptPubKey in this input source script to show that the source transaction was transferred to the current initiator's account address. Second, the transaction initiator calculates the hash value of the temporary transaction record and uses his private key to sign this temporary record, and then the signature and the transaction initiator's public key will be filled into the position where in the previous step scriptSig is put as a temporary value.

2.3 Data Structure of Blocks

After receiving the transaction records written by initiators, the miners will aggregate the transaction records collected from the entire network to form a public, global, and only-increasing allowed book, i.e., the blockchain. In this way, the currency is guaranteed not to be reused. Specifically, each block will contain a combination of all existing transaction records through the Merkle tree, and a new block forms part of the entire blockchain if it passes through the mining process, which is, one of the miners needs to find a random number *nonce* that makes the hash of a block's header less than a given target value, as expressed by the formula

$$hash(header \| nonce) < target,$$

wherein the block header *header* comprises the following parts:

Integer nVersion: version number, comprising 32 bits;
hashPrevBlock: hash value of the previous block, which indicates the identity of the block, comprising 256 bits;
hashMerkleRoot: hash value computed from all transaction records by the Merkle tree hash operation, comprising 256 bits;
nTime: timestamp, comprising 32 bits; and
nBits: upper bound target value, comprising 32 bits

The mechanism of the process above is PoW; that is, the probability of generating a new block is proportional to the miner's computational power, and because the miners can get the transaction fee from this, they are hence motivated to perform these operations to confirm transaction information by generating valid blocks.

3 The Trojan Message Attack

3.1 Model of Trojan Message Attack

In 2009, Andreeva et al. proposed a new attack method for the hash function, the "Trojan" message attack [28]. The basic idea behind such attack is as follows: First, attacker A constructs in advance a Trojan message string and provides it to the victim V. V arbitrarily chooses a message prefix P from a limited set, cascades $P \| S$ to form a message, calculates the hash value $hash(P \| S)$, and sends it to A or to the public. Since the Trojan message is constructed by attacker A, if it can satisfy some specific properties, then A can successfully give a second preimage of the message.

Based on the above idea, we will show how to construct a Trojan message attack on the transaction record's data structure in Bitcoin's P2PKH protocol. It should be noted that this method will be used to generate new transaction records and blocks, rather than existing blocks. If the attack is successful, the attacker can make a transaction record in which the victim signs to transfer currency to some malicious address controlled by the attacker without the victim's knowledge, and, at the same time, the transaction record can also get through the miners' verification and hence the attacker can spend coins from it as a source input of subsequent transactions.

Our attack applies to the following scenario: Adversary A and user V reach an agreement that V will transfer Bitcoins to some designated legal accounts in a transaction, and user V uses the P2PKH-type protocol and chooses one of his own available source transactions as the input of the transaction; user V has N source transactions that can be used as an input. According to the working principle of the blockchain, the source transactions are publicly visible, but before the attack adversary A does not know which one user V will choose; adversary A cannot know the private key of user V, and, for a given message, the probability that adversary A can forge a signature is negligible.

Such a situation can occur easily as: (1) adversary A can be one of the participants in the Bitcoin blockchain system who have different accounts while others cannot tell which accounts in the whole system belong to A because of Bitcoin's pseudo-anonymity; (2) adversary A can communicate with user V so that user V agrees to transfer currency to some legitimate, visible addresses, fill in a transaction record, and then sign it; and (3) because the key management mechanism generally requires that user V's private key be isolatedly saved, adversary A needs not to know the user's private key. These conditions are not hard to achieve for attacker A practically.

3.2 Steps of the Attack

The attack focuses on the step when calculating the hash value of the temporary transaction record before calculating the script scriptSig, and it will produce the effect that adversary A can construct another temporary transaction record with the same hash value, which has the same source input transaction and output amounts as the target temporary record but different output addresses. With this attack, adversary A can replace the output list of the transaction record and broadcast it to the network. Because the miner nodes do not confirm the information with the initiator during the verification of transaction records (and in fact the miner nodes only use the initiator's public key to verify whether the information received in the transaction records can be calculated according to the corresponding signature) and the information is first compressed by the hash function into a fixed length and then signed, the miner nodes would consider the modified transaction records to be valid as the two temporary transaction records have the same hash value. At the same time, the application scenario of the attack bypasses the conditions for the existential unforgeability of ECDSA, so that adversary A can get the signature of another message without knowing the private key of user V.

Similar to the Trojan message attack of Andreeva et al. [28], in our attack, we need to use an identical prefix collision search algorithm, which takes one intermediate value of the iteration hash function as an input parameter to produce a pair of messages that start with the intermediate value and compute the same hash output value.

If we denote by H^f the hash function SHA256's iterative compression function [29, 30] and define $|x|$ as the length of bit string x, where the symbol $||$ indicates concatenation of the bit strings, then the attack process of adversary A proceeds as follows:

(1) Fill user V's available transaction sources in the data structure of the temporary transaction record, which includes nVersion (32 bits), prevout (288 bits), and scriptSig (192 bits; actually, it is the script scriptPubKey to which a transaction's output *prevout* corresponds) and denote the filled information by $P^i, i = 1, 2, \cdots, N$.

(2) Arbitrarily select n_0 addresses as the output addresses and amounts in the transaction, fill each of the n_0 address and amount information into the CtxOut class object, and denote this by S_0, which takes a space of $224 \cdot n_0$ bits such that $|P_i| + 224 \cdot n_0$ is an integer multiple of 512, as 512 is the block size of input to each SHA256's iterative compression function according to the Merkle–Damgard construction.

(3) Use H^f to calculate the iterated compression values $h_0^i, i = 1, 2, \cdots, N$ for $P^i || S_0, i = 1, 2, \cdots, N$.

(4) Use the following method to calculate N pairs of messages $(S_i, T_i), i = 1, 2, \cdots, N$ that can generate collisions:

For each $i = 1$ to N

    Construct candidate lists $List_S, List_T$;

    Choose $S_i \in List_S, T_i \in List_T$ such that $H^{n_2, f}(h_{i-1}^i, S_i) = H^{n_2, f}(h_{i-1}^i, T_i)$;

    For each $j = 1$ to N

        $h_i^j \leftarrow H^{n_2, f}(h_{i-1}^j, S_i)$;

    The loop ends

The loop ends

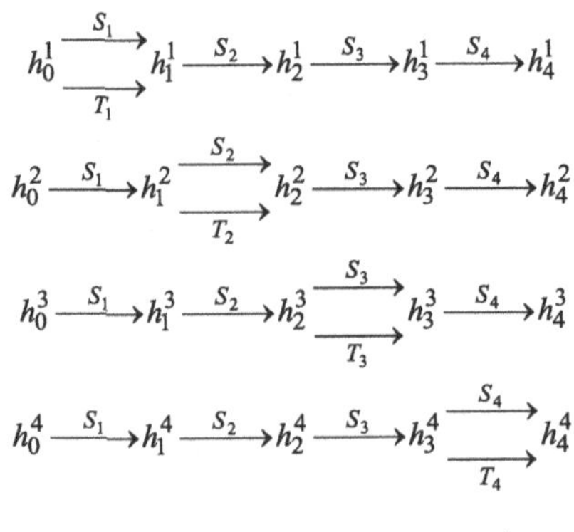

$$h_0^1 \xrightarrow[T_1]{S_1} h_1^1 \xrightarrow{S_2} h_2^1 \xrightarrow{S_3} h_3^1 \xrightarrow{S_4} h_4^1$$

$$h_0^2 \xrightarrow{S_1} h_1^2 \xrightarrow[T_2]{S_2} h_2^2 \xrightarrow{S_3} h_3^2 \xrightarrow{S_4} h_4^2$$

$$h_0^3 \xrightarrow{S_1} h_1^3 \xrightarrow{S_2} h_2^3 \xrightarrow[T_3]{S_3} h_3^3 \xrightarrow{S_4} h_4^3$$

$$h_0^4 \xrightarrow{S_1} h_1^4 \xrightarrow{S_2} h_2^4 \xrightarrow{S_3} h_3^4 \xrightarrow[T_4]{S_4} h_4^4$$

Fig. 2. Computation of each h_i^j.

Specifically, for each $i = 1$ to N, first, when the candidate list $List_S$ is being constructed, each candidate S_i contains n_1 CtxOut class objects; that is, it contains n_1 legal output addresses and amounts $v_j, j = 1, 2, \cdots, n_1$, where n_1 satisfies that $224 \cdot n_1$ is an integer multiple of 512 (where we denote $\frac{224 \cdot n_1}{512} = n_2$, and n_2 is an integer, for example, if $n_1 = 16$ is selected, then $n_2 = 7$) and $\sum_{j=1}^{n_1} v_j < \frac{V_i}{N}$ (where V_i is the amount of Bitcoins available in the source input corresponding to P^i); second, when the candidate list $List_T$ is being constructed, each candidate T_i also contains n_1 CtxOut class objects, where the 160-bit address in one of them is controlled by attacker A and the other $n_1 - 1$ addresses are random legal ones, and the output amounts are also $v_j, j = 1, 2, \cdots, n_1$. After that, by using a sort-and-match technique, for each element T in $List_T$, calculate $H^{n_2 f}(h^i_{i-1}, T)$ and test whether there is an element S in $List_S$ such that $H^{n_2 f}(h^i_{i-1}, S)$ equals the value; if there are any, take out the pair of elements and denote them by (S_i, T_i), where the symbol $H^{n_2 f}(h^i_{i-1}, x)$ represents the hash value of message x computed by using H^f as the iterative compression function, h^i_{i-1} as the initial value, and n_2 as the number of iteration times; then, as shown in Fig. 2, taking S_i, which have just been found as the message, compute each $h^j_i \leftarrow H^{n_2 f}(h^j_{i-1}, S_i)$, in which h^{i+1}_i will be used for the next collision message search.

(5) For $i = 1, 2, \cdots, N$, calculate the remaining amount that needs to be transferred to the last output address (that is, the address of user V) according to $P^i, S_0, S_1, \cdots, S_N$, nLockTime, the padded bits of hash function's requirements, and denote these as message block S^i_{N+1}. Calculate the final inner hash value $h^i_{N+1} = H^f(h^i_N, S^i_{N+1})$ of the temporary transaction records by taking each P^i as the prefix message and the outer hash values $SHA256(h^i_{N+1})$.

(6) Adversary A sends to user V a string of output addresses and amounts $S_0, S_1, \cdots, S_N$. Because these addresses are meaningful and legal, adversary A can make user V agree to transfer the Bitcoin currency to these target accounts.

(7) User V chooses an available transaction source (numbered i_0) and completes the filling in of the temporary transaction record, i.e., getting $P^{i_0} \| S_0 \| S_1 \| \cdots \| S_N \| S^{i_0}_{N+1}$, calculating its hash value with the function SHA256 (SHA256 (.)), and uses this hash value for subsequent operations including formal scriptSig signature generation, filling in the complete transaction record, and sending the final record to the network.

(8) After this transaction record sent by user V is collected into the blockchain by miners, adversary A can see the transaction record and obtains the information that user V has selected the transaction source of number i_0. At this time, the adversary can forge a new temporary transaction record $P^{i_0} \| S_0 \| S_1 \| \cdots \| T_{i_0} \| \cdots \| S_N \| S^{i_0}_{N+1}$. According to the above process, its signature is the same as the formal scriptSig signature sent by user V, and hence adversary A has obtained a forged transaction record. At this time, it is equivalent to say that user V has transferred coins into the address in T_{i_0}.

Figure 3 shows the whole flow of the attack:

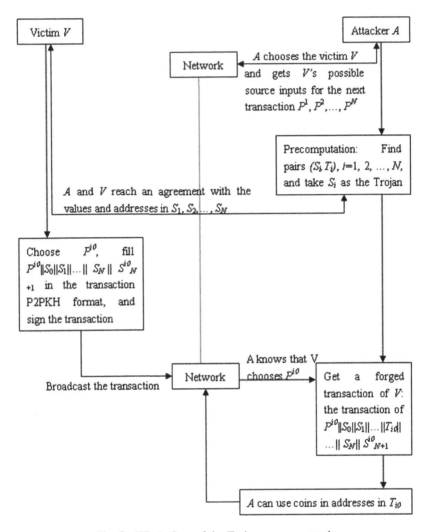

Fig. 3. Whole flow of the Trojan message attack.

3.3   Complexity of the Attack

In the following, we analyze the complexity of the attack method described above. It can be seen that, in the above attack, except for step (4), the other steps are direct steps such as filling and modifying that do not need additional calculations. Consequently, the entire attack requires nontrivial complexity for step (4) only; hence, we need to analyze the complexity of this step. According to the birthday attack principle (balanced case), for each $i = 1$ to N, if we want to find a collision that satisfies the condition, the number of elements included in either of the candidate lists should be greater than $2^{n/2}$, for the compression function H^f of n-bit output length (where, in SHA256, $n = 256$). That is, adversary A can select $|List_S| = |List_T| = 2^{n/2}$, so the complexity of the collision search phase is also $2^{n/2}$. In addition, in this step, also the computation $h_i^j \leftarrow H^{n_2,f}(h_{i-1}^j, S_i)$ is conducted N times; that is, it is an n_2 times of H^f compression function evaluation operation. In summary, the time complexity of the attack algorithm is $N \cdot 2^{n/2} + N^2 \cdot n_2 = O(N \cdot 2^{n/2})$.

It can be seen that the above attack constructs a new temporary transaction record that has the same hash value as the original temporary transaction record. Therefore, the above attack can also be regarded as a second preimage attack, for which the complexity $N \cdot 2^{128}$ is much lower than the security strength setting 2^{256} of the blockchain as the hash function used is SHA256.

Although the complexity seems to be high and impractical at present, the attack proposed still makes sense. The first reason is that cryptographic primitives usually break gradually, instead of abruptly breaking completely, as also mentioned by Giechaskiel et al. [26]. Theoretically, in cryptanalysis an attack is called successful if its complexity is less than that of a brute-force attack. Hence, as a second preimage attack with complexity of order 2^{128}, which is exponentially much less than 2^{256} (the complexity of a brute-force attack), the attack proposed in this paper is meaningful. The second reason is that no plan or adequate mechanism for such an attack has been built into Bitcoin or even considered for updates of Bitcoin in the future. Consequently, with the rapidly increasing computational power, it will be dangerous to leave a gap between the attack and current-version Bitcoin alone without deploying a proper treatment.

In addition, if there is a more efficient identical prefix collision search algorithm for the SHA256 function to be used in step (4), such as Stevens [16–18] mentioned, the complexity of such a collision search algorithm is 2^{16} for the hash function MD5, which also has a Merkle–Damgard iteration structure, and for the hash function SHA-1 in the same SHA series the complexity of this type of collision search algorithm is $2^{77.1}$, which is much lower than the security strength setting, so the attack method in this paper will be more effective. Another piece of evidence to indicate that such attacks might be potentially practical is the result shown by Mendel et al. [31] that collisions exist for 31/64-steps reduced number of rounds SHA256 with $2^{65.5}$ operations and the improvements shown by Kortelainen et al. [32] that Trojan message attacks can be conducted in more efficient ways.

4   Conclusions

In summary, we have constructed the steps for and studied the theoretical complexity of a Trojan message attack, the new kind of cryptanalysis attack to Bitcoin. Such an attack is based on the fact that all users' candidate input transactions are open to the attacker and employs a combination of the Bitcoin transaction structure with standard Merkle–Damgard extension vulnerabilities. Conditions for an attacker to launch the attack have been identified, revealing that they are not difficult to reach for malicious participants in Bitcoin's blockchain system. Because of the potential practicability and harmful effects that the attack brings, appropriate and effective contingency plans for updating Bitcoin's P2PKH protocol are needed. Also, it is crucial to anticipate the impact of partial breakage or weakening of a cryptography primitive caused by data format and other public information in the blockchain when revising Bitcoin and designing other cryptocurrency systems in the future.

References

1. Nakamoto, S.: bitcoin: A Peer-to-Peer Electronic Cash System (2008)
2. Bonneau, J., Miller, A., Clark, J., et al.: SoK: research perspectives and challenges for bitcoin and cryptocurrencies. In: 2015 IEEE Symposium on Security and Privacy, pp. 104–121. IEEE (2015)
3. Garay, J., Kiayias, A., Leonardos, N.: The bitcoin backbone protocol: analysis and applications. In: Oswald, E., Fischlin, M. (eds.) EUROCRYPT 2015. LNCS, vol. 9057, pp. 281–310. Springer, Heidelberg (2015). https://doi.org/10.1007/978-3-662-46803-6_10
4. Miers, I., Garman, C., Green, M., et al.: Zerocoin: anonymous distributed e-cash from bitcoin. In: 2013 IEEE Symposium on Security and Privacy, pp. 397–411. IEEE (2013)
5. Sasson, E.B., Chiesa, A., Garman, C., et al.: Zerocash: decentralized anonymous payments from bitcoin. In: 2014 IEEE Symposium on Security and Privacy, pp. 459–474. IEEE (2014)
6. Eyal, I., Sirer, E.G.: Majority is not enough: bitcoin mining is vulnerable. In: Christin, N., Safavi-Naini, R. (eds.) FC 2014. LNCS, vol. 8437, pp. 436–454. Springer, Heidelberg (2014). https://doi.org/10.1007/978-3-662-45472-5_28
7. Velner, Y., Teutsch, J., Luu, L.: Smart contracts make bitcoin mining pools vulnerable. IACR Cryptology ePrint Archive, 2017:230 (2017)
8. Kwon, Y., Kim, D., Son, Y., Choi, J., Kim, Y.: Doppelganger in bitcoin mining pools: an analysis of the duplication share attack. In: Choi, D., Guilley, S. (eds.) WISA 2016. LNCS, vol. 10144, pp. 124–135. Springer, Cham (2017). https://doi.org/10.1007/978-3-319-56549-1_11
9. Dmitrienko, A., Noack, D., Yung, M.: Secure wallet-assisted offline bitcoin payments with double-spender revocation. In: Proceedings of the 2017 ACM Asia Conference on Computer and Communications Security, pp. 520–531. ACM (2017)
10. Gervais, A., Ritzdorf, H., Karame, G.O., et al.: Tampering with the delivery of blocks and transactions in bitcoin. In: Proceedings of the 22nd ACM SIGSAC Conference on Computer and Communications Security, pp. 692–705. ACM (2015)
11. Heilman, E., Kendler, A., Zohar, A., et al.: Eclipse attacks on bitcoin's peer-to-peer network. In: USENIX Security Symposium, pp. 129–144 (2015)
12. Liao, K., Katz, J.: Incentivizing blockchain forks via whale transactions. In: Brenner, M., et al. (eds.) FC 2017. LNCS, vol. 10323, pp. 264–279. Springer, Cham (2017). https://doi.org/10.1007/978-3-319-70278-0_17
13. Bartoletti, M., Pompianu, L.: An analysis of bitcoin OP_RETURN metadata. In: Brenner, M., et al. (eds.) FC 2017. LNCS, vol. 10323, pp. 218–230. Springer, Cham (2017). https://doi.org/10.1007/978-3-319-70278-0_14
14. McCorry, P., Shahandashti, S.F., Hao, F.: Refund attacks on bitcoin's payment protocol. In: Grossklags, J., Preneel, B. (eds.) FC 2016. LNCS, vol. 9603, pp. 581–599. Springer, Heidelberg (2017). https://doi.org/10.1007/978-3-662-54970-4_34
15. Bonneau, J.: Why buy when you can rent? In: Clark, J., Meiklejohn, S., Ryan, P.Y.A., Wallach, D., Brenner, M., Rohloff, K. (eds.) FC 2016. LNCS, vol. 9604, pp. 19–26. Springer, Heidelberg (2016). https://doi.org/10.1007/978-3-662-53357-4_2

16. Stevens, M., Lenstra, A.K., De Weger, B.: Chosen-prefix collisions for MD5 and applications. Int. J. Appl. Cryptogr. **2**(4), 322–359 (2012)
17. Stevens, M., et al.: Short chosen-prefix collisions for MD5 and the creation of a rogue CA certificate. In: Halevi, S. (ed.) CRYPTO 2009. LNCS, vol. 5677, pp. 55–69. Springer, Heidelberg (2009). https://doi.org/10.1007/978-3-642-03356-8_4
18. Stevens, M.: New collision attacks on SHA-1 based on optimal joint local-collision analysis. In: Johansson, T., Nguyen, P.Q. (eds.) EUROCRYPT 2013. LNCS, vol. 7881, pp. 245–261. Springer, Heidelberg (2013). https://doi.org/10.1007/978-3-642-38348-9_15
19. Bhargavan, K., Leurent, G.: Transcript collision attacks: breaking authentication in TLS, IKE, and SSH. In: Network and Distributed System Security Symposium, NDSS 2016 (2016)
20. Mavrogiannopoulos, N., Vercauteren, F., Velichkov, V., et al.: A cross-protocol attack on the TLS protocol. In: Proceedings of the 2012 ACM Conference on Computer and Communications Security, pp. 62–72. ACM (2012)
21. Vaudenay, S.: Security flaws induced by CBC padding—applications to SSL, IPSEC, WTLS.... In: Knudsen, L.R. (ed.) EUROCRYPT 2002. LNCS, vol. 2332, pp. 534–545. Springer, Heidelberg (2002). https://doi.org/10.1007/3-540-46035-7_35
22. Zheng, Z., Zhao, C., Fan, H., et al.: A key backup scheme based on bitcoin. IACR Cryptology ePrint Archive, 2017:704 (2017)
23. Abusalah, H., Alwen, J., Cohen, B., Khilko, D., Pietrzak, K., Reyzin, L.: Beyond Hellman's time-memory trade-offs with applications to proofs of space. In: Takagi, T., Peyrin, T. (eds.) ASIACRYPT 2017. LNCS, vol. 10625, pp. 357–379. Springer, Cham (2017). https://doi.org/10.1007/978-3-319-70697-9_13
24. Dinur, I., Nadler, N.: Time-memory tradeoff attacks on the MTP proof-of-work scheme. In: Katz, J., Shacham, H. (eds.) CRYPTO 2017. LNCS, vol. 10402, pp. 375–403. Springer, Cham (2017). https://doi.org/10.1007/978-3-319-63715-0_13
25. Biryukov, A., Khovratovich, D.: Egalitarian computing. In: Holz, T., Savage, S. (eds.) 25th USENIX Security Symposium, USENIX Security 16, Austin, TX, USA, 10–12 August 2016, pp. 315–326. USENIX Association (2016)
26. Giechaskiel, I., Cremers, C., Rasmussen, K.B.: On bitcoin security in the presence of broken cryptographic primitives. In: Askoxylakis, I., Ioannidis, S., Katsikas, S., Meadows, C. (eds.) ESORICS 2016. LNCS, vol. 9879, pp. 201–222. Springer, Cham (2016). https://doi.org/10.1007/978-3-319-45741-3_11
27. bitcoincore.org. bitcoin core. https://github.com/bitcoin/bitcoin
28. Andreeva, E., Bouillaguet, C., Dunkelman, O., et al.: Herding, second preimage and Trojan message attacks beyond Merkle-Damgård. Sel. Areas Cryptogr. **5867**, 393–414 (2009)
29. Menezes, A.J., Van Oorschot, P.C., Vanstone, S.A.: Handbook of Applied Cryptography. CRC Press, Boca Raton (1996)
30. Standard SH: Federal Information Processing Standard Publication 180-2, US Department of Commerce, National Institute of Standards and Technology (NIST) (2002) csrc.nist.gov/publications/fips/fips180-2/fips180-2withchangenotice.pdf
31. Mendel, F., Nad, T., Schläffer, M.: Improving local collisions: new attacks on reduced SHA-256. In: Johansson, T., Nguyen, P.Q. (eds.) EUROCRYPT 2013. LNCS, vol. 7881, pp. 262–278. Springer, Heidelberg (2013). https://doi.org/10.1007/978-3-642-38348-9_16
32. Kortelainen, T., Kortelainen, J.: On diamond structures and Trojan message attacks. In: Sako, K., Sarkar, P. (eds.) ASIACRYPT 2013. LNCS, vol. 8270, pp. 524–539. Springer, Heidelberg (2013). https://doi.org/10.1007/978-3-642-42045-0_27

Blockchain-Based Implementation of Smart Contract and Risk Management for Interest Rate Swap

Xiaowei Ding[1,3]([✉]) and Hongyao Zhu[2,3]

[1] School of Information Management, Nanjing University,
163 Xianlin Road, Nanjing 210023, China
dingxiaowei@nju.edu.cn
[2] Kuang Yaming Honors School, Nanjing University,
163 Xianlin Road, Nanjing 210023, China
[3] Inclusive & Rural Financial Technology Innovation Research Center,
Nanjing University, 163 Xianlin Road, Nanjing 210023, China

Abstract. Blockchain is a decentralized infrastructure that has attracted more and more attention from financial institutions due to its irreplaceable advantages. We implemented a blockchain solution for interest rate swap based on the Corda platform. Based on Andersen et al. [8], we derive a risk estimation model for blockchain empowered interest rate swap trading. We conjecture that most of problems in today's derivative markets could potentially be relieved. For example, through our numerical experiment, we find that with blockchain, both the expected risk exposure and dynamic initial margin decrease significantly, which reduces the risk in interest rate swap trading and increases market liquidity. At the same time, we expect the Effective Expected Positive Exposure (EEPE) in the Basel III standard to decrease. Next, we plan to conduct more mathematical and numerical analysis and continue working on improving our blockchain based trading implementation and risk management model.

Keywords: Blockchain · R3 · Corda · Risk Weighted Assets (RWA) · Effective expected positive exposure(EEPE) · Dynamic initial margin · Variation margin · Interest rate swap · Risk management · Basel III

1 Introduction

Blockchain is the technology foundation of Bitcoin, which first appeared in Satoshi Nakamoto's "Bitcoin: a peer-to peer electronic cash system" [1].

In traditional financial industry, data are segregated in silos. Synchronizing data between different ledgers requires a large amount of manual work, which is time-consuming and costly, not to say conducting "big data analysis" effectively. It is said the "data silo challenge" might be one of the root causes for the 2008 financial crisis. Blockchain technology may help eliminate a large part of this problem [2]. Besides, due to low margining frequency, the risk of interest rate swap derivatives is high even when banks and financial institutions post large initial and variation margin to protect themselves from risk. This leads to high default risk and low market liquidity. Our blockchain

X. Si et al. (Eds.): CBCC 2019, CCIS 1176, pp. 210–219, 2020.
https://doi.org/10.1007/978-981-15-3278-8_14

approach could hopefully alleviate these problems. Moreover, as our blockchain-based implementation substantially simplifies the traditional default process and time-line, we expect the risk management process will change accordingly. Therefore we developed a risk estimation model in accordance to our blockchain approach. Our experiment shows that not only the default process is substantially simplified, but also the risks are reduced and hence the margins needed are reduced significantly.

Our work is based on Corda platform. It can handle arbitrary data types so many kinds of smart contracts can be implemented on this platform. Besides, the contract only contains functions, so contracts do not "have any kind of mutable storage" [2].

The remainder of the paper is structured as follows. In Sect. 2 we introduce the background of our problem. In Sect. 3 we overview related works. In Sect. 4 we present the challenges in the current market. In Sect. 5 we present our approach. In Sect. 6 we present the evaluation and discuss the results, along with our thoughts on future works. We conclude with Sect. 7.

2 Background

2.1 Interest Rate Swap

In the derivatives market, the rise of blockchain may help reduce costs and increase efficiency [3]. According to Basel III, banks will have to report the Effective Expected Positive Exposure (EEPE) to the regulatory authorities to calculate the Risk Weighted Assets (RWA). The definition of EEPE is given in formula (1).

$$\text{EEPE(t)} = \frac{1}{t} \int_0^t \max_{u \in [0,s]} \mathbf{E}[E(u)] ds \tag{1}$$

Here, $\mathbf{E}[E(u)]$ is the expected positive exposure of certain derivatives. Regulatory authorities usually require that the ratio of core capital and RWA of a bank be greater than 10%. If we reduce the expected exposure of certain derivatives, the bank will have to lock-up less core capital and thus its asset liquidity can increase.

In this article, we focus on interest rate swaps. An interest rate swap is a forward contract in which two parties sign a series of future interest payments to be exchanged based on a specified notional amount. Interest rate swap usually involves exchange of a float interest for a fixed rate at the specified time in accordance with the contract [4, 5]. It is very effective as an interest rate hedging instrument and a liability management tool [4], and can also help reduce financing costs [6]. As a result, the total notional amount of interest rate swap has increased gradually since 1999 [7], and it has become one of the most important financial products.

Here, we define a set of terminology and notions [8]:

- B: The bank side. All the subsequent calculations and definitions are based on the perspective of the bank.
- C: The counterparty, that is, the party that may default.
- Risk exposure: The quantified potential for loss as a result of an investment.
- Expected risk exposure: The expected value of risk exposure in the model.

- Fixed leg: The party who will be paying the fixed rate.
- Floating leg: The party who will be paying the floating rate.
- Counterparty risk: The risk to parties in the contract that the counterparty will not fulfill its obligations.
- VM: Variation margin. It is a variable margin paid by participants to their respective clearing houses in a transaction because of the adverse price movements of the futures contracts they hold.
- IM: Initial margin. It provides additional default protection for banks. Typically, it is calculated at the beginning of the trade.
- Dynamic IM: Dynamically refreshed IM to "cover portfolio-level close-out risk" [8].

2.2 Corda Platform

The Corda platform is a distributed ledger developed by R3 Alliance consisting mutually untrusted nodes.

Compared to Bitcoin, the Corda platform can handle with any typed data rather than only the quantities of bitcoin in a Bitcoin transaction. Besides, only one part of the contracts is used to synchronize the whole system so that the function is "pure and stateless" [2]. Also, the platform will "operate under the assumption of an adversarial security environment" [2], which means we must consider the condition of growing threat of cybercrime.

The Corda platform supports smart contracts defined by Clack, Bakshi, and Braine [9]. Smart contracts are generally executed automatically but also support manual input and control. Smart contracts can link business logic and data to relevant laws and regulations so that financial contracts on the platform have legal enforcement [2]. The Corda platform is based on contract states objects as shown in Fig. 1. It ensures that all participants can maintain consensus when the contract state changes.

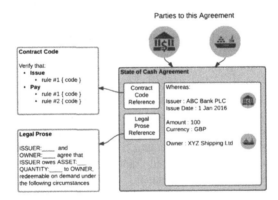

Fig. 1. Diagram of a state object representing a cash claim of £100 against a commercial bank, owned by a fictional shipping company [2].

The Corda platform updates the records of state objects through transactions. Each transaction overwrites the existing state object and generate new state objects [2].

3   Related Work

Prior to our research, there was also a program implementation for interest rate swap in the case of non-blockchain [10]. However, the interest rate curve was pre-set and could not be updated in real time. There were also papers about "central bank money on blockchain" [11] but they only discuss possible scenarios without an actual implementation. In [12] the authors discussed secure derivative contracts for Ethereum. It allows certain derivative contracts to be traded but it lacks precise timing due to Ethereum's causal timestamps. In [13], blockchain based currency forward contract were implemented and it was observed to reduce concentration and counterparty risk.

There are also many models capturing the risk exposure and market value of interest rate swap products, but these models have many problems. Sometimes, in order to simplify the mathematical derivation, or to speed up the calculation, many assumptions and simplifications are made in modeling, such as assuming zero default risk in the transaction process [14], or assuming symmetrical risk of both sides in the transaction [15]. However, the details of OTC (over-the-counter) derivatives trading are complicated. Simplification of models may lead to model errors or model risks, resulting in a great difference between the model predictions and the actual data [16–20].

4   Challenges

Currently, without blockchain technology, time-consuming and manual effort are necessary to keep disparate ledgers synchronized, which may be replaced with blockchain transformation. Besides, due to the low margining frequency, the risk exposure of interest rate swaps is still high even with the protection of large IM, which decrease the liquidity of banks and financial institutions.

There are two kinds of cash flows, which are transaction flows and margin flows, between the parties involved in an interest rate swap. Transaction flow is brought by transaction itself, including contract cash flow, physical settlement, etc. According to ISDA/CSA, once delay happened in a transaction flow, which is regarded as a serious credit event, it will lead to a default alert, or even a transaction interruption. However, when the two parties exchange margin flows, there may be delay due to disputes. In the current market, margin disputes not only have subjective reasons, but also have objective reasons including the inconsistency of valuation models of bilateral transactions mentioned above. The subjective reason is that some counterparties will deliberately use margin disputes to procrastinate the transaction time, which is often the prelude to default. But banks are often reluctant to immediately take unilateral measures and make a default warning.

Since the 2008 financial crisis, most large financial institutions recalculate their VM values on a daily basis and have required margin calls from counterparties based on the results. In practice, however, it often takes a few days for financial institutions to actually acquire the collateral after the valuation and calculation of the collateral. Take banks as an example. Suppose the bank collects and solidifies the market data after the market closes on day 1. Usually it can only evaluate the collateral during the working hours and notify the counterparty on day 2, and successfully collect the collateral at least on day 3. This is one of the main reasons why the collateral VM cannot completely offset the risk of the counterparty's default. There are also a number of simplified models in practical applications that assume that the bank's daily calculated collateral is real-time, and the collateral's coverage and protection is real-time and sufficient, and such idealized simplification leads to great model risks.

Based on Andersen, Pykhtin and Sokol [8], we analyze the risk exposures theoretically from the perspective of banks. In this work, we take the risks caused by the inability to clear the collateral in a timely manner into consideration.

5 Our Blockchain Approach

Next, we propose a solution based on blockchain.

1. Assume that cash flow operations such as trade flows and margin flows occur on an integer lattice of Δ (For example, assume that Δ equals to one hour).
2. Both parties confirm the jointly accepted valuation model and margin model before the transaction begins, and write the smart contract to be solidified into the blockchain. It will run automatically, so there will be no dispute in the future.
3. Smart contracts automatically perform real-time valuations (here assuming the portfolio valuation is fast enough) every Δ hours and transfer corresponding assets instantly.
4. After entering the breach procedure, the smart contract may call other smart contracts to execute operations that have been agreed in the contract.
5. Suppose that the parties agree to give a grace period of ϕ for such delay as default. (For example, assume that $\phi = 2\Delta$).

We can first implement the automatic adjustment of the interest rate swap transaction flow based on externally provided market rate data. Based on this, hourly atomic payment operations are implemented according to the atomic payment process designed as follows.

Algorithm 1: Framework of atomic swap in our system

Input: *Data class* : *Contract with hash(key), cash to pay*
Output: *Transaction*
1 *B generates and sends the Contract to C*;
2 **if** *Contract.cash $\equiv$ cash to pay* **then**
3   C pays the cash flow;
4 **if** *The amount of money B received $\equiv$ cash to pay* **then**
5   B sends the key to C;
6 **else**
7   B sends 0 to C;
8 **if** *hash(the key C received) $\equiv$ Contract.hash(key)* **then**
9   C redeems the Contract;

Here, the password can be either artificially input or automatically generated by transaction time. The atomic payment process is shown in Fig. 2.

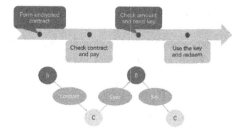

Fig. 2. Sketch map for atomic swap process.

In Corda platform, the atomic swap starts when B begins to generate and send encrypted smart contract to C. After C automatically checks the amount of the payment according to the contract and market rate data provided, C will transfer cash to B. Then B will check the cash flow and send C the key. Finally, C will use the key to redeem the contract to obtain B's cash flow.

The implementation of atomic swap process is combination of two advantages of the Corda platform. First, *EventScheduling* method is used in this smart contract. Smart contracts can inherit the *SchedulableState* class and implement the *nextScheduledActivity* function, enabling it to automatically run events at a specified time. There are two kinds of timed events. One is to update the floating rate floating leg needs to pay based on the provided market rate data. The other is to exchange cash flows according to the schedule in the contract. Second, in the Corda platform, when two parties in the transaction communicate, if one cannot receive the required information (cash flows or password transmissions for atomic payment process), the process stops and the platform reports an error. These features make sure that Corda smart contracts can run atomic swaps according to the above timeline.

In a non-blockchain scenario, the atomic payment process can only be achieved by a trusted third party, because the two steps of checking cash amount and sending redemption password cannot be bounded. The cash and password need to be handed over to the trusted third party first. This will lead to delay in trading and higher counterparty and concentration risks. Blockchain implementations make sure that receiving cash and sending redemption passwords are bounded together, thus achieving point-to-point real-time transactions, increasing the speed of transactions and reducing the risk.

However, in current blockchain implementation, after errors are reported, the electronic notification letters sent by the smart contract may not have legal-binding effect. In this sense, the operation of smart contracts has to be semi-automatic. With the rise of Internet Court [21], the process can become more and more automatic gradually.

In our design, cash flow transactions are scheduled for the working hours of both parties (assumed here to be between 9 a.m. and 5 p.m. local time). Once an error occurs, it can be guaranteed that a staff member will promptly handle it and notify the transaction parties to terminate the transaction in advance and proceed to the next step. Moreover, electronic legal notice that are recognized by the Internet Courts can be used.

6 Evaluation and Discussion

In response to the characteristics of blockchain atomic payment, we have retrofitted the traditional default timeline. Here we assume that the grace period $\phi = 2\Delta$.

1. Time $T - \Delta$: C paid the cash flow in full for the last time, including margin and transaction flow.
2. Time T: At this time, a suspected breach of contract occurred in C, failing to submit the deposit or delivery transaction in full and on time. At this point, the smart contract begins to report errors, and B must issue an electronic reminder letter in time. As explained in the smart contract feature above, the payment is an atomic operation, and C does not update the margin at the same time, and temporarily deducts all transaction flow operations.
3. Time $T + \Delta$: No operations while both sides are waiting for the solution.
4. Time $T + 2\Delta$: At this time, our assumed grace time has been up. If C's problem is solved, the margin flow and transaction flow will resume as usual; if C's problem has not been solved, the default procedure will be entered, and an electronic notification letter with legal effect will be issued to notify the parties of the transaction to terminate early. At this point, we can call other smart contracts to automatically inquire on the block chain and seek the average. Other operations that are agreed upon at the contract can also be executed in order to clear, settle and transfer fund immediately.

Based on Andersen, Pykhtin & Sokol [8], we take the time required for one party to fail to pay the margin until the other party confirms the counterparty's default as a model parameter. Then, using Local Gaussian Approximation, we can get an effective ratio of IM, that is, expected risk exposure with IM divided by expected risk exposure without IM. In Local Gaussian Approximation, we can define IM in formula (2).

$$IM(t) = Q_q(V(t) - V(t - 3\Delta)|\mathcal{F}_{t-3\Delta}) \tag{2}$$

Here q is the confidence of quantile Q, V(t) is the market value of interest rate swap. Based on Andersen, Pykhtin and Sokol [8], the risk exposure is defined in formula (3).

$$E(t) = [V(t) - V(t - 3\Delta) - IM(t)]^+ \tag{3}$$

We can calculate the risk exposure of the same interest rate swap twice, one under the current market practice and the other under our blockchain approach. At present, the Monte Carlo method is commonly used to calculate the IM and risk exposure for each example (path). In the calculation process, a method of simulating the risk factor and the transaction flow at a daily frequency is usually employed [22–26].

The risk exposure can be calculated using Open Source Risk Engine which is an open source software for financial quantitative analysis [29, 30]. The software offers a Monte Carlo framework to calculate V(t) of given derivative so that we can do the simulation using our own model.

After increasing the margining frequency, it can be expected that the aforementioned problems in current industry practice can be greatly alleviated. In particular, there will be smaller risk peaks in risk exposure due to unilateral payments, as shown in our numerical simulation [27, 28].

In the simulation, the notional amount is $10,000,000 with 0.02 fixed interest rate, fixed legs and floating legs are paid quarterly. The following plots were obtained by comparing our simulation results with the data in the literature [8].

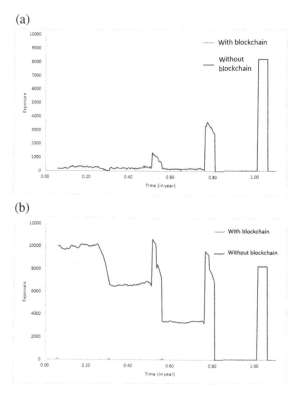

Fig. 3. (a). Expected exposure with IM protection with and without blockchain. (b). Expected exposure without IM protection with and without blockchain.

We can see from Fig. 3a and b that the expected risk exposure of interest rate swaps is lower than that of traditional market models regardless of protection by IM. Especially in the case with IM protection, the expected exposure approaches 0 in blockchain circumstance.

As the expected risk exposure is an estimation of the risk of a financial derivative, we can see from the plots that in general, the interest rate swap trading under our blockchain approach has lower risk than under current market practice. There are peaks near transaction flows because B is always the net payer when transaction flow exists, which leads to the upward peaks in the exposure value. When the counterparty does not post the margin, the party must continue to pay the transaction flow and submit the collateral without the counterparty paying the collateral because it cannot confirm whether it has really defaulted. In case of transaction expiration, etc., the party even has to return the collateral that the counterparty has paid. And peaks will appear in the numerical plot. When the peaks appear, the dealer lost protection and increase exposure. These greatly reduce the effectiveness of margin. And with atomic swap, such unilateral payment will reduce and risk peaks will be smaller.

In summary, thanks to the atomic swap, blockchain helps increase margining frequency and makes near-real time clearing possible. Under our blockchain model, the interest rate swaps will be safer and banks will have to pay less IM to protect the derivative. As a result, banks can reduce risk and improve liquidity while trading. Next, we plan to conduct more mathematical and numerical analysis and continue working on improving our blockchain based trading and risk management implementation.

7 Conclusion

Under current industry practice, there are a number of issues in interest rate swap trading, clearing and risk management. There are inaccurate pricing problems for existing interest rate swap products, and there is also large risk exposure due to low margining frequency. It can be shown intuitively thru numerical simulations: there is an upward spike in the expected risk exposure near each trading flow, which necessitates a higher initial margin amount. Despite of the larger initial margin amount, the interest rate swap is still not well protected.

One of our main contributions is that we implemented a blockchain program to realize atomic swap for interest rate swap. We also ran numerical simulations to show that blockchain does help alleviate problems mentioned above. By using blockchain, we can not only automatically adjust the transaction cash flow to be paid by both sides according to the floating interest rate announced by the market periodically, but also design an atomic transaction process to increase margining frequency. As a result, with blockchain, we can reduce the required initial margin amount and the expected risk exposure of the transaction.

In addition, since all transaction records are stored in the blockchain, the transaction process is more convenient for government regulation, which renders fair, transparent and near-real time penetrative supervision possible.

References

1. Nakamoto, S.: Bitcoin: a peer-to peer electronic cash system. https://bitcoin.org/bitcoin.pdf
2. Brown, R.G., Carlyle, J., Grigg, I., et al.: Corda: An introduction. R3 CEV, August 2016
3. Swan, M.: Blockchain: Blueprint for a New Economy. O'Reilly Media Inc., USA (2015)
4. Bicksler, J., Chen, A.H.: An economic analysis of interest rate swaps. J. Financ. **41**, 645–655 (1986). https://doi.org/10.1111/j.1540-6261.1986.tb04527.x
5. Brigo, D., Mercurio, F.: Interest Rate Models-Theory and Practice: with Smile, Inflation and Credit. Springer Finance. Springer Science & Business Media, Heidelberg (2007). https://doi.org/10.1007/978-3-540-34604-3

6. Wall, L.D.: Interest rate swaps in an agency theoretic model with uncertain interest rates. J. Bank. Financ. **13**(2), 261–270 (1989)
7. BIS statistics Explorer: Table D7. https://stats.bis.org/statx/srs/table/d7. Accessed 01 Oct 2018
8. Andersen, L.B.G.. Pykhtin, M., Sokol, A.: Rethinking Margin Period of Risk (2016). https://ssrn.com/abstract=2719964
9. Clack, B., Braine, L.: Smart Contract Templates: foundations, design landscape and research directions (2016). http://arxiv.org/abs/1608.00771
10. Mosler, W.B., McCauley, W.P., Sherman, J.M.: Method, system, and computer program product for trading interest rate swaps. Patent 6,304,858. 2001-10-16, U.S
11. Bott, J.: Central bank money and blockchain: a payments perspective. J. Paym. Strategy Syst. **11**(2), 145–157 (2017)
12. Biryukov, A., Khovratovich, D., Tikhomirov, S.: Findel: secure derivative contracts for Ethereum. In: Brenner, M., et al. (eds.) FC 2017. LNCS, vol. 10323, pp. 453–467. Springer, Cham (2017). https://doi.org/10.1007/978-3-319-70278-0_28
13. Pennington, W.: The collateral-linked currency forward (CLCF) contract: blockchain-enabled OTC currency forward market infrastructure. J. Index Invest. **9**(2), 27–33 (2018)
14. Grinblatt, M.: An analytic solution for interest rate swap spreads. Int. Rev. Financ. **2**(3), 113–149 (2001)
15. Duffie, D., Singleton, K.J.: An econometric model of the term structure of interest-rate swap yields. J. Financ. **52**(4), 1287–1321 (1997)
16. Brown, K.C., Van Harlow, W., Smith, D.J.: An empirical analysis of interest rate swap spread. Boston University, School of Management (1991)
17. Liu, J., Longstaff, F.A., Mandell, R.E.: The market price of credit risk: An empirical analysis of interest rate swap spreads. National Bureau of Economic Research (2002)
18. Sun, T.S., Sundaresan, S., Wang, C.: Interest rate swaps: An empirical investigation. J. Financ. Econ. **34**(1), 77–99 (1993)
19. Eom, Y.H., Subrahmanyam, M.G., Uno. J.: Credit risk and the yen interest rate swap market (2000)
20. Minton, B.A.: An empirical examination of basic valuation models for plain vanilla US interest rate swaps. J. Financ. Econ. **44**(2), 251 (1997)
21. Liangyu.: China Focus: China launches first Internet court in e-commerce hub. Xinhua. https://www.xinhuanet.com//english/2017-08-18/c-136537234.htm
22. Glasserman, P.: Monte Carlo Methods in Financial Engineering. Stochastic Modelling and Applied Probability. Springer-Verlag, New York (2004). https://doi.org/10.1007/978-0-387-21617-1
23. Gibson, M.: Measuring counterparty credit exposure to a margined counterparty. In: Pykhtin, M. (ed.) Counterparty Credit Risk Modelling. Risk Books, London (2005)
24. Hull, J., White, A.: Numerical procedures for implementing term structure models i: single factor models. J. Deriv. Fall **2**, 7–16 (1994)
25. Hull, J., White, A.: Using Hull-White interest rate trees. J. Deriv. Winter **3**(3), 26–36 (1996)
26. Hull, J., White, A.: The general Hull-White model and super calibration. Financ. Anal. J. **57**, 34–44 (2001)
27. Ostrovski, V.: Efficient and Exact Simulation of the Hull-White Model (2013). Available at SSRN. https://ssrn.com/abstract=2304848
28. Black, F., Scholes, M.: The pricing of options and corporate liabilities. J. Polit. Econ. **81**(3), 637–654 (1973). https://doi.org/10.1086/260062
29. ORE User Guide Quaternion Risk Management (2017). https://github.com/OpenSourceRisk/Engine/blob/master/Docs/UserGuide/userguide.tex
30. Quantlib Homepage. http://www.quantlib.org. Accessed 30 Aug 2018

Overview and Thoughts on Standardization of China's Blockchain Technology

Ming Li[1], Jingjing Yang[2,4], and Xiaowei Ding[3,4(✉)]

[1] China Electronics Standardization Institute, Beijing 100007, China
[2] School of Business, Nanjing University,
163 Xianlin Road, Nanjing 210023, China
[3] School of Information Management, Nanjing University, 163 Xianlin Road,
Nanjing 210023, China
dingxiaowei@nju.edu.cn
[4] Inclusive & Rural Financial Technology Innovation Research Center,
Nanjing University, 163 Xianlin Road, Nanjing 210023, China

Abstract. As an emerging technological field, Blockchain has developed rapidly in recent years. However, its overall development is still at a premature stage. Due to the lack of standards, a series of problems have surfaced, arresting the further development of this industry. Therefore, standardization of Blockchain technology is called for in order to solve these problems. By reviewing the international and domestic status quo of Blockchain standardization, we identify the problems that need to be solved under the current situation, and then we present our Systems Engineering Methodology based approach for standardizing the Blockchain technology.

Keywords: Blockchain · Distributed Ledger Technology (DLT) ·
Standardization · Systems engineering

Since 2016, the innovation and entrepreneurship in the Blockchain field have become a favorite pursuit of various industries. *White Paper on China Blockchain Technology and Application Development (2016)* released by the China Blockchain Technology and Application Forum (CBD-Forum) in October 2016 clarifies the basic concepts, main features, key technologies and areas of applications of Blockchain. Meanwhile, Blockchain was also incorporated the first time into the national Thirteenth Five-Year Plan for National Informatization.

1 The Problems that Need to Solve

The *White Paper on China's Blockchain Technology and Application Development (2016)* pointed out that according to the layout of standardization for National Information Technology Service Standard (ITSS), Cloud Computing, Big Data, Intelligent Manufacturing and so on, the standardized system should serve the functions of discovering and solving problems, and guiding the development of standards and application. The standardization system should also focus on the following issues:

- Establish standardized terminology for Blockchain in order to build up a unified understanding of Blockchain;
- Unify the basic development platform and application programming interface of the Blockchain to support the development, porting and interoperability of Blockchain;
- Unify the links between different Blockchains and establish an interoperable basis between Blockchain;
- Create a secure and credible environment for standardizing services based on Blockchain, and make it favorable for application and development.

2 International Work on Blockchain Standardization

In 2016, the international Blockchain standardization started. At that time, organizations involved in the Blockchain standardization are ISO, IEEE, ITU, W3C etc.

Different organizations have different focuses. ISO is more concerned with basic standards and is committed to advancing technological advancement; IEEE focuses more on standards for engineering and specific applications, such as applications in IoT, power engineering, and autonomous driving. It is also actively pursuing projects that use Blockchain to optimize clinical trials and protect patients, and promote the use of Blockchain in pharmaceutical companies and agriculture. The ITU is committed to developing interoperable decentralized ledger technology standards. The W3C Blockchain Community Group has released a distributed ledger format and protocol.

2.1 ISO

In April 2016, the Australian Standards Association submitted *a New Field of Technical Activity* (NFTA) proposal to the ISO. It proposed the establishment of a new Blockchain technical committee under the ISO to develop Blockchain standardization for interoperability, terminology, privacy, security and other related areas. The proposal was adopted in September 2016 and the ISO appointed the Australian Standards Association as the secretariat of the ISO/Blockchain and DLT Committee. In March 2017, the Office of the National Standardization Administration officially recognized China Electronics Standardization Institute as ISO/TC 307 technical counterparties in China.

The ISO/TC 307 Technical Committee held the first and second plenary meetings in April and November 2017 respectively. In the two plenary sessions, WG1 (Foundation Working Group), SG2 (Use Cases Working Group), WG2 (Security, Privacy and Identity Working Group), SG5 (Smart Contract Working Group), SG6 (Governance of Blockchain and Distributed Ledger Technology Systems Working Group) and SG7 (Interoperability of Blockchain and Distributed Ledger Technology Systems Working Group) were established. Chinese experts mainly participated in the research work of reference architecture, classification and ontology in WG1, completing the reference architecture research report together with experts from the United States, Britain, Russia and other countries. They also actively shared the contents about the role, sub-role, activity and functional structure in China's *Blockchain reference architecture*, contributing our domestic achievements to the international standard pre-research, and actively take part in editing the reference architecture of international standards, classification and ontology technical specifications. In the WG2, by participating in research on privacy and personal information protection, security risks and vulnerabilities, we have gained a comprehensive understanding of the current regulatory tools for Blockchain technology across various countries. For example, the United States currently strengthens regulations and legislations about ICO to improve the security of the Blockchain while the Japanese parliament passed an amendment to the "Financial Closing Algorithm", which officially included "virtual currency" in the legal regulation system. This will help China develop a set of complete, highly applicable security privacy and identification standards. In the future work, SG6 will produce a Blockchain and DLT Governance Guide research report to explain the relationship between the strategic implementation of the Blockchain (including business goals, market, benefits) and Blockchain users or stakeholders, and provide a reference model for system lifecycle management and consensus. As more and more public as well as private organizations adopt Blockchain and DLT solutions to support organizational work, a significantly increasing need for interaction between these solutions will arise in the future. Therefore, the SG7 under TC 307 will conduct further research on inter-chain and inter-system interoperability solutions, providing a standardized framework for facilitating interaction between different technologies while reducing and managing the technical and business complexities within and across industries.

In May 2018, ISO/TC 307 held its third plenary meeting. In the meeting, they discussed about 11 international standards under research (Table 1), including the latest developments and work plans, new work proposals in various fields and issues related to communications with other international standards organizations. By September 2018 [11], ISO/TC 307 has 39 active members with 13 observers. In addition, the meeting decided to establish a Convenors Coordination Group to promote new working projects such as governance guidelines, interoperability, and to promote communications with multiple organizations or to form joint working groups.

Table 1. 11 Standards under research [11]

1	ISO/CD 22739 terminology
2	ISO TR 23244 Overview of privacy and personally identifiable information (PII) protection
3	ISO TR 23245 Security risks and vulnerabilities
4	ISO TR 23246 Overview of identity management using Blockchain and distributed ledger technologies
5	ISO 23257 Reference architecture
6	ISO TS 23258 Taxonomy and Ontology
7	ISO TS 23259 Legally binding smart contracts
8	ISO/CD TR 23455 Overview of and interactions between smart contracts in Blockchain and DLT systems
9	ISO TR 23576 Security of digital asset custodians
10	ISO TR 23578 Discovery issues related to interoperability
11	ISO TS 23635 Guidelines for governance

According to the analysis of the ISO/TC 307 Special Business Strategic Plan Working Group, international standardization work contributes a lot to the global economic and social development. The development and deployment of Blockchain applications lack standardized guidance and evaluation tools for security, reliability, and interoperability. In response to these challenges, countries and industries need international Blockchain standardization to reach consensus. It will provide solutions to the common challenges to different industries, and thus the sharing of technology and experience will be truly realized, laying the foundation for large-scale application of Blockchain. According to *ISO/TC 307 Strategic Business Plan*, the committee's goal is to develop a set of international standards and technical specifications by 2021, which includes terminology, reference architecture, security, interoperability and so on [9].

2.2   IEEE

IEEE Standards Association (IEEE-SA), a globally recognized standards-setting body within IEEE, has been actively pursuing blockchain standardization through launching various activities in multiple industry sectors. IEEE has initiated the following Blockchain projects:

- C17-012 Supply chain technology and implementation
- P2418 Standard for the Framework of Blockchain Use in IoT
- P825 Guide for Interoperability of Transmissive Energy Systems based on Electric Power Infrastructure
- P2418.2 Standard Data Format for Blockchain Systems
- P2418.3 Standard for the Framework of DLT Use in Agriculture (Preparing)
- P2418.4 Standard for the Framework of DLT Use in Connected and Autonomous Vehicles (CAVs) [12]

On July 27, 2018, experts from China Electronics Technology Standardization Institute and IEEE successfully held the first meeting of the IEEE P2418.2 project in Beijing.

2.3   ITU

ITU standardization department has established a focus group for Distributed Ledger Technology (FGDLT). In accordance with its charter, the group will take into account the ongoing activities of ITU, as well as other standardization development organizations, forums and groups, in order to develop a standardized route map for interoperable distributed ledger-based services [6].

ITU's current work items include:

- Security architecture for DLT
- Security capabilities and threats of DLT
- Privacy and security considerations for using DLT data in identity management
- Security assurance for DLT
- Security threats and requirements for digital payment services based on DLT
- Security services based on DLT
- Security threats to online voting using DLT [14]

2.4 W3C

W3C is a non-profit international standardization organization whose member organizations work together to set network standards. They launched a Blockchain community group and current work includes:

- Generate message format standards for Blockchain;
- Guidelines for the use of stocks including seeds, public and private Blockchain, side chains and CDNs;
- Research and evaluate new technologies and new uses, such as inter-bank communications [13].

3 China's Blockchain Standardization Work

3.1 Background of China's Blockchain Standardization

In order to give full play to the role of standardization in the allocation of market resources and advance standardization work, China Electronics Standardization Institute has carried out the standardization work of Blockchain under the guidance of State Administration for Market Regulation and State Standardization Management Committee and relying on the standardization working group under the Forum of Blockchain Technology and Industry Development. First, the Institute carried out research work on the Blockchain standard system and proposed the standard system of Blockchain and applications to provide guidance for the development of subsequent standards. Second, the Institute developed and issued the two standards *Blockchain Reference Architecture* and *Blockchain Data Format Specification*, actively promoting the transformation from group standards to national standards and industry standards.

3.2 2016.10 White Paper on Blockchain Technology and Application Development in China (2016)

The *White Paper on China's Blockchain Technology and Application Development (2016)* was compiled by the China Electronics Standardization Institute, with a focus on the Blockchain standardization roadmap and the Blockchain standard system framework. the Blockchain standards are divided into five categories: Basic Standards, Processes and Methods, Trusted and Interoperability, Business and Applications, Information Security.

3.3 2017.5 Blockchain Reference Architecture

Blockchain, Reference Architecture is the first Blockchain standard in China and is a group standard jointly compiled by members of the China Blockchain Technology and Industry Development Forum Board. Based on this standard, the *Information Technology Blockchain and DLT Reference Architecture* has been approved as the first national standard in the Blockchain field. This is an effective practice of transforming the existing group standard into a national standard with conditional availability.

Meanwhile, *Blockchain Reference Architecture* was incorporated in the 100 Group Standard Application Demonstration Project and the 2017 China Standardization. Most Concerned Standard by the Ministry of Industry and Information Technology in 2017.

3.4   2017.12 Blockchain Specification for Data Formats

Blockchain Specification for Data Formats is the second Blockchain group standard jointly compiled by members of the China Blockchain Technology and Industry Development Forum Board. It provides the data structure, data classification and interrelationships of Blockchain technology, and data format requirements for data elements. It intends to provide a reference of data format for organizations using Blockchain to build Blockchain system, and for the intermediate service organization in the construction process of Blockchain system. It also guides the Blockchain service organization to establish the Blockchain system data structure. The release of this standard helps to provide a reference for the data structure design of Blockchain systems as well as a unified data standard for Blockchain industry applications.

3.5   2018.3 Proposal for the Establishment of National Blockchain and DLT Standardization Technical Committee

According to the preparation application, the organizational structure of this committee will be based on the organizational structure of TC 307. The detailed professional areas of the proposed national standards are as follows (Fig. 1):

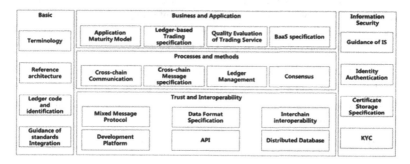

Fig. 1. Blockchain and distributed ledger standard system [5]

4   Thoughts on the Standardization of Blockchain

4.1   Methods of Blockchain Standardization

Research the Standard Architecture using Systems Engineering Methodology.
Systems engineering deals with large and complex systematic issues based on system ideas and methods that includes both quantitative and qualitative measures. Both the design and establishment of a system as well as the management can be regarded as a

kind of engineering practice, collectively referred to as systems engineering. The basic methods of systems engineering include: system analysis, system design and comprehensive evaluation of the system (performance, cost and time, etc.), employing the system ideas including both quantitative and qualitative methods to deal with the problems of large complex systems.

Hall three-dimensional structure, also known as Hall's systems engineering, is a systems engineering methodology proposed by American systems engineering expert Hall (Alfred Daniel Hall) in 1969. With the three-dimensional structure, Hall's model vividly describes the framework of systems engineering research. Each stage and step can be further developed into a hierarchical tree system (Fig. 2).

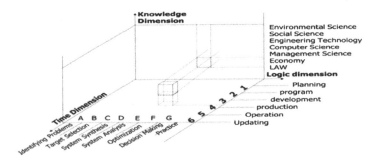

Fig. 2. Systems engineering-3D structure graph

Analyze the Standard Architecture with Reference to International Standards and Best Practices. We should learn from the best international practices, draw on the industry's general methodology and important ideas to promote the integrity and operability of the research results of the standard system.

Establish a Standard Architecture Based on National Standards and Industry Characteristics. The standard system framework is based on national standards and absorbs the relevant practices of the industry. The national standards that can be referred to are as follows:

- GB/T13016 *Principles and Requirements for the Compilation of Standard System Tables*
- GB/T13017 *Guidelines for the Compilation of Enterprise Standard System Tables*

Knowledge Dimension - Standard System Framework. The knowledge dimension refers to the various professional and managerial knowledge required to accomplish the goal. The reference model contains sets, domains, and classes, which summarize the relevant content from the perspective of standardization through strategy and business, and decompose layer by layer with modular ideas. The standard system framework corresponds to the reference model of the standard system, mainly showing the knowledge domain covered in the standard system. Through the standard system hierarchy, the standardized objects are organized and systematically composed into a systematic tree structure (Fig. 3).

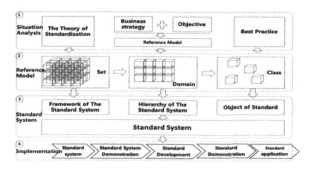

Fig. 3. Project implementation methodology

Logical Dimension - Implementation Method.

- Current Situation Analysis: Through the analysis of business status and information technology development, combined with the best practices both at home and abroad, we should carry out the analysis of the status quo under the guidance of standardization theory;
- Establish a standardized reference model based on the status quo analysis and build a standard system framework;
- Establish a standard system based on the standardized reference model and the standard system framework, and establish a standard system table at the same time;
- Take the standard system as the starting point, design the implementation path of the standard system, and illustrate the development, demonstration and application process of key standards.

Time Dimension - Implementation Method. In the process of implementing the standard system, we need to:

- Clarify the objectives and principles of the implementation of the standards system, based on strategic and business needs;
- Accord to the principle of "Urgency First" and address key and urgent issues in the process of implementing the standard system, and gradually put in place the necessary standards;
- Formulate relevant elements such as personnel, resources, and technology to ensure that the information standard system is implemented as originally planned.

The procedure of implementation path is shown in Fig. 4.:

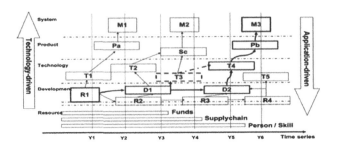

Fig. 4. Project implementation time series

4.2   The Work Plan of Standardization

In the future, China's standardization work will be primarily focused on Blockchain and DLT standards system. Taking into consideration the trend of Blockchain technological development and applications, we should provide orientations for the work of standardization that not only directly reflects the characteristics of the Blockchain, but also guides and standardizes Blockchain-related technology and product development including service design, deployment and delivery. Moreover, it will effectively address issues such as data exchange, information security and privacy protection to guide the establishment and formulation of specific standards. In addition to developing specific standards, the following work will also be carried out based on the results of standardization:

- **Carry Out Standard Verification and Application Pilot Programs.**
  Relevant organizations should timely summarize the effective practices and the acquired experiences of the pilot organizations of each standard. The interaction between provinces and cities should be strengthened to form a joint force. Ensure that key standards are thoroughly applied and support Informatization and Software Service Industry Department to organize exchange meetings on standard verification and application pilot programs. Moreover, they will accelerate the research and development to achieve wider application, fostering new modes and new formats such as BaaS, distributed data storage, and big data transactions, and promoting the integration of Blockchain and industry applications.
- **Accelerate the Construction of Independent Open Source Communities.**
  China should build independent open source community operation mechanism, promote the entry and application of advantageous projects of various forms such as development competition, hackathon, and excellent project contest, and cultivate a group of internationally competitive technology projects at the base level. Through the promotion of establishing incubators and demonstrating application, we expect to build a development platform for all and application solutions that are application-oriented and conform to the reference architecture standards.
- **Carry Out Various Forms of Training on Standardization.**
  Based on the results of standard development and application research in conjunction with local governments such as Jiangsu, Wuxi and Hangzhou and relevant associations, relevant organizations should continue to organize training camps for

Blockchain developers and entrepreneurs, and provide sufficient intellects for the construction of open source communities. Meanwhile, we should invest in the training of high-end development and entrepreneurial intellects in order to enhance our capabilities to research and develop core Blockchain technologies independently. By accelerating the industrialization of Blockchain and solving the problem of the intellect shortage, we can secure a safe development path of Blockchain development and applications.

- **Participate In and Lead International Standardization Work.**
  We should actively participate in Blockchain standardization activities of ISO and strengthen international exchanges and cooperation in this respect. Making full use of our advantage which is supported by the completion of two documents of group standards *Blockchain Reference Architecture* and *Blockchain Specification for Data Formats*, the research group should continue to work on better reports, strengthen international communication and update China's standards. We will fulfill our duties in joint editing and classifying Blockchain and DLT reference architecture international standards and specifying ontological technical standards. At the same time, we will keep track of and also participate in the work of international standardization in smart contracts, Blockchain governance, interoperability as well as other related fields, so as to further promote China's technologies and standardization results to the world, and increase China's influence in international Blockchain standardization.

References

1. Ministry of Industry and Information Technology of the People's Republic of China: White Paper on Blockchain Technology and Application Development in China (2016)
2. Ministry of Industry and Information Technology of the People's Republic of China: China Electronics Standardization Institute: Blockchain Reference Architecture (2017)
3. Ministry of Industry and Information Technology of the People's Republic of China: China Electronics Standardization Institute: Blockchain Specification for Data Formats (2017)
4. Ping, Z., Xiaodan, T.: Current condition and development trends of blockchain standardization. Inf. Technol. Stand. 18–21 (2017)
5. Ministry of Industry and Information Technology of the People's Republic of China: Application for the preparation of the National Technical Committee for Professional Standardization (2018)
6. Anjum, A., Sporny, M., Sill, A.: Blockchain standards for compliance and trust. IEEE Cloud Comput. 4(4), 84–90 (2017)
7. Gramoli, V.: Mark Staples: Blockchain Standard: Can We Reach Consensus? http://gramoli.redbellyblockchain.io/web/doc/pubs/blockchain_standards.pdf
8. Hyland-Wood, D., Khatchadourian, S.: A Future history of international blockchain standards running head suggestion: future blockchain standards. J. Br. Blockchain Assoc. 1 (1), 1–10 (2018)
9. ISO/TC307 Committee: Strategic Business Plan ISO/TC 307. https://isotc.iso.org/livelink/livelink/fetch/2000/2122/687806/ISO_TC_307__Blockchain_and_distributed_ledger_technologies_.pdf?nodeid=19772644&vernum=-2

10. Standards Australia: Roadmap for Blockchain Standards, March 2017. https://www.standards.org.au/getmedia/ad5d74db-8da9-4685-b171-90142ee0a2e1/Roadmap_for_Blockchain_Standards_report.aspx
11. ISO Homepage. https://www.iso.org/committee/6266604.html. Accessed 04 Oct 2018
12. IEEE Homepage. https://ieeexplore.ieee.org/document/8328731/. Accessed 04 Oct 2018
13. W3C Mission. https://www.w3.org/Consortium/mission. Accessed 05 Oct 2018
14. European Commission: ITU Blockchain standards (2017)

Routing Optimization for High Speed Photon State-Channel Architecture

Xiaowei Ding[1,7(✉)], Litai Ren[2,7], Zizhou Sang[3,7], Zijie Zhang[4,7],
Yifan Du[4,7], and Peter Yan[5,6(✉)]

[1] School of Information Management, Nanjing University,
163 Xianlin Road, Nanjing 210023, China
dingxiaowei@nju.edu.cn
[2] School of Chemistry, Nanjing University,
163 Xianlin Road, Nanjing 210023, China
[3] School of Engineering Management, Nanjing University,
163 Xianlin Road, Nanjing 210023, China
[4] School of Mathematics, Nanjing University,
163 Xianlin Road, Nanjing 210023, China
[5] SmartMesh Foundation Pte. Ltd., Singapore, Singapore
peter@smartmesh.io
[6] MeshBox Foundation Pte. Ltd., Singapore, Singapore
[7] Inclusive & Rural Financial Technology Innovation Research Center,
Nanjing University, 163 Xianlin Road, Nanjing 210023, China

Abstract. Compared with mainstream payment systems such as Visa, the biggest obstacles to blockchain based technologies such as Bitcoin and Ethereum becoming mainstream means of payment in human daily life lie in their low transaction rate and slow response time. A potentially promising solution is the state channel architecture. State channels are more general than payment channels, which provide off-chain transaction settlement without much need for expensive on-chain operations. We investigate the routing optimization problem for Photon, a state channel network for Spectrum, which is similar to Raiden being a 2nd layer state channel network on top of Ethereum. Yet Photon possesses interesting characteristics that Raiden lacks. Extensive simulations show our proposed algorithm can effectively achieve high success rate and throughput with low deposit lockup.

Keywords: Blockchain · Bitcoin · Ethereum · Lightning Network · Raiden Network · Spectrum · Photon Network · Payment channel network · State channel network

1 Introduction

Blockchain networks, such as Bitcoin and Ethereum, are notorious for having low transaction rate and slow response time. Bitcoin can process no more than 7 transactions per second [1] and it takes tens of minutes to confirm a transaction. Even if the parameters of blockchain (such as block size and block interval) are optimized, it is still difficult to exceed 100 transactions per second [2]. In contrast, mature payment systems such as Visa can process thousands of transactions per second with only a few seconds' latency.

Many contributions tackle the above-mentioned challenges from various angles, such as modifying consensus mechanisms, sharding, sidechains, and state (or payment) channels. While these methods may potentially expand the overall transaction capability, only the state channel networks, such as the Lightning Network and Raiden Network, also simultaneously improve on the cost and latency fronts [3–13]. The state channel network technology aims to build a second layer on top of the blockchain network, e.g. Bitcoin or Ethereum and establish bilateral "channels" between nodes of the blockchain network, and the main blockchain is then only used to setup channels, close channels and handle abnormal situations. Between two nodes with a channel established, two-way payments can be performed at high speed, and the bilateral accounts are only updated off-chain, within the channel. Thus, state channels improve transaction throughput because most transactions do not need to be written onto the blockchain. State channels can be further interconnected to form networks, which can be used to transfer funds between nodes with no direct connections.

In July 2018, it was reported that Lightning Network launched an experiment involving more than 100 merchants [14]. High-quality routing in a state channel network is technically challenging, especially when facing dynamically changing unstructured network topologies. The challenge is even more prominent when the scale of the network reaches the level of everyday human transactions [15]. The path-finding optimization problem in state channel networks bears certain similarities to that in traditional communication networks. However, since blockchains transfer value, the challenges are not only technical, but also of profound economic and financial connotations.

The main contribution of our work is summarized as follows. We study the routing optimization problem for the Photon Network. Photon is similar to Raiden yet with the following unique and distinct differences:

- Photon routing will be optimized with Transactive Real-time AI Negotiator (TRAIN), which can make the Transfer-Matrix to be more smooth and predictable, and therefore improves the performance of Photon.
- We have MeshBoxes [17] acting as Photon Infrastructure Nodes which can create channels with deposits. Thus, for Photon, we as the designer have control in terms of deposits, channels and network topology. For others, they don't have such control since they use public nodes on Internet which are controlled by normal users.

Against this background, as the first step in a series of research undertakings, we analyze the routing performance vs. deposit requirements for Photon and propose a few algorithms for routing and rebalancing. Our research contributes to the understanding of the tradeoffs in various design choices for the Photon State Channel Architecture.

The remainder of the paper is structured as follows. In Sect. 2 we introduce the background. In Sect. 3 we overview related works. In Sect. 4 we present our approach. In Sect. 5 we present evaluation. We conclude with Sect. 6.

2 Background

The state channel allows a peer-to-peer direct payment highway to be established between the two parties in a transaction. When establishing a payment channel, both parties are required to submit certain deposits. Both parties maintain the private bilateral ledger without having to write all transactions to the blockchain. At the same time, the channel guarantees that the parties will not have bad behavior, or the misbehavior will be punished. At the end, if off-chain transactions are no longer needed, or if one party proposes to close the state channel, or if the available balance is exhausted, the channel is closed and settled and the final state is recorded back onto the blockchain. If arbitration is needed for misbehavior, the blockchain will also be resorted to. One of the advantages of the state channel is that it can avoid on-chain transactions, and the throughput is limited only by the bandwidth between the two parties. Another advantage is that no miner service is required, so transaction costs can be saved.

In a state channel network, the path-finding algorithm must guarantee atomicity. If for an intermediate node, no outgoing channel adjacent to it has sufficient balance to service the fund transfer, then the path-finding failure at this node will cause the entire path to fail automatically. The path-finding algorithm can then explore other paths. The balance or capacity of the channel on a path is either updated simultaneously or not updated at all. There can be no partial updates because partial updates can result in loss of funds. The Lightning Network uses Hash Time-Lock Contract (HTLC) to solve this problem. In a state channel network, the path-finding algorithm must achieve the highest possible throughput and success rate using as little capital locked in the network as possible. In addition, it is also necessary to provide certain economic incentives to users, especially service providers and intermediate nodes that provide routing services. Unlike traditional network routing algorithms, state channel network routing algorithms focus on finding a path with sufficient available balance to support the funds to be transferred, rather than the traditional shortest path. In addition, routing algorithm is faced with constantly changing available balances on channels. Last but not the least, security and privacy protection are extremely important.

Spectrum is a Proof-of-Capability based public chain. In Spectrum, nodes that contribute more resources to the system will get more capability scores, giving them more opportunities to do the bookkeeping on the blockchain [16]. Important members of the Spectrum network are the Meshbox (indoor) and MeshBox++ (outdoor) wifi routers [17]. When a MeshBox (++) owner contributes bandwidth and disk space to the system, the node's capability score also increases.

3 Related Work

Research on state (payment) channel networks focuses on multiple dimensions such as performance, security and privacy.

Flare [6] is a beacon-based hybrid source-based routing scheme in Lightning Network, which borrowed ideas from the routing of mobile ad hoc networks. Due to the design decisions such as the adoption of beacons, this routing algorithm is probabilistic, that is, there is no guarantee that a path will be found between the sender and the receiver. This is acceptable for Lightning Network because when difficulties in path-finding arise, the network architecture allows a new channel to be opened to increase the connectivity of the network and also allows for funds to be transferred thru the main blockchain. Such a retry or fallback mechanism can also be integrated into the Lightning Network clients. The authors estimate that Flare can support millions of users.

In [19], the authors argued that single path routing schemes have a number of problems, with the most severe problem being the low utilization of available capabilities. The authors modelled payment channel networks as flow networks. They leveraged flow network algorithms to effectively utilize available capacities by aggregating multiple paths. They proposed an extended push-relabel algorithm and demonstrated that their algorithm could meet the demands when single-path based approaches fail.

SpeedyMurmurs [13] is an embedding-based or distance-based routing algorithm. It provides formal privacy guarantee in fully distributed environment and reduces the overhead of routing a transaction by more than a factor of two.

SilentWhispers [21] is a landmark-based routing algorithm. It achieves a number of privacy properties (sender, receiver, link, and value privacy). The use of highly linked Ripple-like gateway nodes is vital to make the system efficient, robust, and scalable.

Spider [18] is a packet-switched payment channel network: it breaks down the payment amount into transmission units and transmits them over multiple paths, using congestion control and in-network scheduling mechanisms. Spider features imbalance-aware routing. The authors derived decentralized algorithms for solving optimization problems taking into account the rate-imbalance constraints. In performance evaluation, for the same amount of funds locked in the network, Spider completes 10–45% more transactions than SpeedyMurmurs and SilentWhispers. In an ISP-like topology, Spider performs 5–15% more transactions than the traditional max-flow algorithm.

Revive [20] focuses on rebalancing. When the available balance of a channel is exhausted, such as in the case of a large number of asymmetric transactions, it is necessary to close the channel first, and then re-open and refund the channel. This is a very expensive operation. Revive proposed to refund the depleting channels thru rebalancing.

There are other related contributions. Due to limitation in space, our list of related works might be incomplete, for which we sincerely apologize.

4 Our Approach

Currently existing solutions assume that the network is defined by users in terms of nodes, channels, and deposits. For these existing solutions, they are given the network topology (connectivity) and deposits, and they try to route as best as they can. Usually deposits will be small, the amount which can be transferred is limited, and failure rates can be high, because users must put their own personal deposit onto channels, and other users will use up this deposit. Unless users are significantly incentivized, there is little reason they will lock up their own funds into channels which are used by others.

These is a major difference in our scenario, which is a niche. Since we have MeshBoxes, and invest significant deposits which can be several orders of magnitude more than in the above-mentioned user defined channel situation into the Infrastructure Channels (between MeshBoxes), we have control over the Infrastructure Nodes, Channels and the network topology, and deposits that are put onto the Infrastructure Channels. This should allow us to achieve a better solution than for the arbitrary networks.

In our architecture, user (initiator) nodes only make a channel to a core node, and a core node must make a channel to each user which can be a target. For networks with "super nodes", such super nodes are similar to our core nodes. However, there is still a big difference between a few "super nodes" being instantiated, and our entire core networks, which is a regular topology of Meshbox Core Nodes with high deposit channels.

Our goal is to find the best rebalancing routing algorithm, but specifically for our Infrastructure network and pre-defined topology, and high-deposits. These are unique assumptions we have because we have control over Meshboxes. We should be able to reach much higher Transaction Per Second (TPS) and much higher success rate than others, given a certain distribution for the amount to be transferred (e.g. Uniform [1,100]) and given various symmetric and asymmetric Transfer Matrices (TM). In Fig. 1, on the left, we show the Photon Architecture, on the right, we show how funds transfer from User node a1 to User node h3. In this example, each link between a pair of nodes represents two uni-directional State-Channels: e.g. a channel from A to B (with Available Balance 100), and channel from B to A (with Available Balance 200). Figure 2 shows that a channel's low available balance might be the cause of "failure".

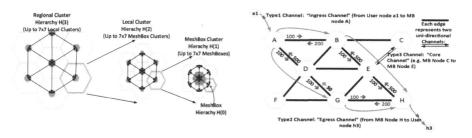

Fig. 1. **Left**: three levels of "fractal" hierarchies for the Photon Networks. **Right:** funds transfer thru Core Channels (Nodes), or Infrastructure Channels (Nodes).

4.1 Rebalancing Algorithms

Let us define:

$D_{i,j}$: (initial) deposit on channel $C_{i,j}$.

$A_{i,j}$: available balance on channel $C_{i,j}$.

$Y_{i,j}$: locked funds on channel $C_{i,j}$ during transaction.

$X_{i,j}$: total amount of successfully transmitted funds on channel $C_{i,j}$.

$D_{i,j}^{\#} = A_{i,j} - A_{j,i}$: difference between forward channel and reverse channel.

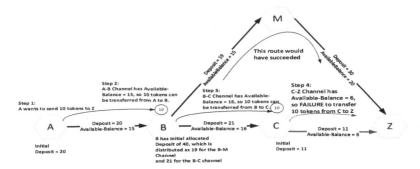

Fig. 2. The notion of "channel failure" due to insufficient available balance on channel.

We consider three types of rebalancing algorithms, Algorithm 1 being the foundational.

Algorithm 1 Conjugate Rebalancing

Input: Sender,Receiver,Payment
Output: Updated state matrix A, Y, X

1: **Parameter:** n: number of top shortest routes used, default n=2.
2: i:=Sender; isSuccess:=true;
3: **while** i not equal to Receiver **do**
4:     Call Dijkstra on (i,Receiver) and return top n shortest routes
5:     **for** j:=1 to n **do**
6:         Let k be i's outgoing edge i→k on the j-th shortest route
7:         **if** $A_{i,k} >$ Payment **then**
8:             $Y_{i,k} = Y_{i,k} +$ Payment
9:             $A_{i,k} = D_{i,k} - X_{i,k} + X_{k,i} - Y_{i,k}$
10:            Declear "Channel Success"; i:=k;
11:            **break**
12:        **end if**
13:    **end for**
14:    Declear "Path Failure"
15:    # Reset A along its path, releasing the locked funds, all the way back to this transaction's Sender.
16:    **for** i_k along the path, e.g. $i_0(=\text{Sender}), i_1, i_2, ..., i_n(=i)$ **do**
17:        $Y_{i_{k-1},i_k} = Y_{i_{k-1},i_k} -$ Payment
18:        $A_{i_{k-1},i_k} = D_{i_{k-1},i_k} - X_{i_{k-1},i_k} + X_{i_k,i_{k-1}} - Y_{i_{k-1},i_k}$
19:    **end for**
20:    isSuccess:=false
21:    **break**
22: **end while**
23: Declear "Path Success"
24: **if** isSuccess **then**
25:     # Make updates, releasing the locked funds, along the whole path.
26:     **for** i_k along the path, e.g. $i_0(=\text{Sender}), i_1, i_2, ..., i_n(=\text{Receiver})$ **do**
27:         $X_{i_{k-1},i_k} = X_{i_{k-1},i_k} +$ Payment
28:         $Y_{i_{k-1},i_k} = Y_{i_{k-1},i_k} -$ Payment
29:         $A_{i_{k-1},i_k} = D_{i_{k-1},i_k} - X_{i_{k-1},i_k} + X_{i_k,i_{k-1}} - Y_{i_{k-1},i_k}$
30:         $A_{i_k,i_{k-1}} = D_{i_k,i_{k-1}} - X_{i_k,i_{k-1}} + X_{i_{k-1},i_k} - Y_{i_k,i_{k-1}}$
31:     **end for**
32: **end if**

The heuristics behind Algorithm 2 is that for an edge, if the available balances of the forward and reverse channels differ too much, then we artificially create a series of triangle-looped transactions to rebalance the channels.

Algorithm 2 Circle Rebalancing

1: **Parameter:** θ_1 : threshold1, determines which level of $D_{i,j}^f$ will lead into circle rebalancing, default $\theta_1=0$
2:            θ_2 : threshold2, determines one time's circle rebalancing's least adjusted A, default $\theta_2=50$
3: Insert the following pseudo-code to between line 10 and 11 in Algorithm 1:
4: ...
5: **if** $D_{i,k}^f > \theta_1$ **then**
6:     Delete $C_{i,k}$ from map, then call Dijkstra on (k,i) and return [k,q,i]
7:     $F_s := \text{sum}(A_{k,q},A_{q,i},A_{i,k}) \# F_s$: sum of A of forward channels within rebalancing circle
8:     $R_s := \text{sum}(A_{q,k},A_{i,q},A_{k,i}) \# R_s$: sum of A of reverse channels within rebalancing circle
9:     $\Delta := \frac{F_s+R_s}{6}$
10:     **if** $\Delta > \theta_2$ **then**
11:         $A_{k,q}\text{-}=\Delta$, $A_{q,i}\text{-}=\Delta$, $A_{i,k}\text{-}=\Delta$
12:         $A_{q,k}\text{+}=\Delta$, $A_{i,q}\text{+}=\Delta$, $A_{k,i}\text{+}=\Delta$
13:     **end if**
14: **end if**
15: ...

The heuristics behind Algorithm 3 is that at a node n, we would like to find the next node x, such that we can maximize $\left(A_{n,x} - A_{x,n}\right)$.

Algorithm 3 Heuristic Routing Rebalancing

1: **Parameter:** N_A:the number of candidate paths (from which to choose the best path with max $D_{i,k}^f$),
2:            default $N_A=2$
3:            T_L: limit on the max number of hops for a path, default $T_L=10$
4: Replace line 4 in Algorithm 1 with the following pseudo-code:
5: ...
6: **for** i=1 to n **do**
7:     **if** current hop count $< T_L$ **then**
8:         **for** j = 1 to N_A **do**
9:             Call Dijkstra on (Sender,Receiver) and return the shortest path and the next node k
10:             **if** if at least one shortest path is returned **then**
11:                 **if** $D_{i,k}^f > D_{max}^f$ **then**
12:                     Take this shortest path as the top i-th path
13:                     $D_{max}^f := D_{i,k}^f$
14:                 **end if**
15:             **else**
16:                 Temporarily mask $C_{i,k}$ away from the map
17:             **end if**
18:         **end for**
19:     **end if**
20: **end for**
21: ...

4.2   Utility Optimization

Let us define:

$\mathcal{T}$: Transaction Initiation Rate (TIR), the number of initiated transactions per second in the system.

$\tilde{\mathcal{T}}$: Transaction per Second (TPS), the number of successful transactions per second in the system.

P : Success Rate (SR), the number of successful transactions divided by total number of transactions in the system.

$\mathcal{T}^f := \mathcal{T} - \tilde{\mathcal{T}}$: failed TPS in the Photon system.
$D_S := \sum\limits_{i \neq j} D_{i,j}$:sum of deposits.

Our utility function then can be defined as:

$$U(D,\mathcal{T}) = \frac{w_{Ptps} \cdot \tilde{\mathcal{T}} - w_{Pftps} \cdot \mathcal{T}^f}{D_S} = \frac{\mathcal{T}}{D_S} \cdot \left[-w_{Pftps} + P \cdot \left(w_{Ptps} + w_{Pftps} \right) \right], \quad (1)$$

where the w's represent the weights on the Quality of Experience (QoE) of successful transactions and failed transactions, respectively. The w's are usually set to be constants.

With increasing number of failures per second, a human-being's QoE degrades, therefore, w_{Pftps} could be a function of $\mathcal{T}^f$. In the simplest case, w_{Pftps} could be set to be a linear function of $\mathcal{T}^f$: $w_{Pftps} = a + b \cdot \mathcal{T}^f = a + b \cdot \mathcal{T} \cdot (1 - P)$.

Then the utility optimization problem can be formulated as:

$$U(D,\mathcal{T}) = \frac{\mathcal{T}}{D_S} \cdot \left\{ P \cdot w_{Ptps} + (P - 1) \cdot [a + b \cdot \mathcal{T} \cdot (1 - P)] \right\}, \quad (2)$$

$$\min U(D, \mathcal{T}), s.t. \begin{cases} \mathcal{T} > 0 \\ D_S = \sum_{i \neq j} D_{i,j} \\ \forall i, j, D_{i,j} = D(> 0) \end{cases} \quad (3)$$

4.3   Simulation Setup

To understand the properties of the Photon system, we focused mainly on the 7-node setup. We adopted the Poisson process to model the Transaction Initiations in the system, with the parameter to the Poisson process being the TIR. Each element of the 3-tuple (Sender, Receiver, Payment) was drawn from uniform distribution. Given the uniform distribution (symmetrical Transfer Matrix), in the long run (steady state), assuming the rebalancing algorithms do well, it should be most effective for all the D's to be the same, as that is the long run equilibrium. Therefore we fix the elements of the D matrix to be one single value, which is the long run equilibrium value. In the follow-up studies, we will study the case of asymmetrical Transfer Matrix and non-uniform (Sender, Receiver, Payment) distributions.

In our study, we set $n = 2$ for Algorithm 1, $\theta_1 = 0, \theta_2 = 50$ for Algorithm 2, $N_A = 2, T_L = 10$ for Algorithm 3. And we experimented with various combinations of (w_{Ptps}, a, b) for the utility function and set $w_{Ptps} = 1, a = 1e - 3, b = 1e - 4$ for the plots. For each hop, we set the delay to be 0.002 s.

5   Evaluation and Discussion

In Fig. 3, the left panel shows the Success Rate vs. D given $\mathcal{T} = 20000$. It is seen that Algorithm 1 can achieve the highest Success Rate for relative low Deposit value. At TIR = 20000, even for Deposits that are below 500, the system can still maintain above 90% Success Rate. The right panel shows that we can still reach >90% Success Rate at

25000 TIR. It is expected that Algorithm 1 achieves the highest performance in comparison. For symmetrical Transfer Matrix and uniformly distributed transactions, in the long run equilibrium, this fact is in line with our intuition. This might not hold when we are faced with asymmetrical Transfer Matrix with non-uniformly distributed transactions, which we will study further in the future. In Figs. 4 and 5, we show the Utility Function (notice the negated vertical axis). It is seen that the lower the deposit, the lower the Utility. The higher the TIR, the lower the Utility. It is intuitive to conjecture that the very low TIR will also lower the Utility value and therefore, there might be an optimal TIR point which maximizes the Utility Function. This will be one of our future works.

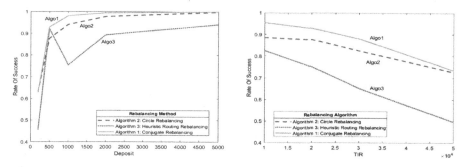

Fig. 3. The Rate of Successes. **Left:** Fix $T = 20000$, $D \in [200, 5000]$. **Right:** Fix $D = 500$, $T \in [10000, 50000]$.

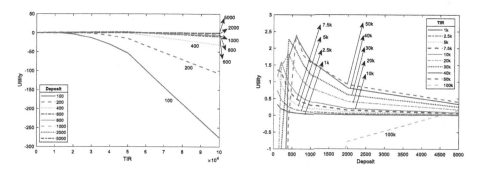

Fig. 4. Utility Function (a = 1e-3, b = 1e-4). **Left:** Fix $D = 100, 200, 400, 600, 800, 1000, 2000, 5000$, $T \in [1000, 100000]$. **Right:** Fix $T = 1000, 2500, 5000, 7500, 10000, 20000, 30000, 40000, 50000, 100000$, $D \in [0, 5000]$.

240 X. Ding et al.

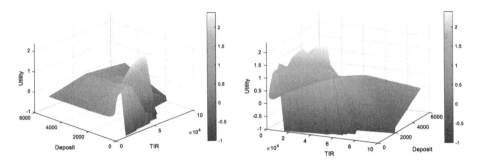

Fig. 5. Utility Function (3D plots, two different views, a = 1e-3, b = 1e-4), $D \in [100, 5000]$, $\mathcal{T} \in [1000, 100000]$.

6 Conclusion

In this work, we investigate the routing optimization problem for Photon. Extensive simulations show that our proposed algorithm can effectively achieve high success rate and throughput of fund-transferring for Photon systems with low deposit lockup.

In the future, we will further deepen our understanding of the system and improve our algorithms. For instance, we will study the case of asymmetrical Transfer Matrix and non-uniform (Sender, Receiver, Payment) distributions. Moreover, to model a more realistic system, Deep Learning can be used with the following considerations: several parameters will change as a function of time, and could be correlated with calendar days (day of the month, day of the week, holidays), time-of-day, local or regional news events, stock market, weather, etc. With enough (big) data, it may be possible to learn how such parameters will vary in advance and configure the parameters (e.g. deposits) proactively in order to maximize the utility function.

Acknowledgements. We greatly appreciate the help from SmartMesh Foundation and MeshBox Foundation.

References

1. Croman, K., et al.: On scaling decentralized blockchains. In: Clark, J., Meiklejohn, S., Ryan, P., Wallach, D., Brenner, M., Rohloff, K. (eds.) FC 2016. LNCS, vol. 9604, pp. 106–125. Springer, Heidelberg (2016). https://doi.org/10.1007/978-3-662-53357-4_8
2. Gervais, A., Karame, G.O., Wüst, K., Glykantzis, V., Ritzdorf, H., Capkun, S.: On the security and performance of proof of work blockchains. In: Proceedings of the 2016 ACM SIGSAC Conference on Computer and Communications Security, pp. 3–16. ACM, October 2016
3. Poon, J., Dryja, T.: The bitcoin lightning network: scalable off-chain instant payments (2016). https://lightning.network/lightning-network-paper.pdf
4. Miller, A., Bentov, I., Kumaresan, R., McCorry, P.: Sprites: payment channels that go faster than lightning. *CoRR abs/1702.05812* (2017)
5. Raiden network. http://raiden.network/

6. Prihodko, P., Zhigulin, S., Sahno, M., Ostrovskiy, A., Osuntokun, O.: Flare: an approach to routing in lightning network. White Paper (2016)
7. Decker, C., Wattenhofer, R.: A fast and scalable payment network with bitcoin duplex micropayment channels. In: Pelc, A., Schwarzmann, A.A. (eds.) SSS 2015. LNCS, vol. 9212, pp. 3–18. Springer, Cham (2015). https://doi.org/10.1007/978-3-319-21741-3_1
8. McCorry, P., Möser, M., Shahandasti, S.F., Hao, F.: Towards bitcoin payment networks. In: Liu, J., Steinfeld, R. (eds.) ACISP 2016. LNCS, vol. 9722, pp. 57–76. Springer, Cham (2016). https://doi.org/10.1007/978-3-319-40253-6_4
9. Malavolta, G., Moreno-Sanchez, P., Kate, A., Maffei, M., Ravi, S.: Concurrency and privacy with payment-channel networks. In: Proceedings of the 2017 ACM SIGSAC Conference on Computer and Communications Security, pp. 455–471. ACM, October 2017
10. Heilman, E., Alshenibr, L., Baldimtsi, F., Scafuro, A., Goldberg, S.: TumbleBit: an untrusted bitcoin-compatible anonymous payment hub. In: Network and Distributed System Security Symposium (2017)
11. Lind, J., Eyal, I., Pietzuch, P., Sirer, E.G.: Teechan: payment channels using trusted execution environments. arXiv preprint arXiv:1612.07766 (2016)
12. Green, M., Miers, I.: Bolt: anonymous payment channels for decentralized currencies. In: Proceedings of the 2017 ACM SIGSAC Conference on Computer and Communications Security, pp. 473–489. ACM, October 2017
13. Roos, S.: Moreno-Sanchez, P., Kate, A., Goldberg, I.: Settling Payments Fast and Private: Efficient Decentralized Routing for Path-Based Transactions. arXiv preprint arXiv:1709.05748 (2017)
14. 100 merchants can now trial Bitcoin's lightning network risk free. https://finance.yahoo.com/news/100-merchants-now-trial-bitcoins-120126391.html. Accessed 07 Oct 2018
15. Engelmann, F., Kopp, H., Kargl, F., Glaser, F., Weinhardt, C.: Towards an economic analysis of routing in payment channel networks. In: Proceedings of the 1st Workshop on Scalable and Resilient Infrastructures for Distributed Ledgers, p. 2. ACM, December 2017
16. Spectrum Foundation.: Parallel Internet Value Transfer Protocol and DAPP Platform. White Paper, July 2018
17. MeshBox Foundation.: MeshBox will create a new distributed routing/storage device standard. White Paper, January 2018
18. Sivaraman, V., Venkatakrishnan, S.B., Alizadeh, M., Fanti, G., Viswanath, P.: Routing Cryptocurrency with the Spider Network. arXiv preprint arXiv:1809.05088 (2018)
19. Rohrer, E., Laß, J.-F., Tschorsch, F.: Towards a concurrent and distributed route selection for payment channel networks. In: Garcia-Alfaro, J., Navarro-Arribas, G., Hartenstein, H., Herrera-Joancomartí, J. (eds.) ESORICS/DPM/CBT -2017. LNCS, vol. 10436, pp. 411–419. Springer, Cham (2017). https://doi.org/10.1007/978-3-319-67816-0_23
20. Khalil, R., Gervais, A.: Revive: rebalancing off-blockchain payment networks. In: Proceedings of the 2017 ACM SIGSAC Conference on Computer and Communications Security, pp. 439–453. ACM, October 2017
21. Malavolta, G., Moreno-Sanchez, P., Kate, A., Maffei, M.: SilentWhispers: enforcing security and privacy in decentralized credit networks. IACR Cryptol. ePrint Arch. 2016, 1054 (2016)

Author Index

Printed in the United States
By Bookmasters